WITHDRAWN

D1266482

for Prune

I would like to thank Frédéric Lavabre, as well as the team from Éditions Sarbacane, who helped me create this book the way I had pictured it.
Guillaume Dégé, Paul Sztulman, Iris Levasseur, Serge Bloch, Pascale Lagautrière and Xavier Mussat for their help, advice and benevolence.
Hadrien Herzog, David Adrien, Gaby Bazin, Nolwenn Vuillier, Sophie Potié, Mathilde Rives, François Lion, Sylvia Letrait, Marianne Baur, Shanti Masud and Dimitri Paz for their friendship and support.
Jean, Aline, Tom and Arthur Harari who always encouraged me to go further, for their unparalleled accompaniment.
And Prune Lion-Letrait for everything that can't be named.

—Lucas Harari

SWIMMING in

DARK

In the heart of the Swiss Alps, the Vals Thermal Baths, the inspiration
behind this graphic novel, were designed by the famous Swiss
architect Peter Zumthor. Born in Basel in 1943, Peter Zumthor earned
the Pritzker Prize in 2009.

Original French edition © 2017 Éditions Sarbacane, Paris
English translation © 2019 David Homel

All rights reserved. No part of this book may be reproduced in any part by any means—graphic, electronic, or mechanical—without the prior written
permission of the publisher, except by a reviewer, who may use brief excerpts in a review, or in the case of photocopying in Canada, a license from Access
Copyright.

ARSENAL PULP PRESS
Suite 202 – 211 East Georgia St.
Vancouver, BC V6A 1Z6
Canada
arsenalpulp.com

This book has received support from the Institut français' Publication Support Programmes.
Cet ouvrage a bénéficié du soutien des Programmes d'aide à la publication de l'Institut français.

Arsenal Pulp Press gratefully acknowledges the support of the Government of Canada and the Government of British Columbia (through the Book Publishing
Tax Credit), for its publishing activities.

Canada BRITISH COLUMBIA | BRITISH COLUMBIA ARTS COUNCIL
An agency of the Province of British Columbia

Arsenal Pulp Press acknowledges the xʷməθkʷəy̓əm (Musqueam), Sḵwx̱wú7mesh (Squamish), and səl̓ilwətaʔɬ (Tsleil-Waututh) Nations, speakers of
Hul'q'umi'num'/Halq'eméylem/hən̓q̓əmin̓əm̓ and custodians of the traditional, ancestral, and unceded territories where our office is located. We pay respect
to their histories, traditions, and continuous living cultures and commit to accountability, respectful relations, and friendship.

Edited by Brian Lam
Proofread by Alison Strobel
Lettering by Oliver McPartlin

This is a work of fiction. Any resemblance of characters to persons either living or deceased is purely coincidental.

Printed and bound in Canada

Library and Archives Canada Cataloguing in Publication:
Title: Swimming in darkness / Lucas Harari ; translated by David Homel.
Other titles: Aimant. English
Names: Harari, Lucas, 1990– author, illustrator. | Homel, David, translator. | Translation of:
    Harari, Lucas, 1990– Aimant.
Description: Translation of: L'aimant.
Identifiers: Canadiana (print) 2019010614X | Canadiana (ebook) 20190106158 | ISBN 9781551527673
    (hardcover) | ISBN 9781551527680 (PDF)
Subjects: LCGFT: Graphic novels.
Classification: LCC PN6747.H37 A7313 2019 | DDC 741.5/944—dc23

NESS

LUCAS HARARI
translated by David Homel

ARSENAL PULP PRESS
VANCOUVER

SWIMMING IN DARKNESS

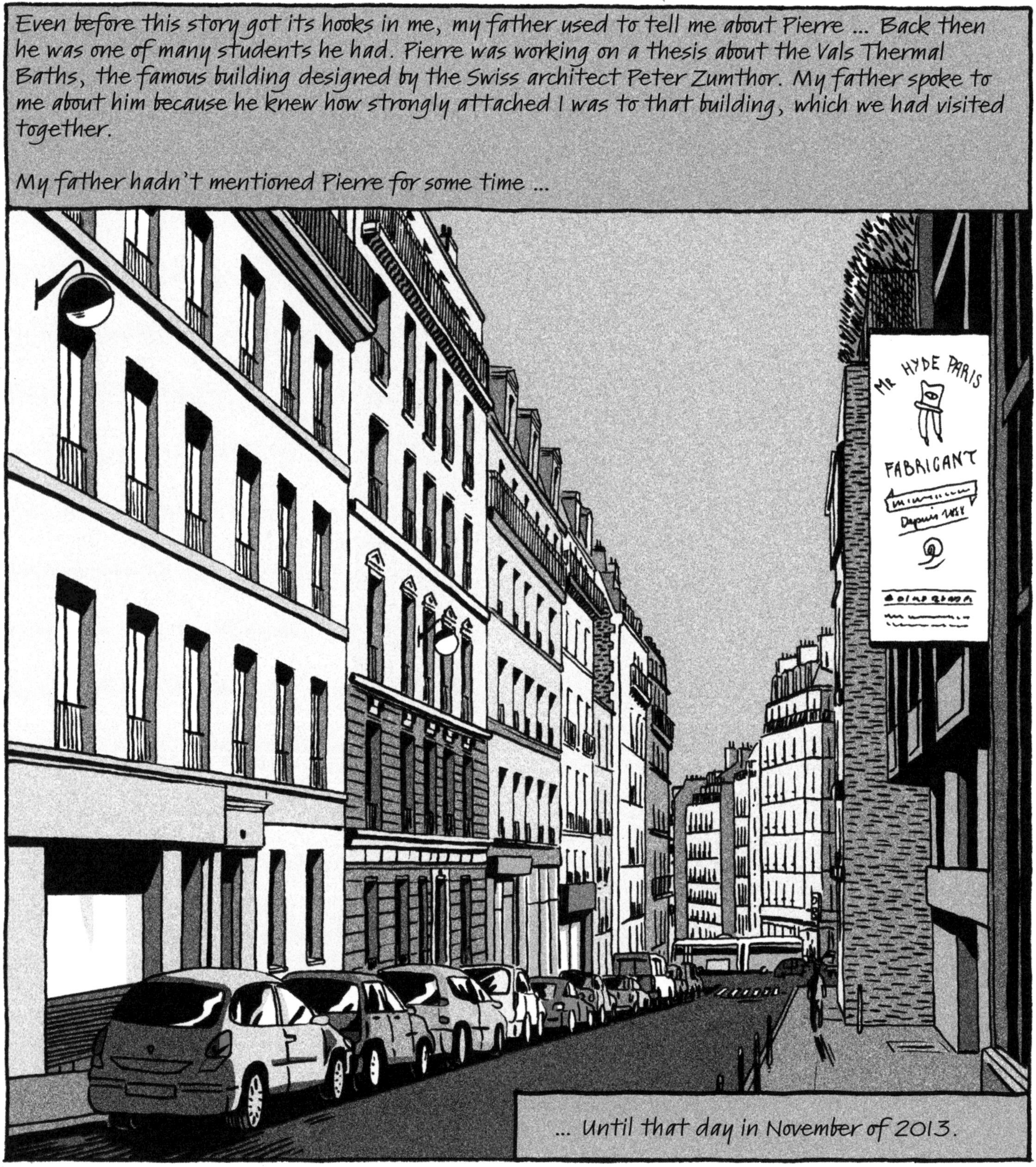
Even before this story got its hooks in me, my father used to tell me about Pierre ... Back then he was one of many students he had. Pierre was working on a thesis about the Vals Thermal Baths, the famous building designed by the Swiss architect Peter Zumthor. My father spoke to me about him because he knew how strongly attached I was to that building, which we had visited together.
My father hadn't mentioned Pierre for some time ...
MR HYDE PARIS
FABRICANT
... Until that day in November of 2013.

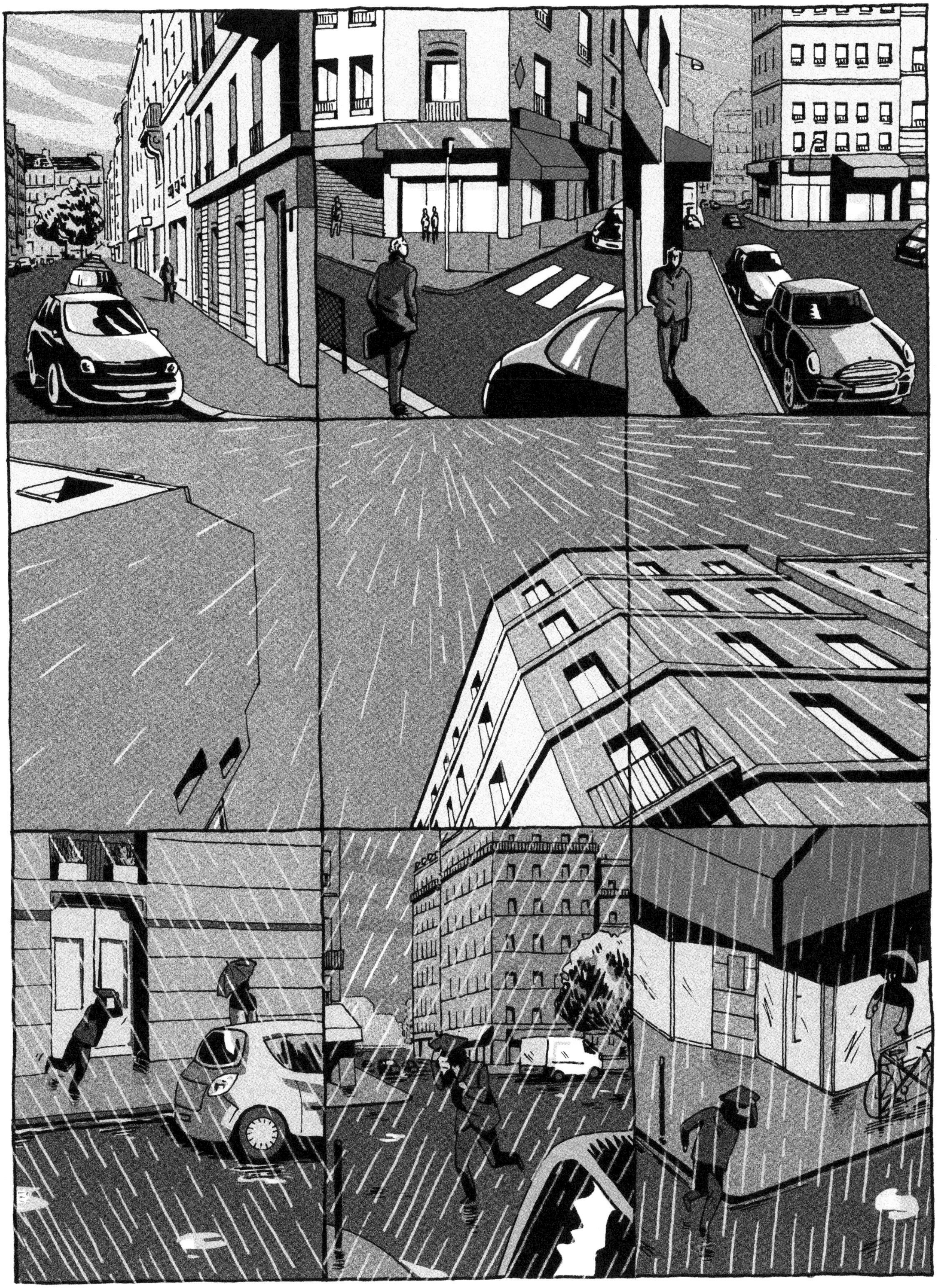

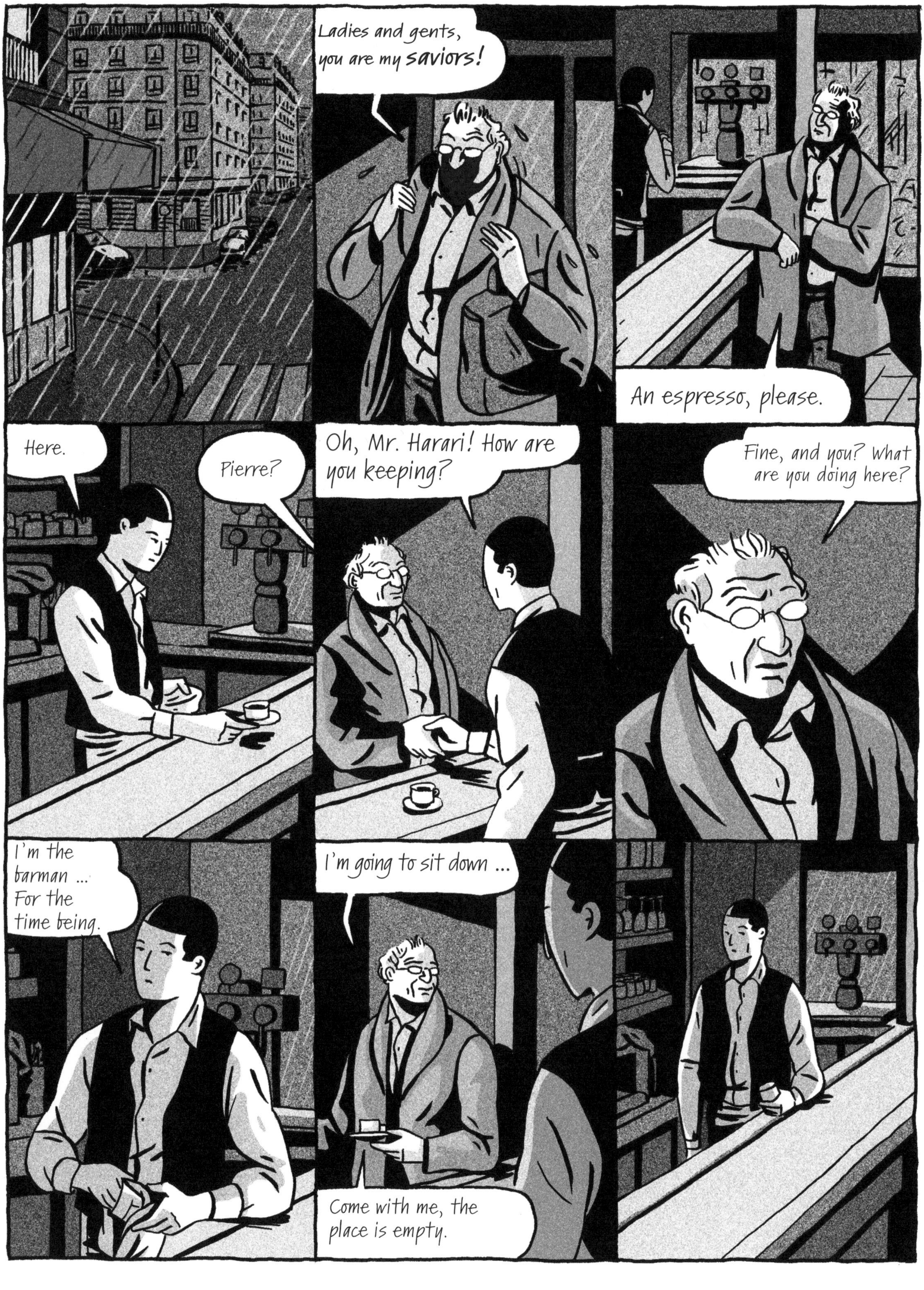
Ladies and gents, you are my saviors!
An espresso, please.
Here.
Pierre?
Oh, Mr. Harari! How are you keeping?
Fine, and you? What are you doing here?
I'm the barman ... For the time being.
I'm going to sit down ...
Come with me, the place is empty.

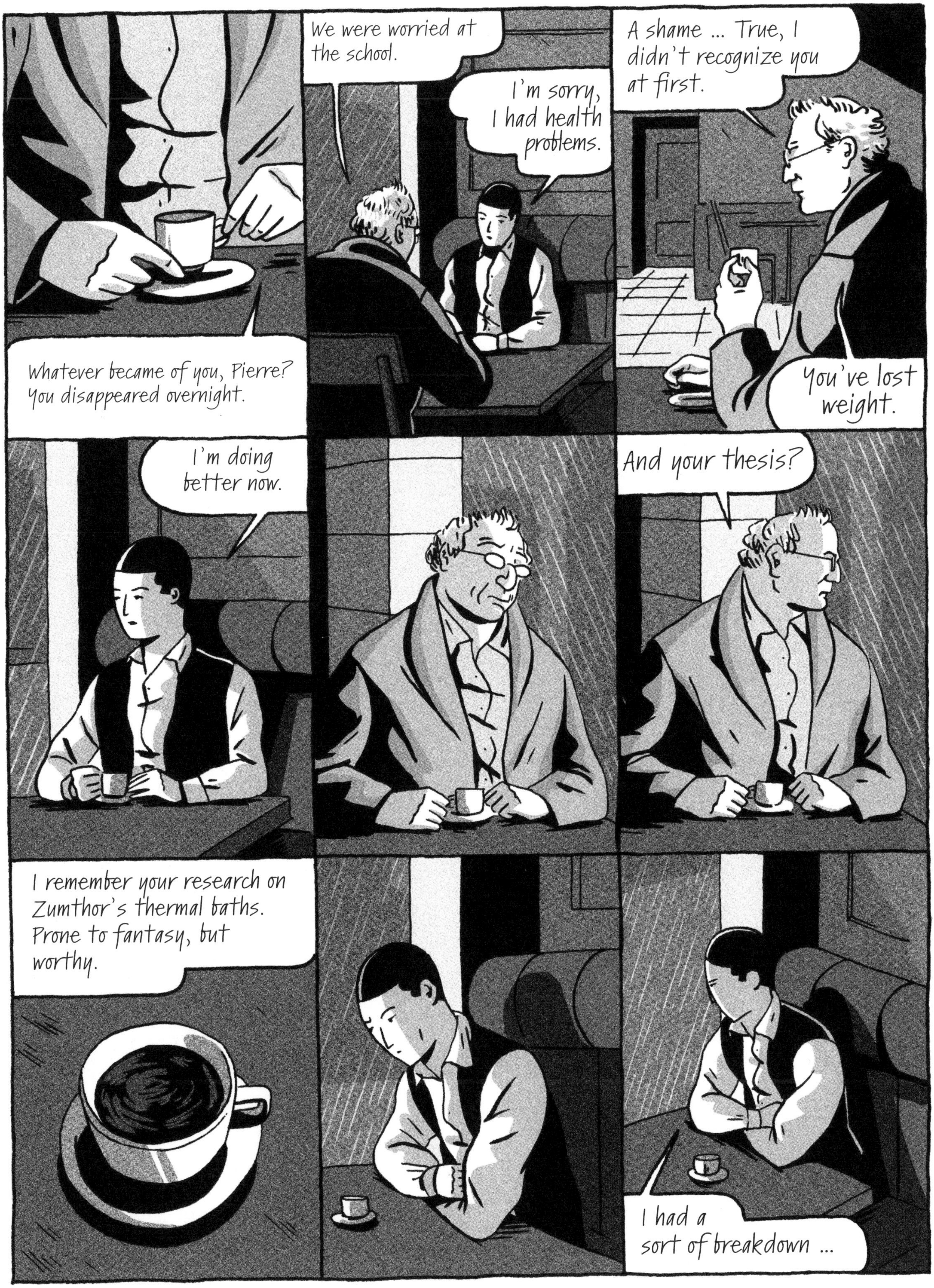
Whatever became of you, Pierre? You disappeared overnight.
We were worried at the school.
I'm sorry, I had health problems.
A shame ... True, I didn't recognize you at first.
You've lost weight.
I'm doing better now.
And your thesis?
I remember your research on Zumthor's thermal baths. Prone to fantasy, but worthy.
I had a sort of breakdown ...

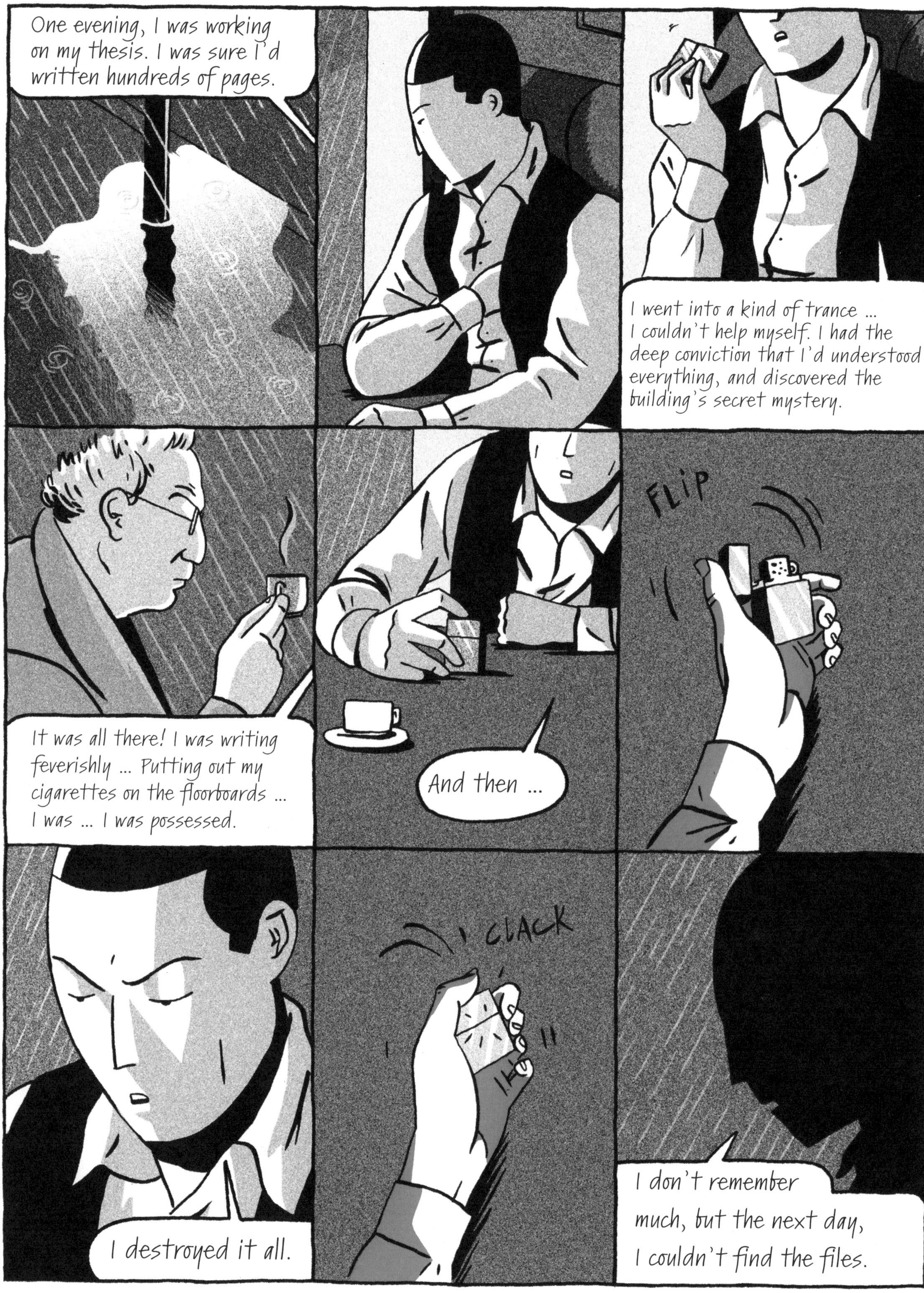
One evening, I was working on my thesis. I was sure I'd written hundreds of pages.
I went into a kind of trance ... I couldn't help myself. I had the deep conviction that I'd understood everything, and discovered the building's secret mystery.
It was all there! I was writing feverishly ... Putting out my cigarettes on the floorboards ... I was ... I was possessed.
And then ...
FLIP
I destroyed it all.
CLACK
I don't remember much, but the next day, I couldn't find the files.

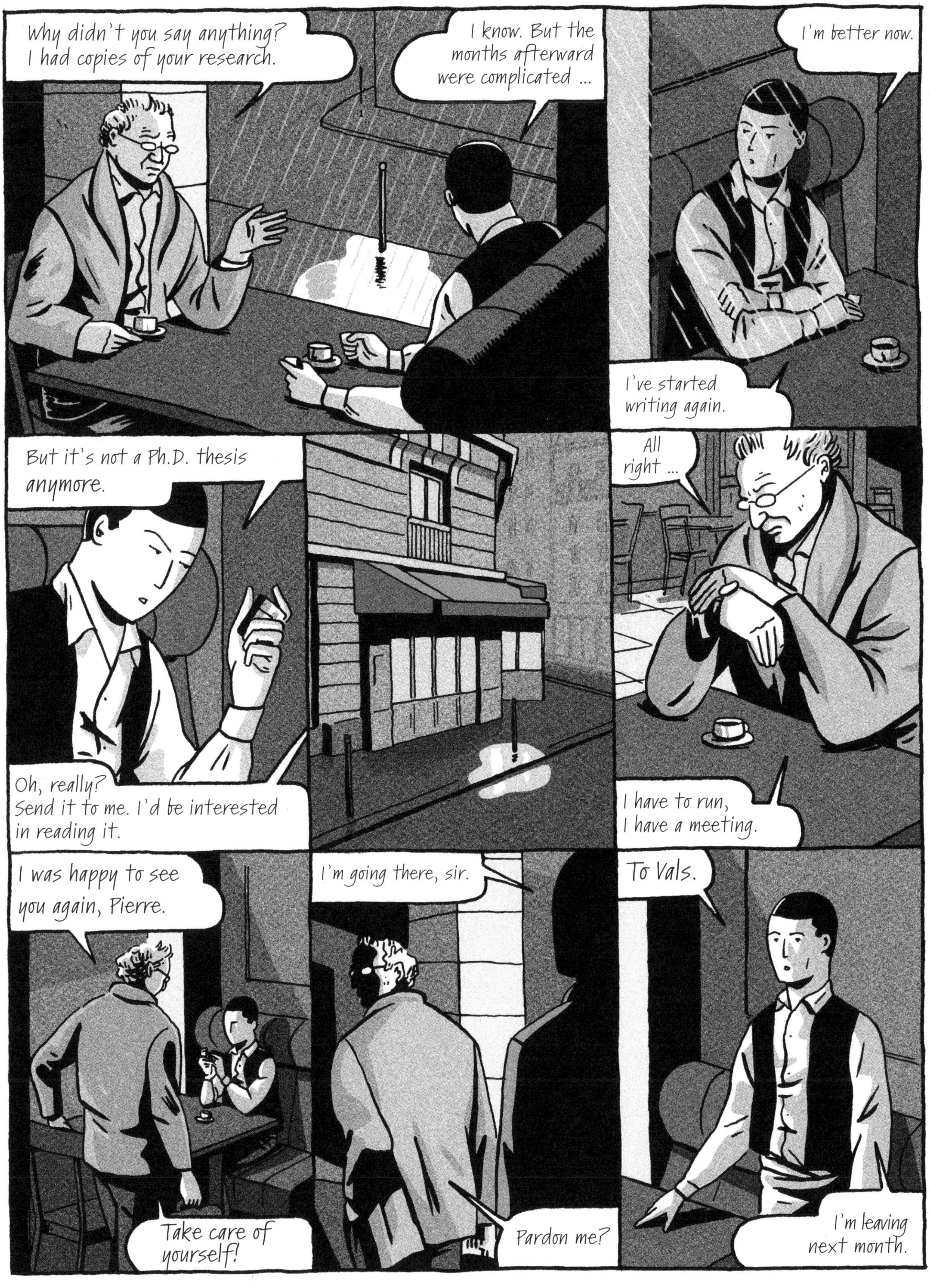
Why didn't you say anything? I had copies of your research.
I know. But the months afterward were complicated ...
I'm better now.
I've started writing again.
But it's not a Ph.D. thesis anymore.
Oh, really? Send it to me. I'd be interested in reading it.
All right ...
I have to run, I have a meeting.
I was happy to see you again, Pierre.
Take care of yourself!
I'm going there, sir.
Pardon me?
To Vals.
I'm leaving next month.

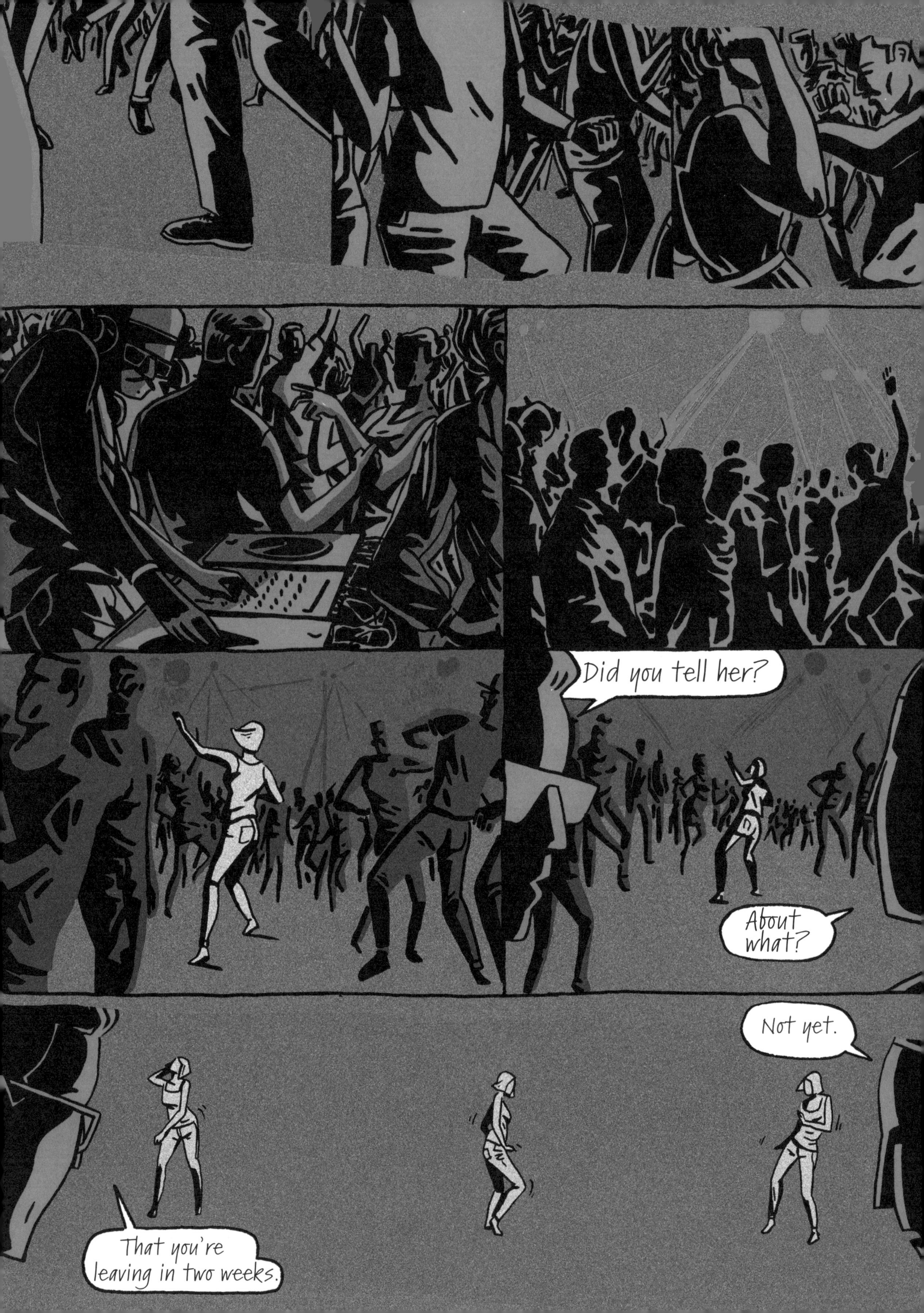
Did you tell her?
About what?
That you're leaving in two weeks.
Not yet.

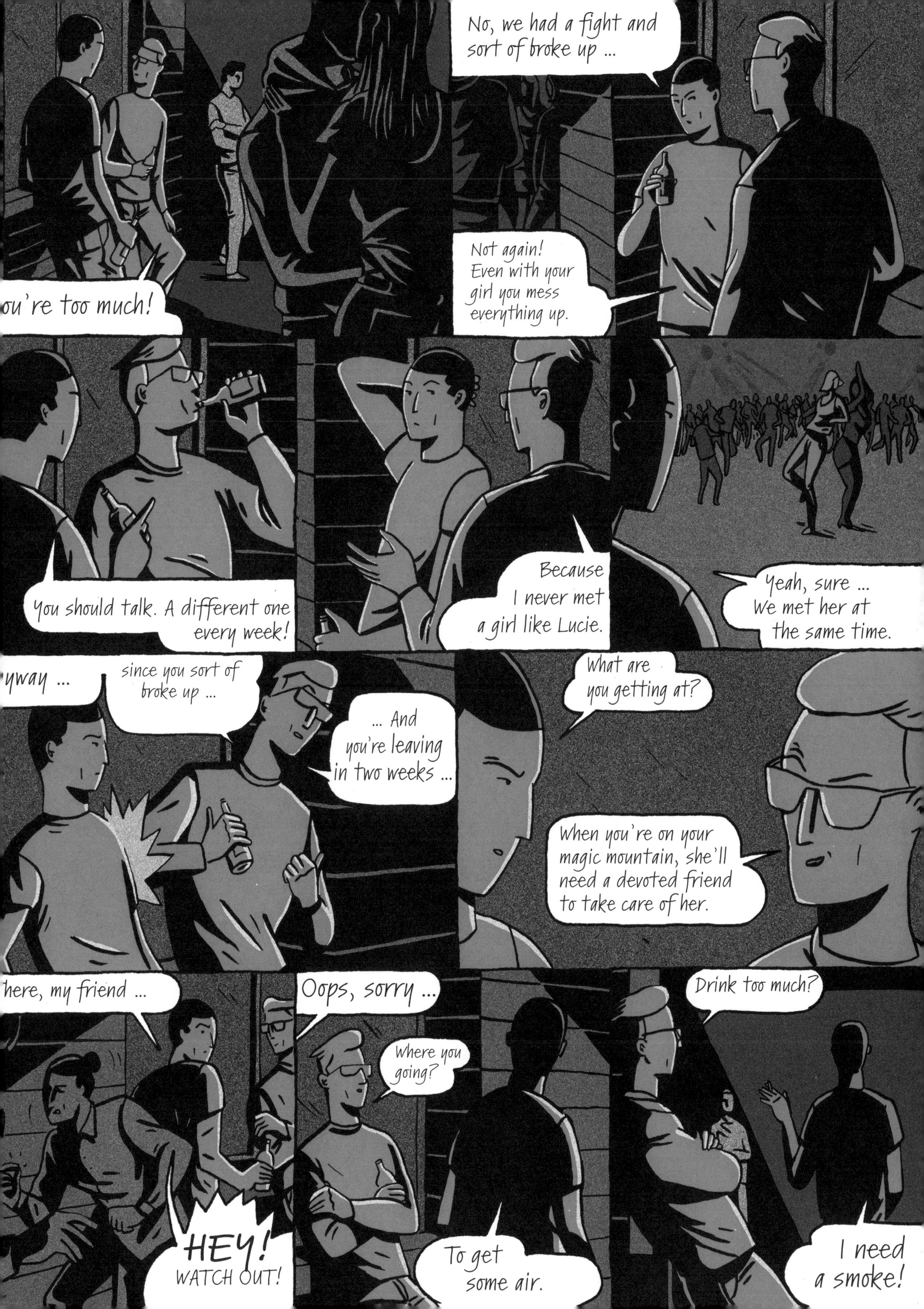
ou're too much!
No, we had a fight and sort of broke up ...
Not again! Even with your girl you mess everything up.
You should talk. A different one every week!
Because I never met a girl like Lucie.
Yeah, sure ... We met her at the same time.
yway ...
since you sort of broke up ...
... And you're leaving in two weeks ...
What are you getting at?
When you're on your magic mountain, she'll need a devoted friend to take care of her.
here, my friend ...
HEY! WATCH OUT!
Oops, sorry ...
Where you going?
To get some air.
Drink too much?
I need a smoke!

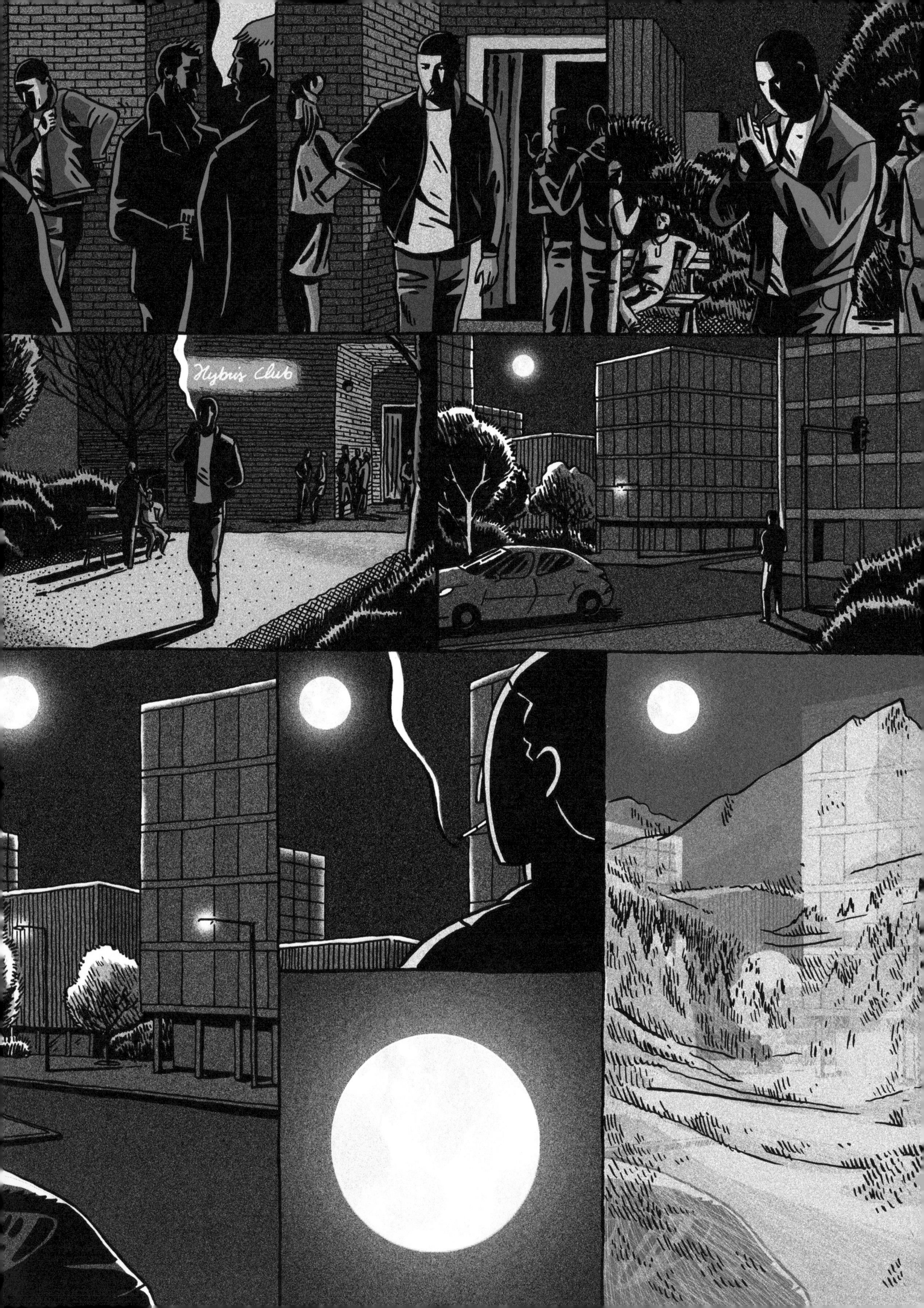
Hybris Club

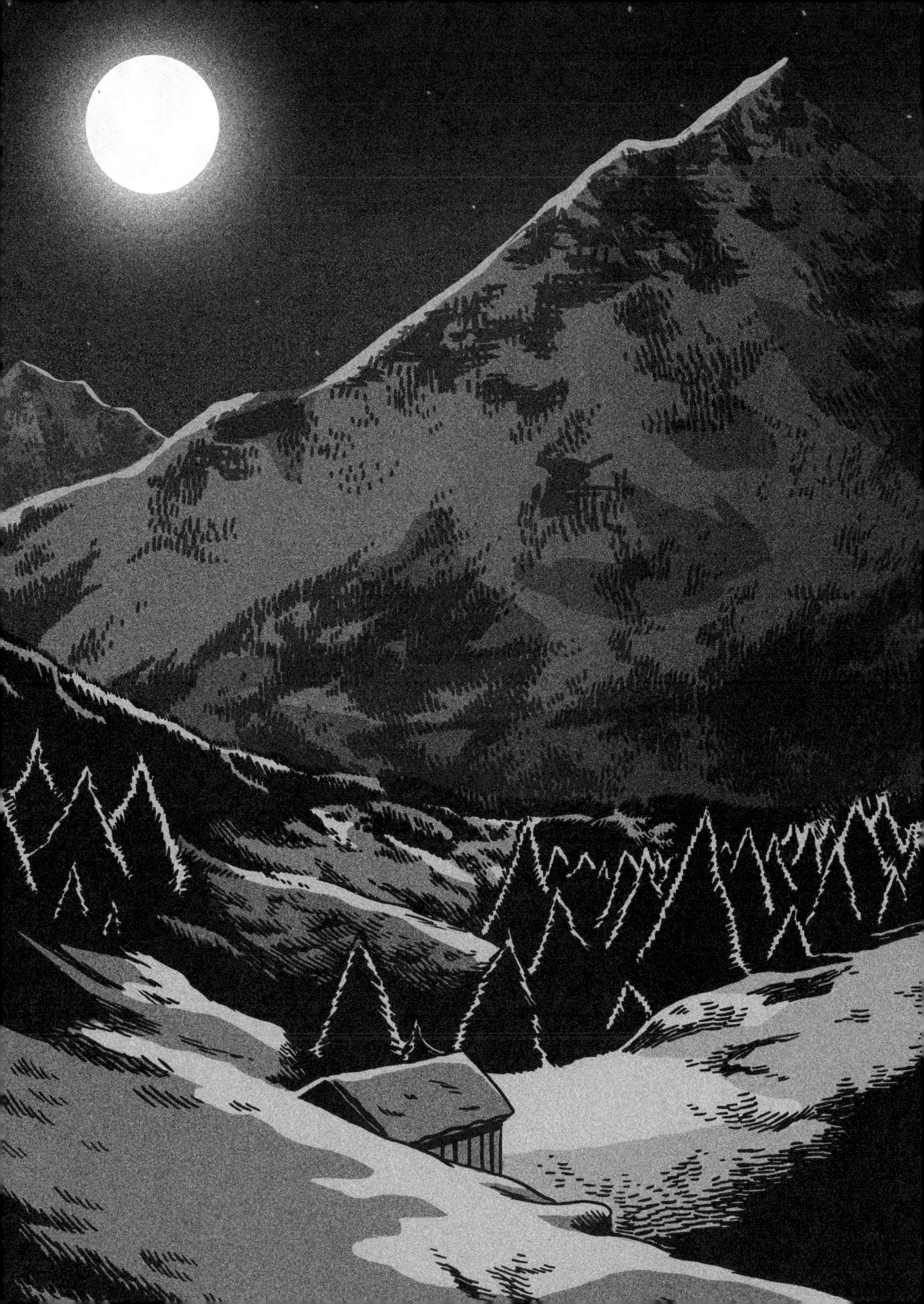

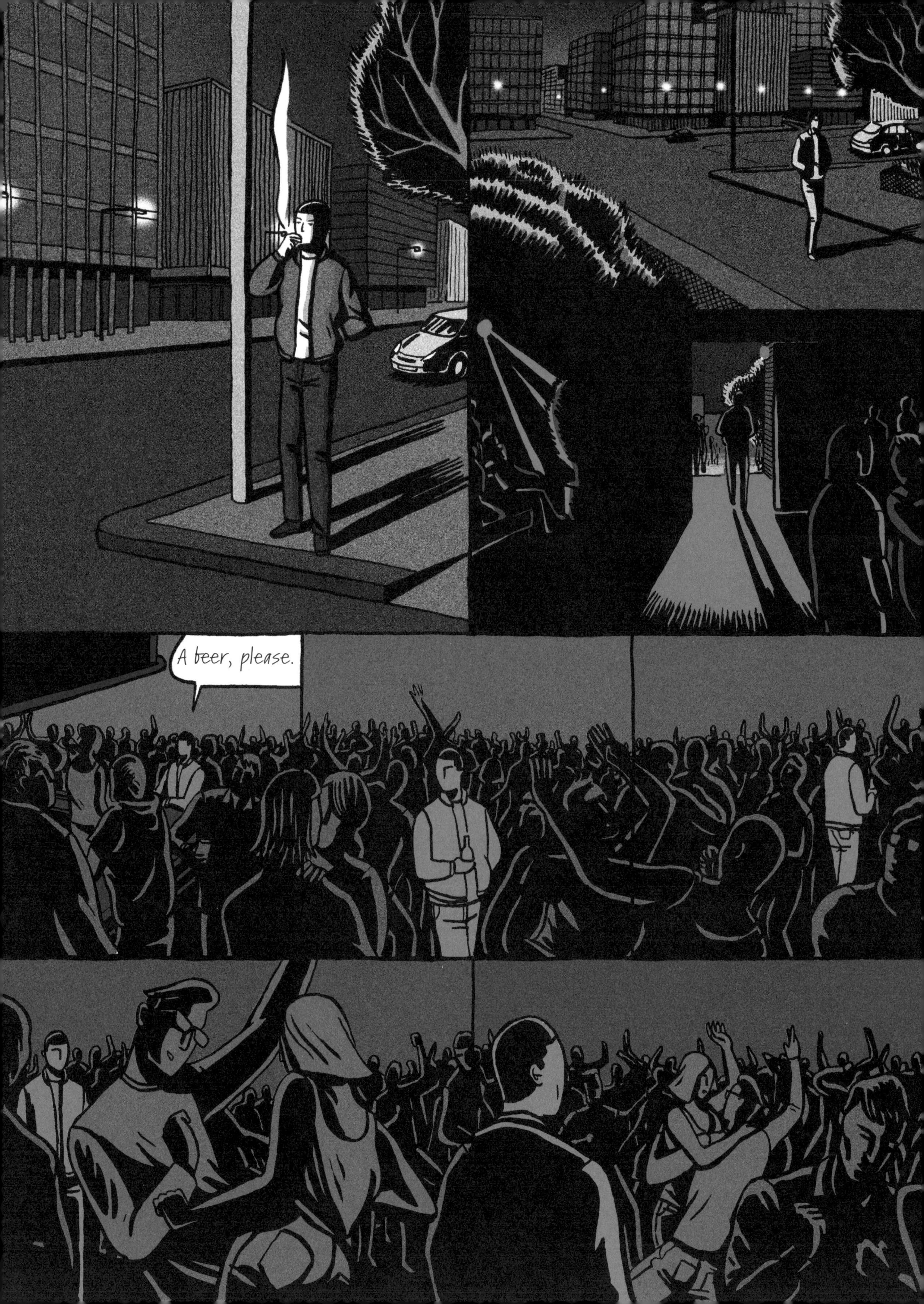
A beer, please.

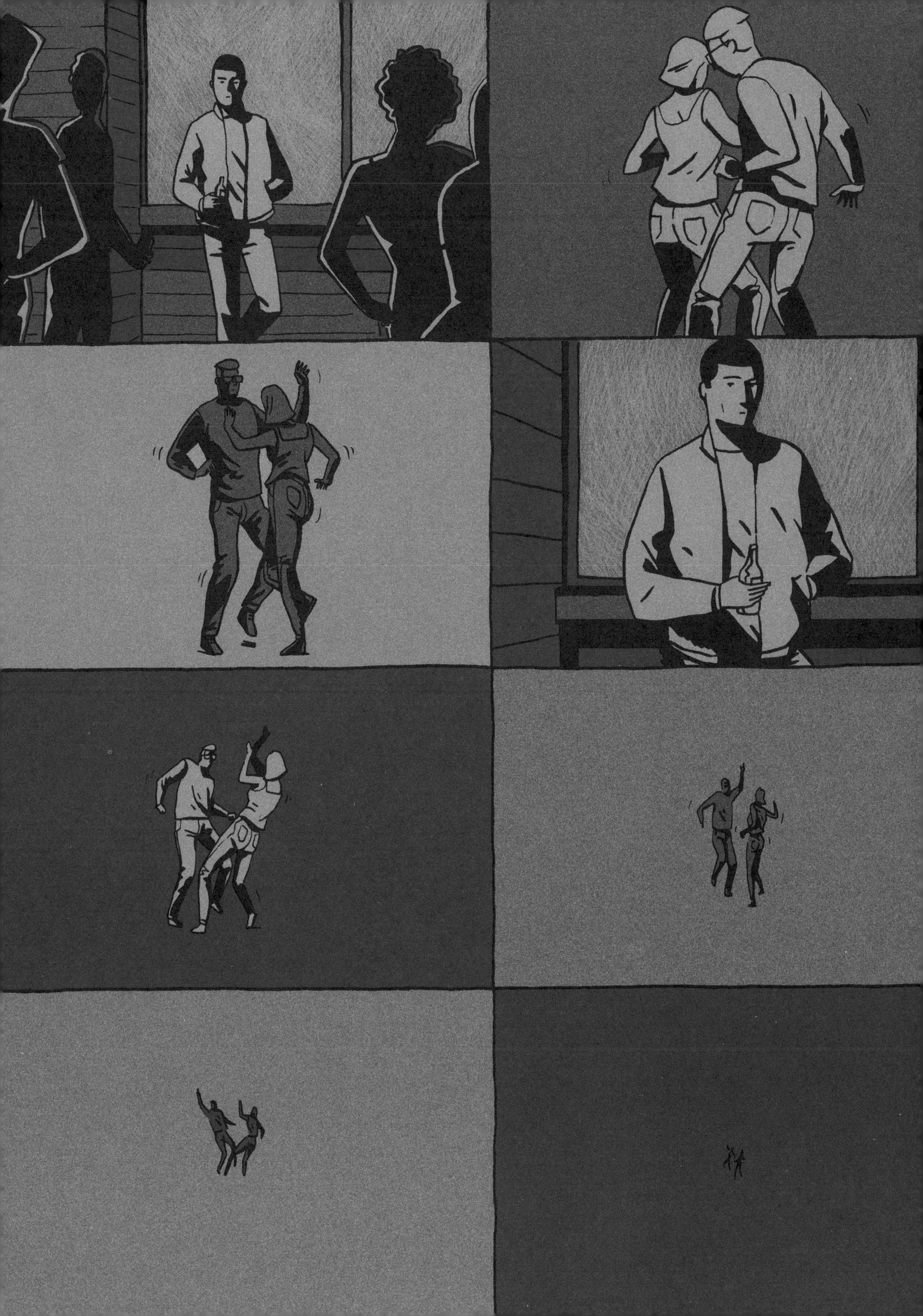

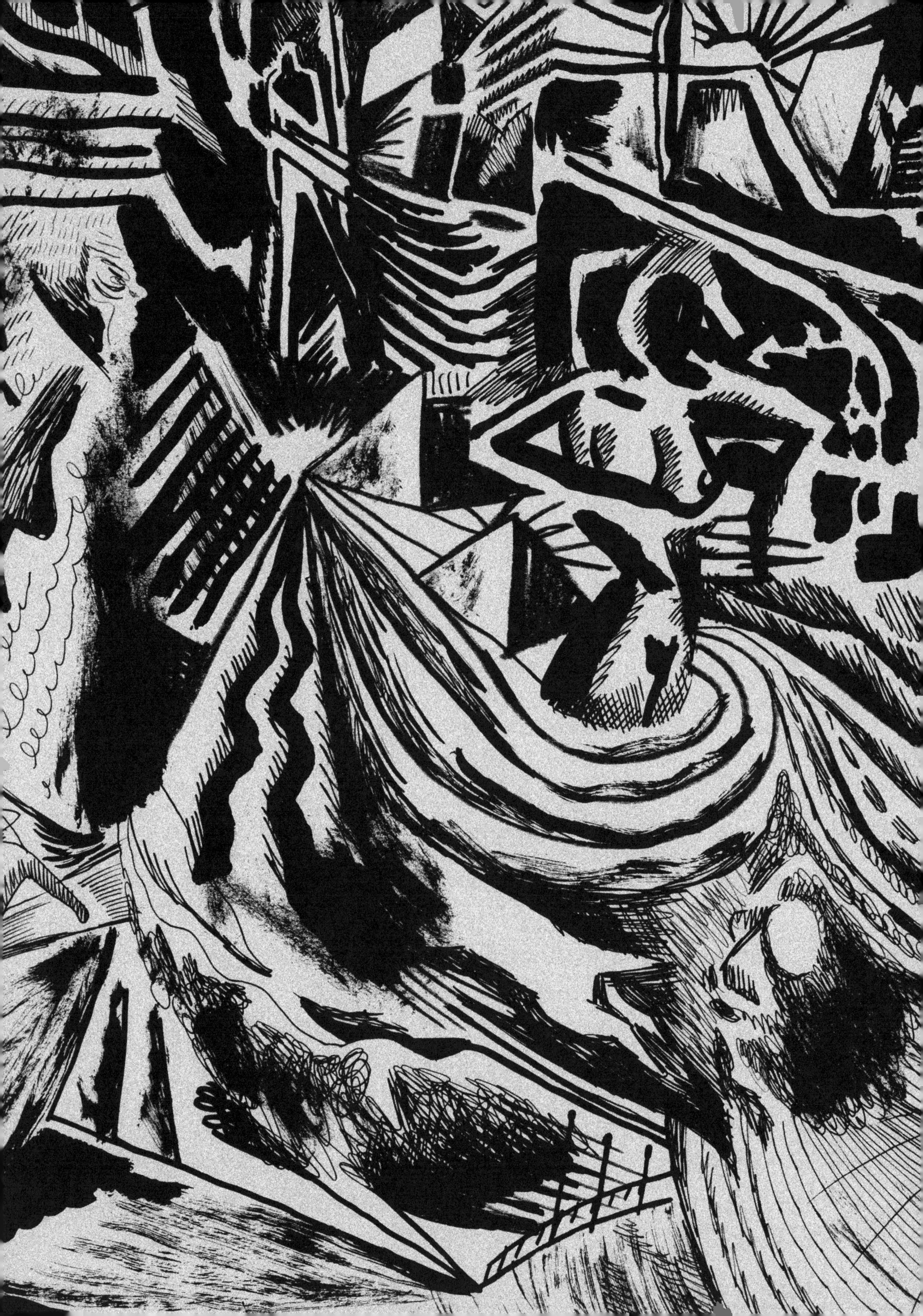

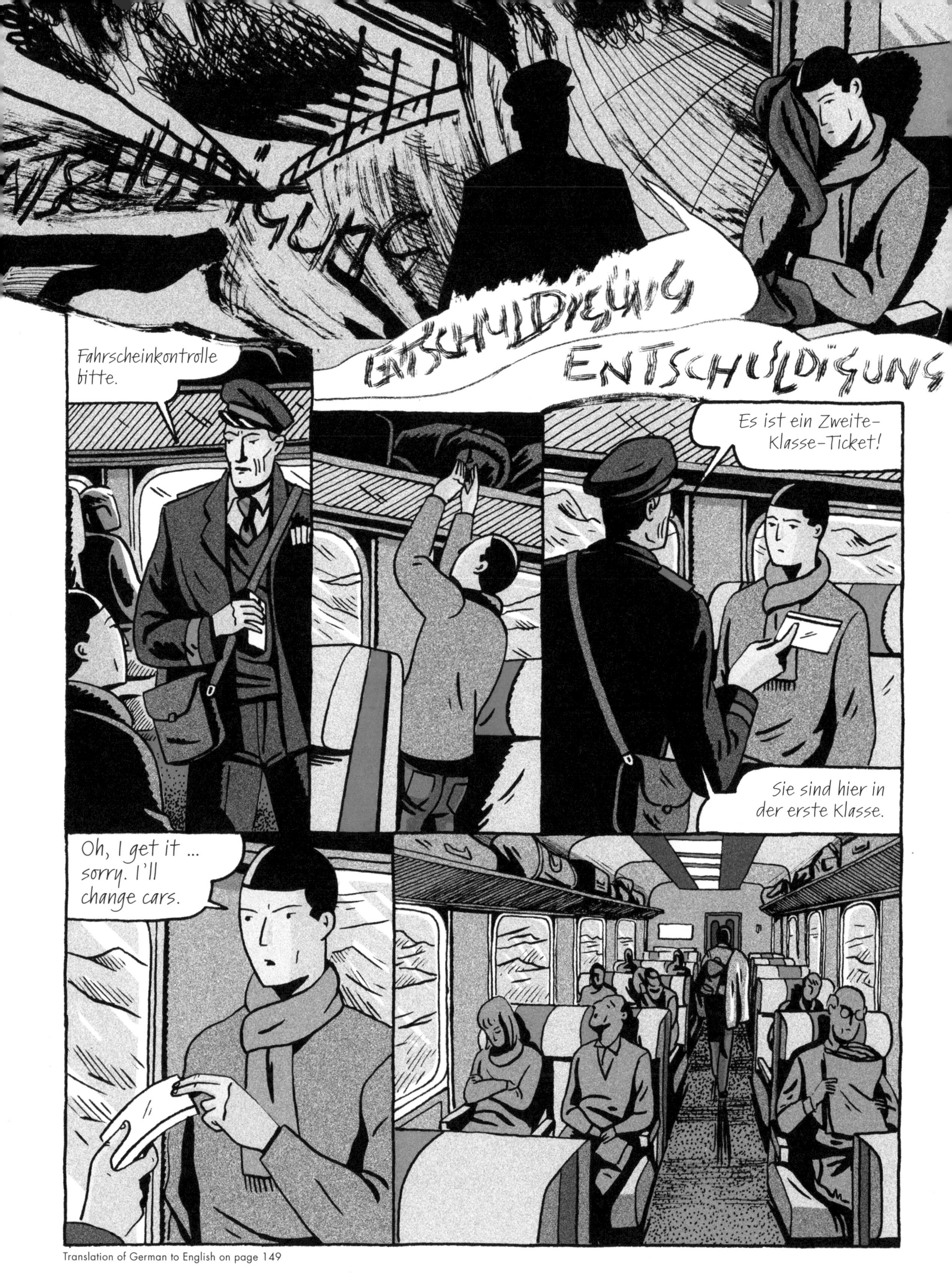
ENTSCHULDIGUNG
ENTSCHULDIGUNG
Fahrscheinkontrolle bitte.
Es ist ein Zweite-Klasse-Ticket!
Sie sind hier in der erste Klasse.
Oh, I get it ... sorry. I'll change cars.

Translation of German to English on page 149

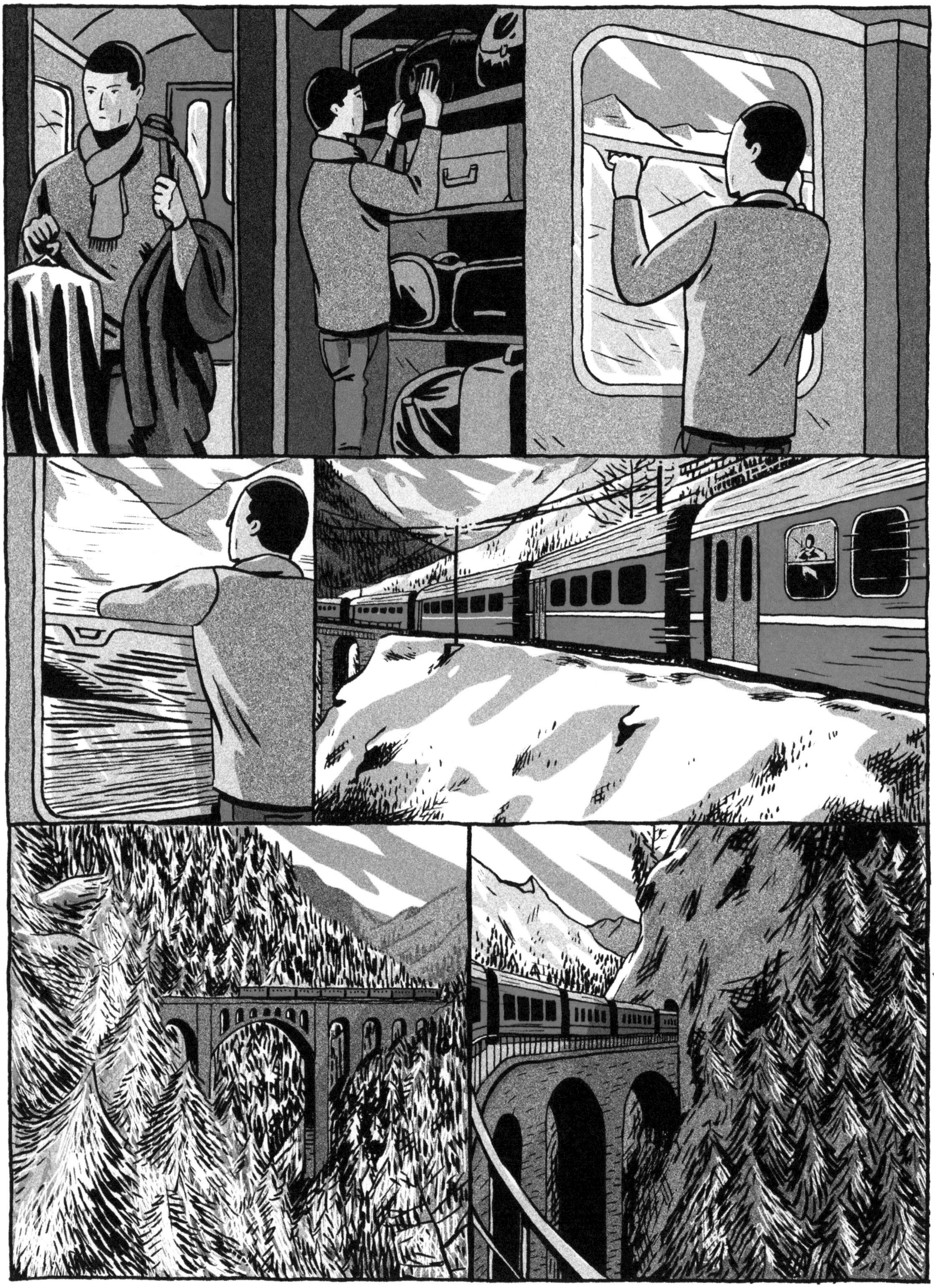

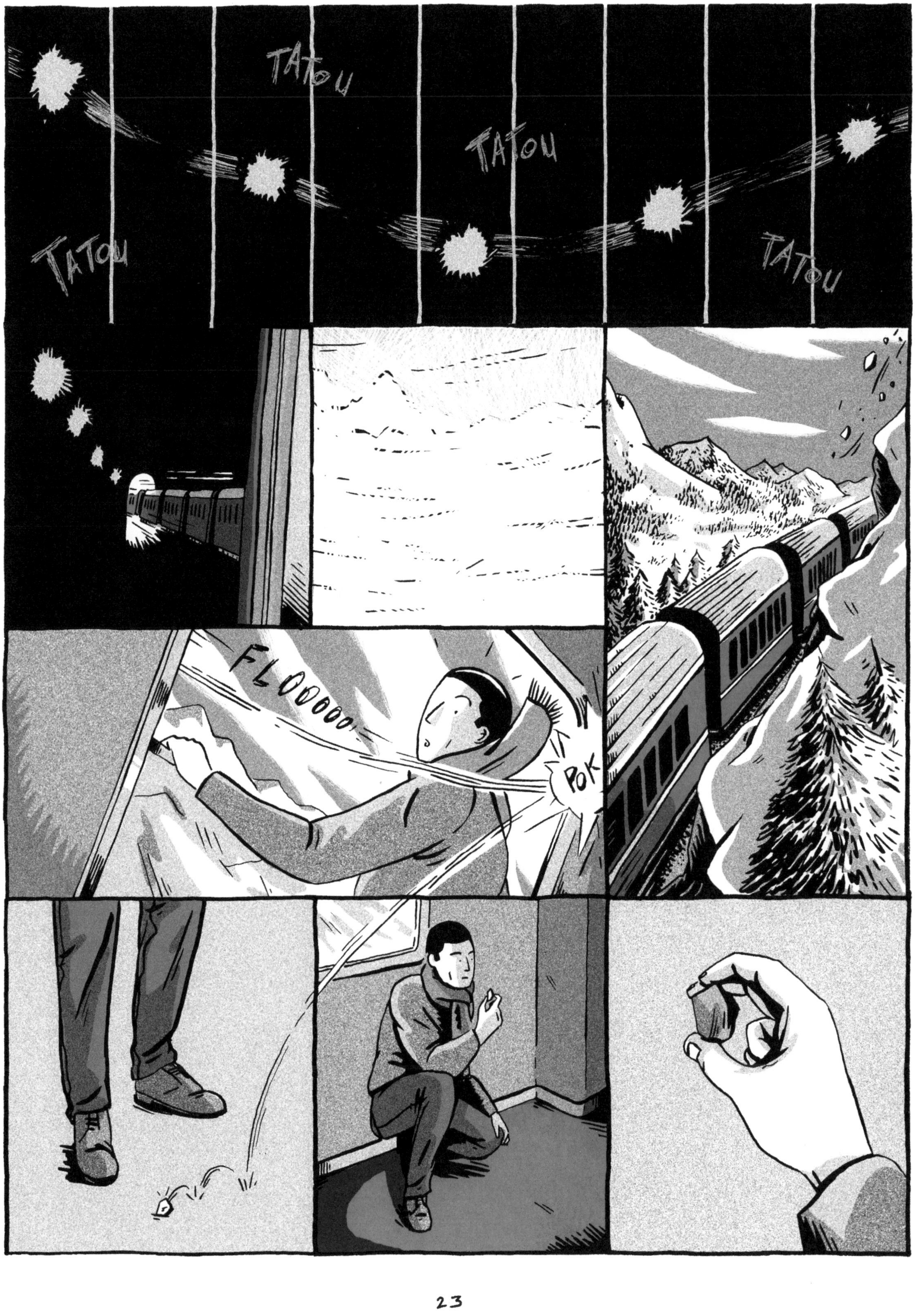
TATOU
TATOU
TATOU
TATOU
FLOOOOOO
POK

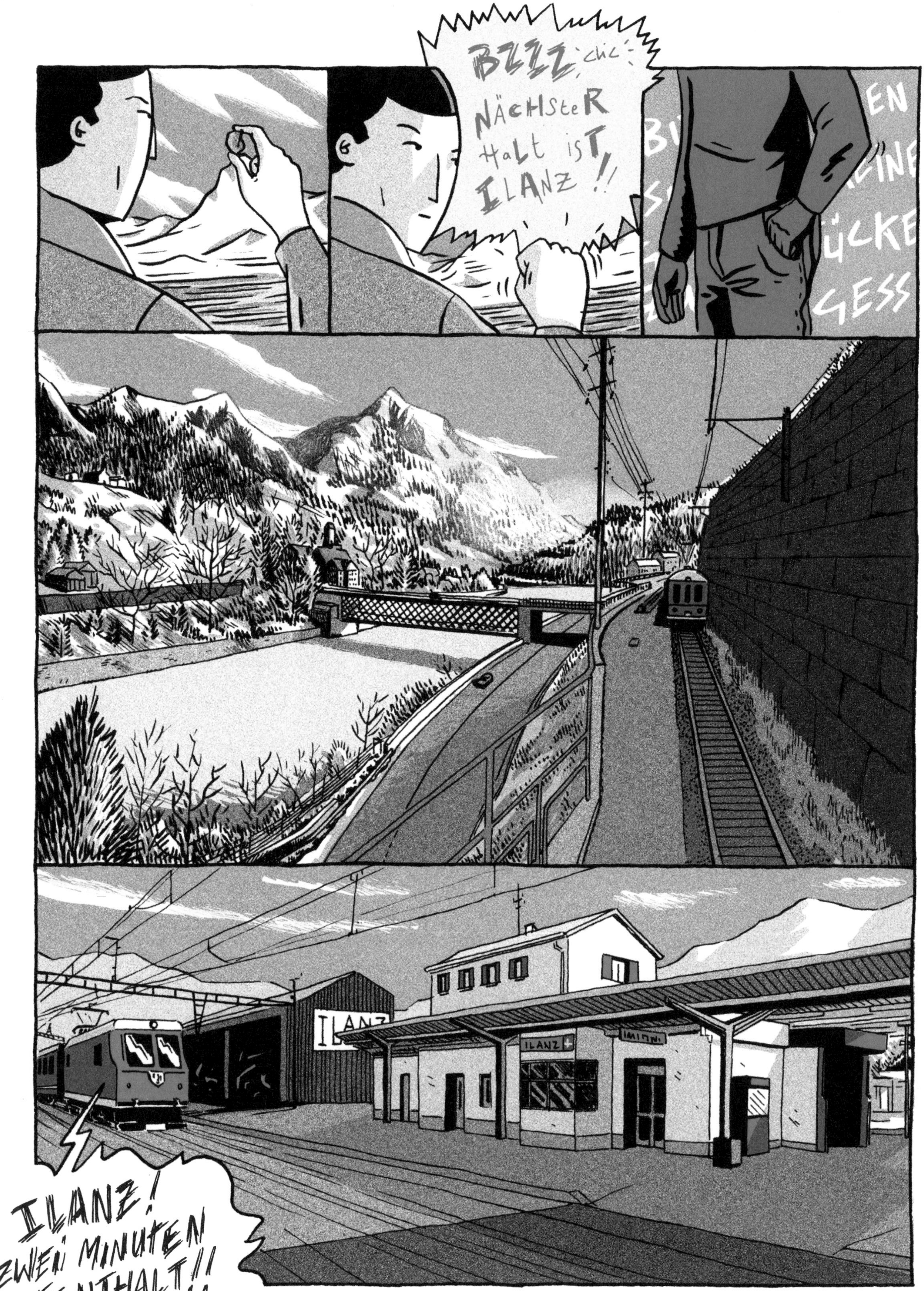
BZZZ
NÄCHSTER HALT IST ILANZ!!
ILANZ
ILANZ
ILANZ! ZWEI MINUTEN AUFENTHALT!!

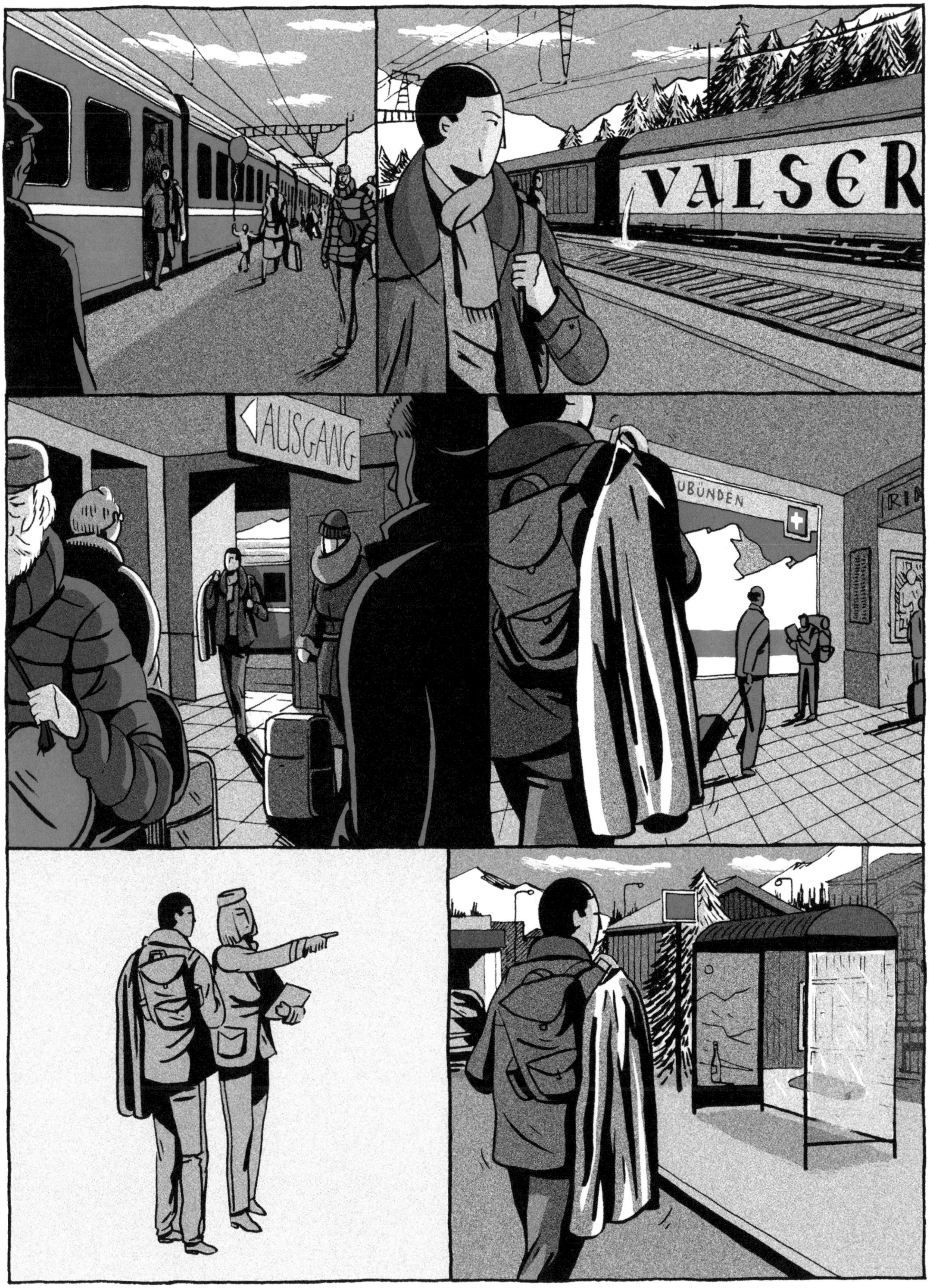
VALSER
AUSGANG

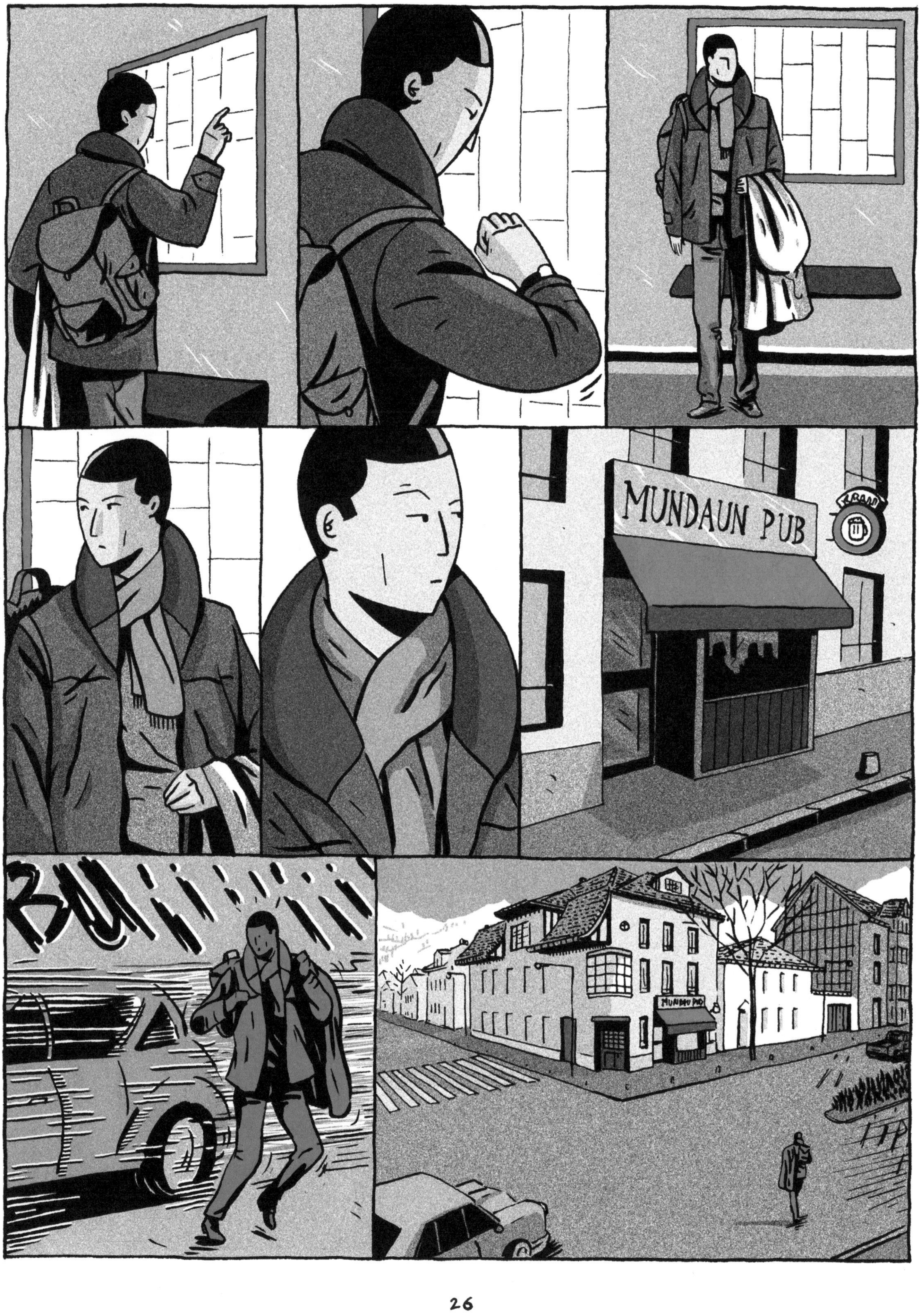
MUNDAUN PUB

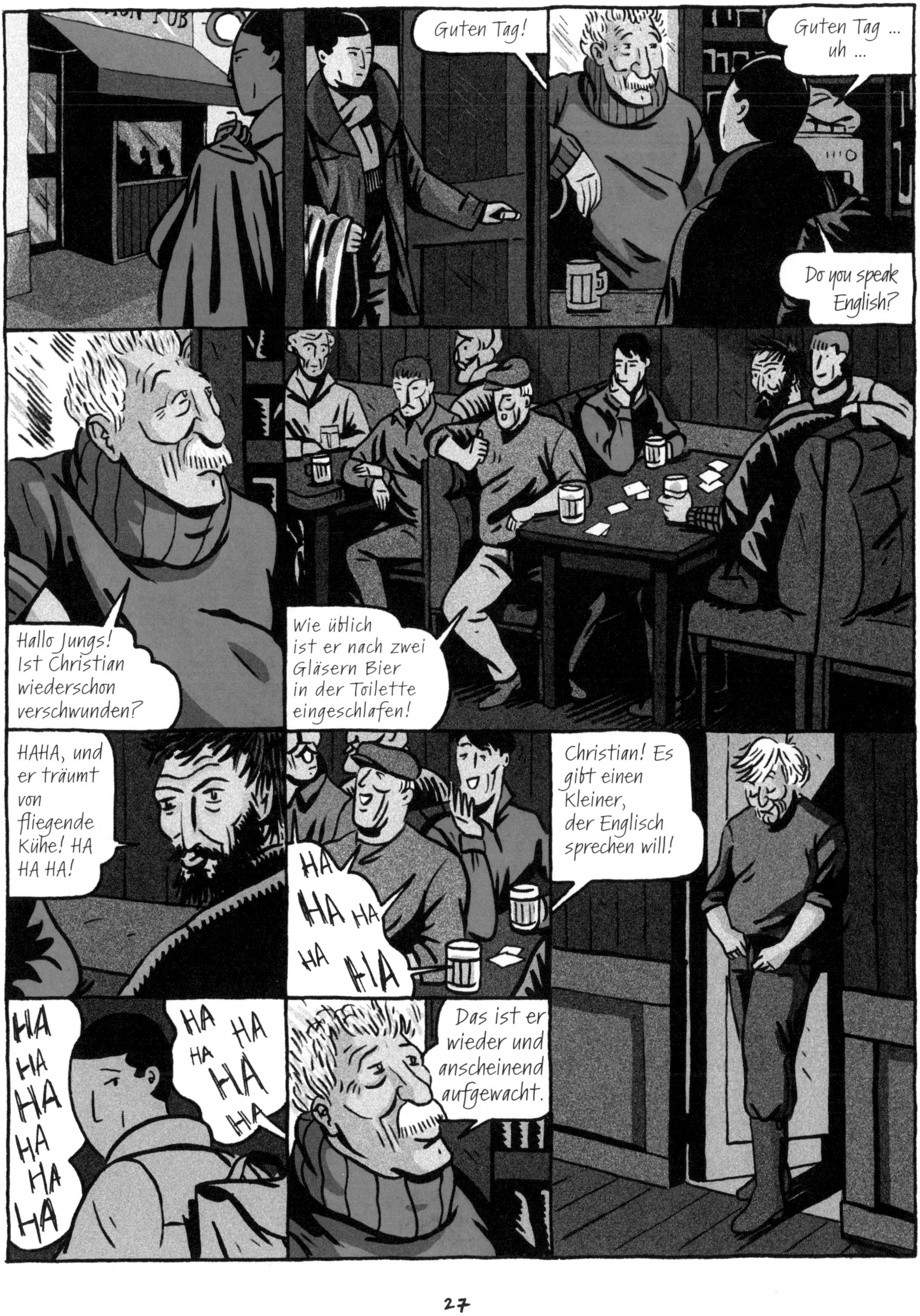
Guten Tag!
Guten Tag … uh …
Do you speak English?
Hallo Jungs! Ist Christian wiederschon verschwunden?
Wie üblich ist er nach zwei Gläsern Bier in der Toilette eingeschlafen!
HAHA, und er träumt von fliegende Kühe! HA HA HA!
HA HA HA HA HA
Christian! Es gibt einen Kleiner, der Englisch sprechen will!
HA HA HA HA HA HA HA
HA HA HA HA HA
Das ist er wieder und anscheinend aufgewacht.

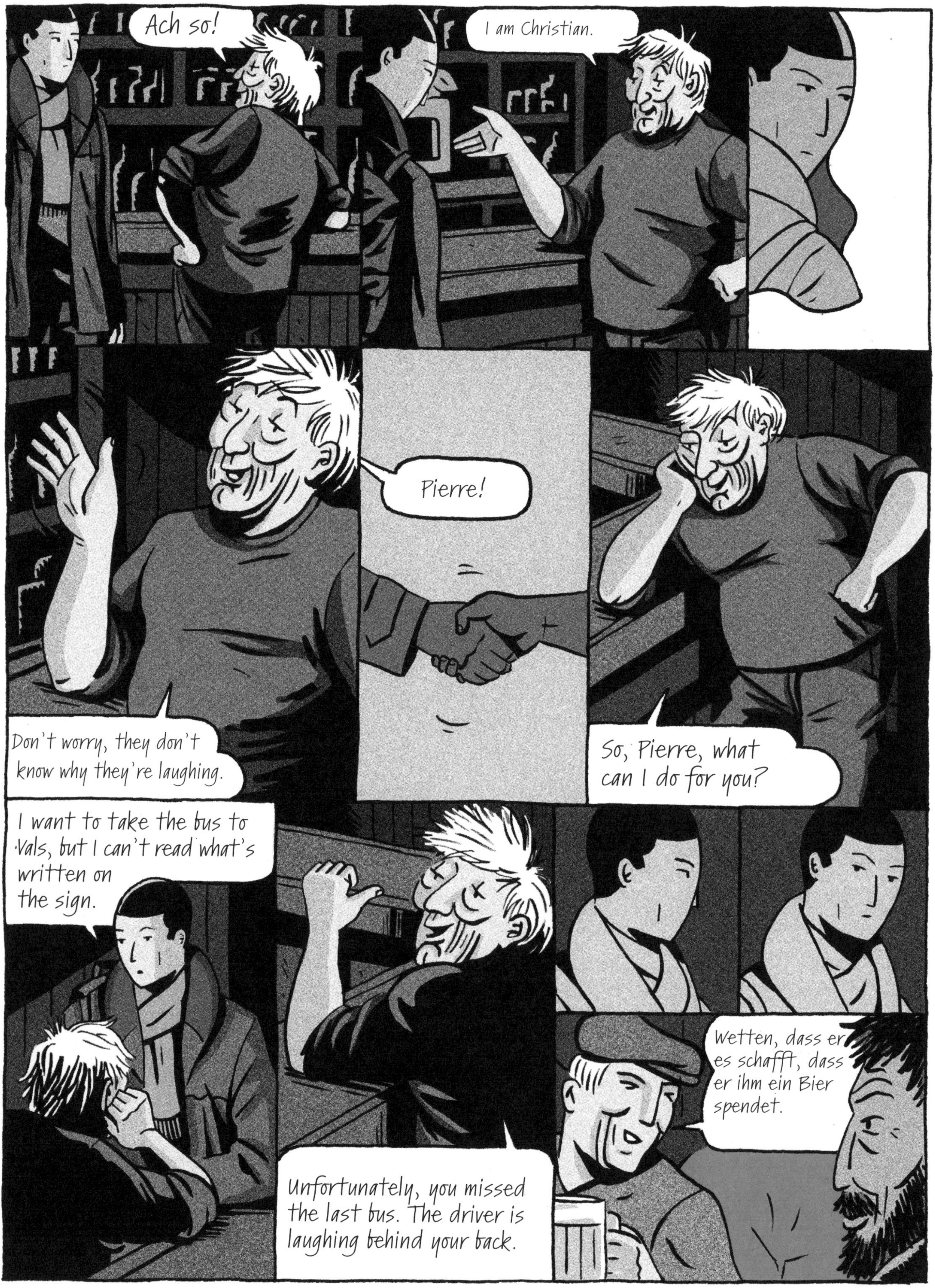
Ach so!
I am Christian.
Pierre!
Don't worry, they don't know why they're laughing.
So, Pierre, what can I do for you?
I want to take the bus to Vals, but I can't read what's written on the sign.
Unfortunately, you missed the last bus. The driver is laughing behind your back.
Wetten, dass er es schafft, dass er ihm ein Bier spendet.

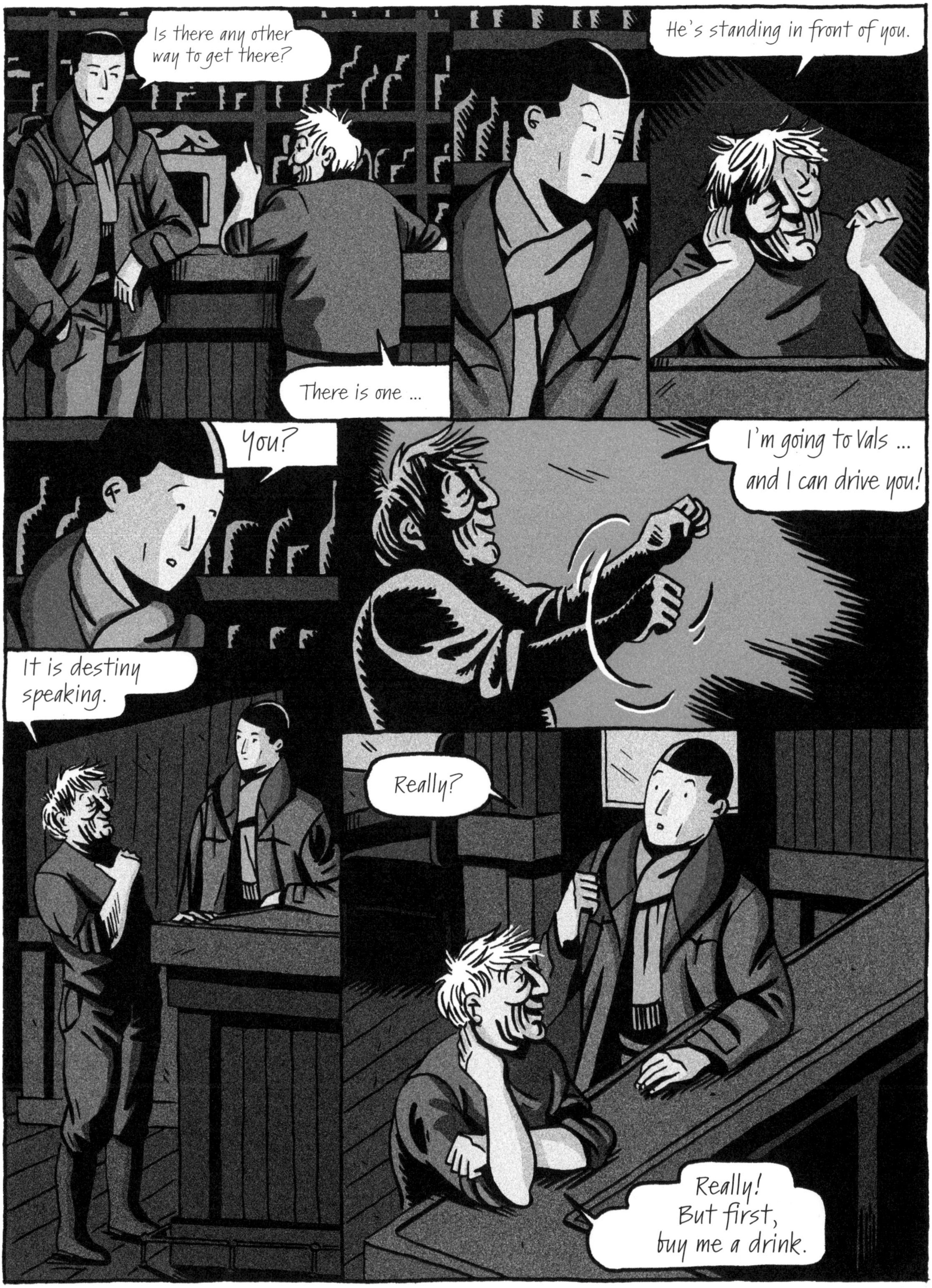
Is there any other way to get there?
There is one ...
He's standing in front of you.
You?
I'm going to Vals ... and I can drive you!
It is destiny speaking.
Really?
Really! But first, buy me a drink.

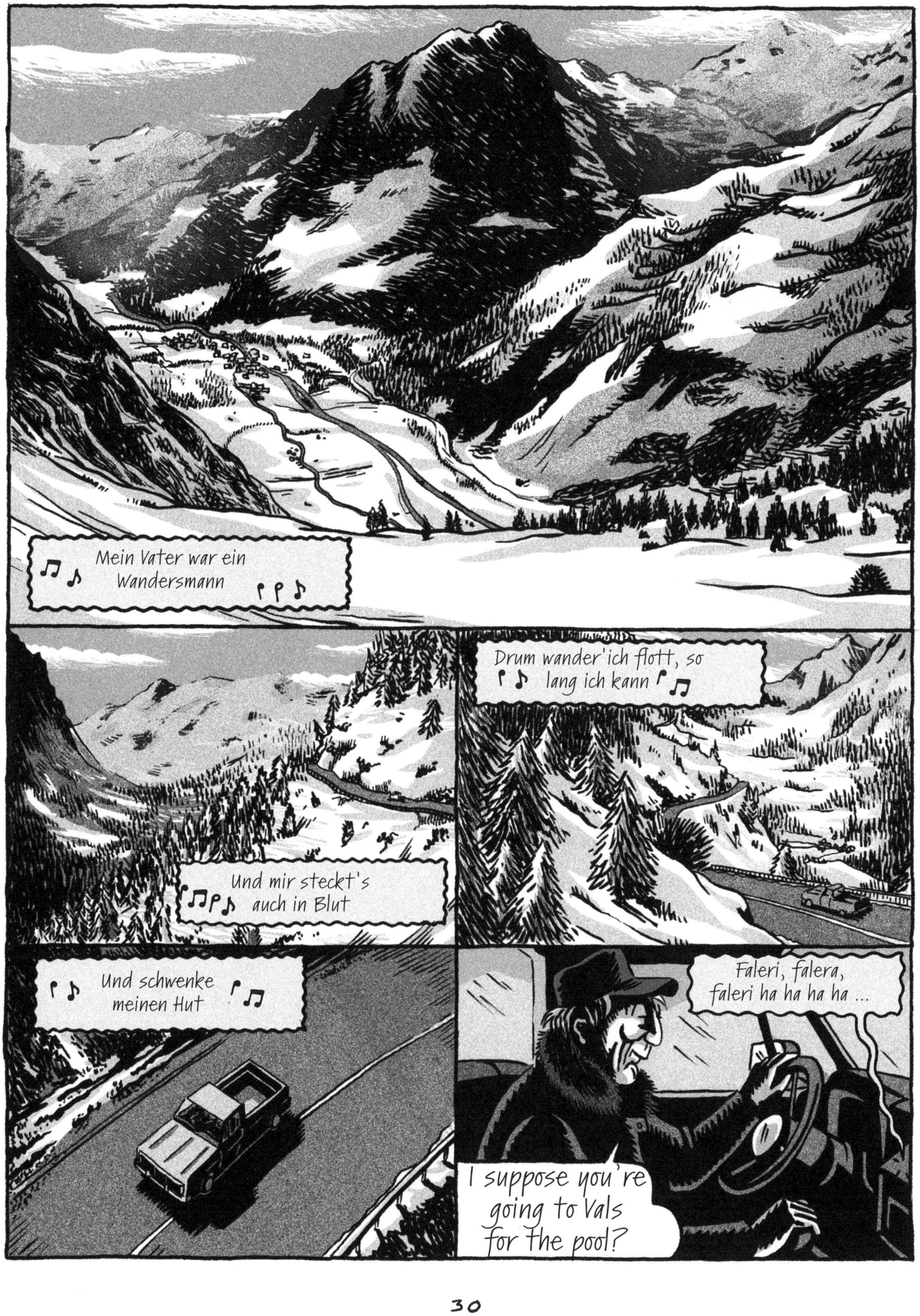
Mein Vater war ein Wandersmann
Und mir steckt's auch in Blut
Drum wander' ich flott, so lang ich kann
Und schwenke meinen Hut
Faleri, falera, faleri ha ha ha ha ...
I suppose you're going to Vals for the pool?

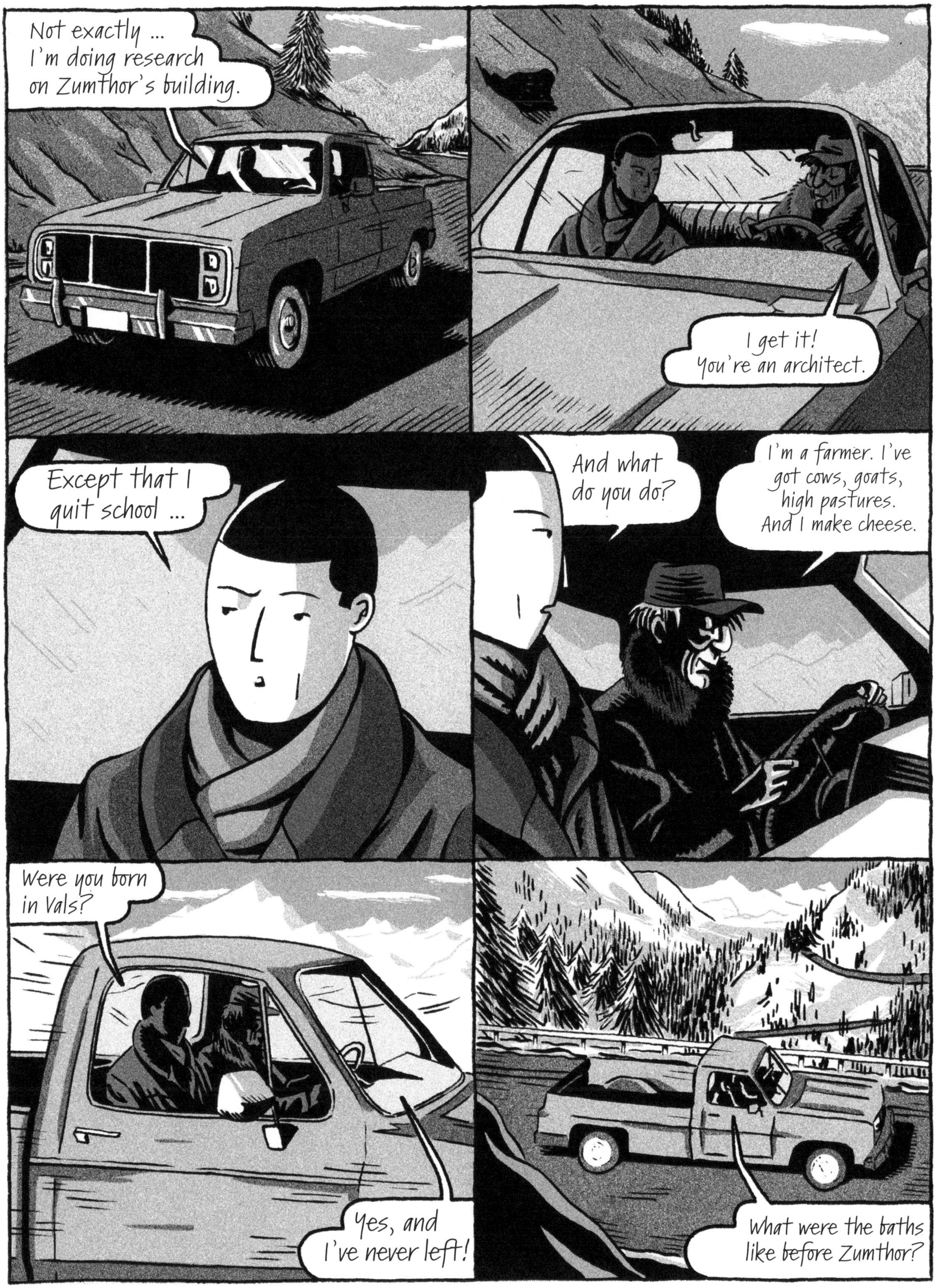
Not exactly ...
I'm doing research on Zumthor's building.
I get it! You're an architect.
Except that I quit school ...
And what do you do?
I'm a farmer. I've got cows, goats, high pastures. And I make cheese.
Were you born in Vals?
Yes, and I've never left!
What were the baths like before Zumthor?

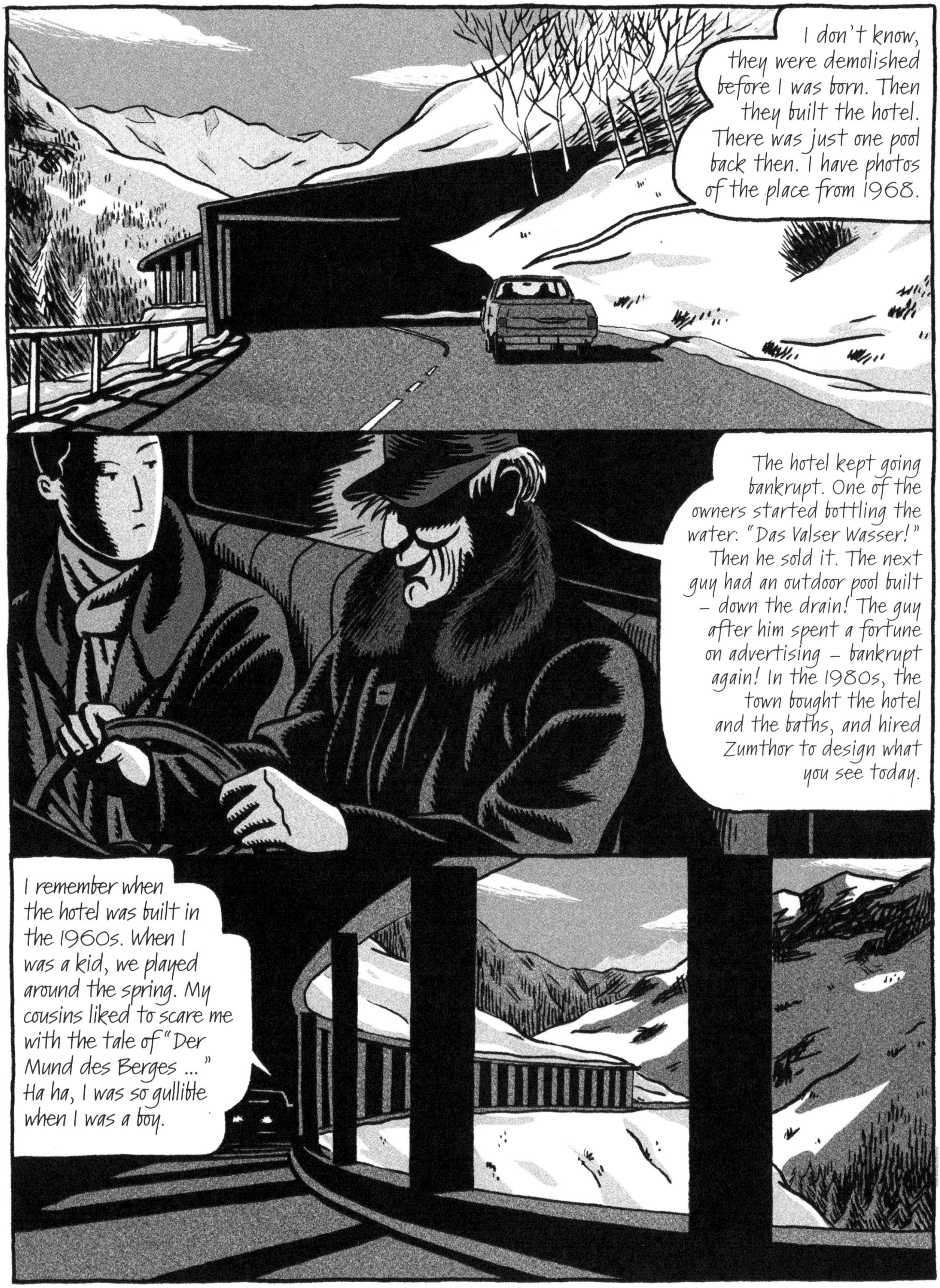
I don't know, they were demolished before I was born. Then they built the hotel. There was just one pool back then. I have photos of the place from 1968.
The hotel kept going bankrupt. One of the owners started bottling the water: "Das Valser Wasser!" Then he sold it. The next guy had an outdoor pool built – down the drain! The guy after him spent a fortune on advertising – bankrupt again! In the 1980s, the town bought the hotel and the baths, and hired Zumthor to design what you see today.
I remember when the hotel was built in the 1960s. When I was a kid, we played around the spring. My cousins liked to scare me with the tale of "Der Mund des Berges ..." Ha ha, I was so gullible when I was a boy.

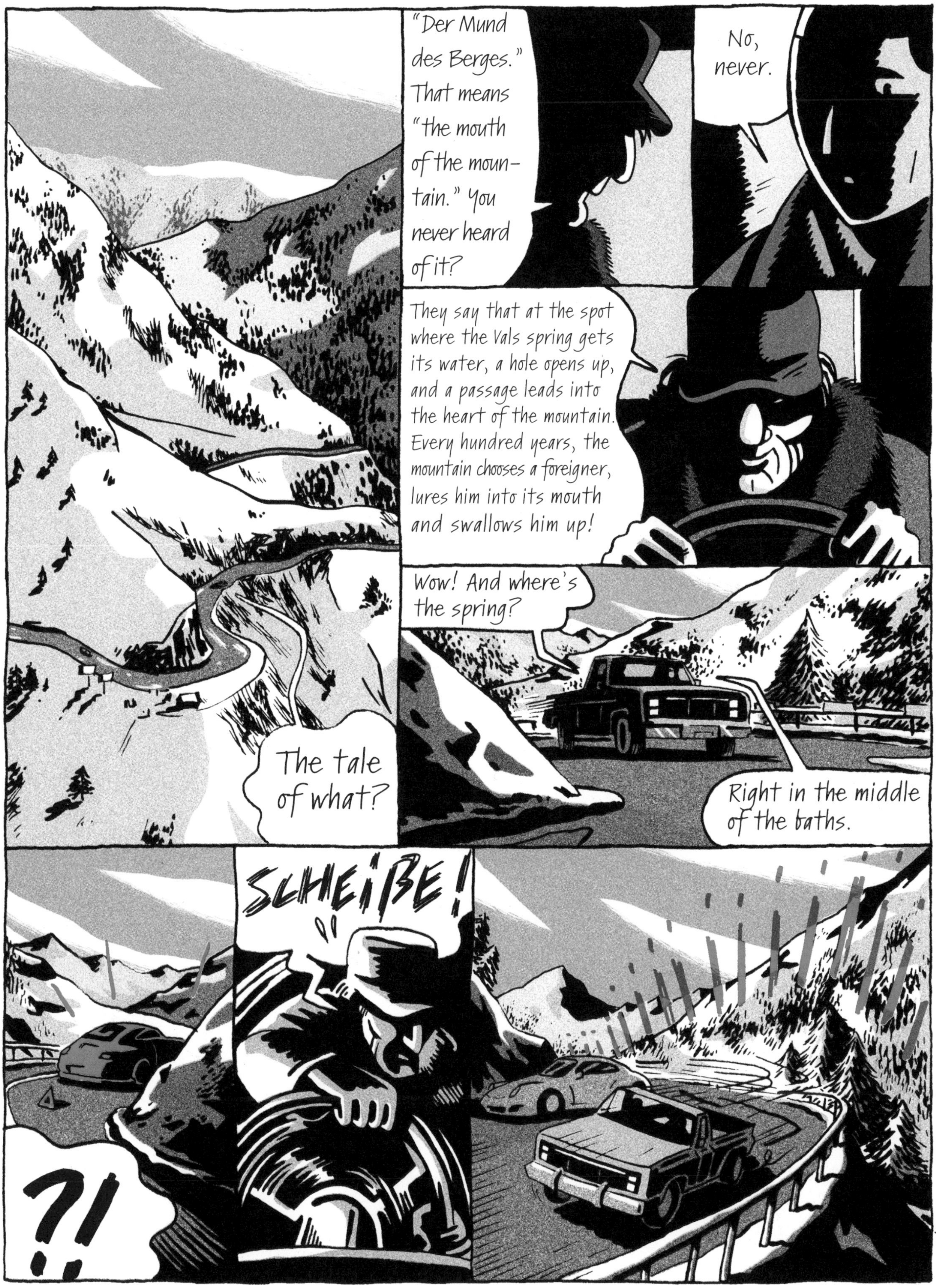
"Der Mund des Berges." That means "the mouth of the mountain." You never heard of it?
No, never.
They say that at the spot where the Vals spring gets its water, a hole opens up, and a passage leads into the heart of the mountain. Every hundred years, the mountain chooses a foreigner, lures him into its mouth and swallows him up!
The tale of what?
Wow! And where's the spring?
Right in the middle of the baths.
?!
SCHEIßE!

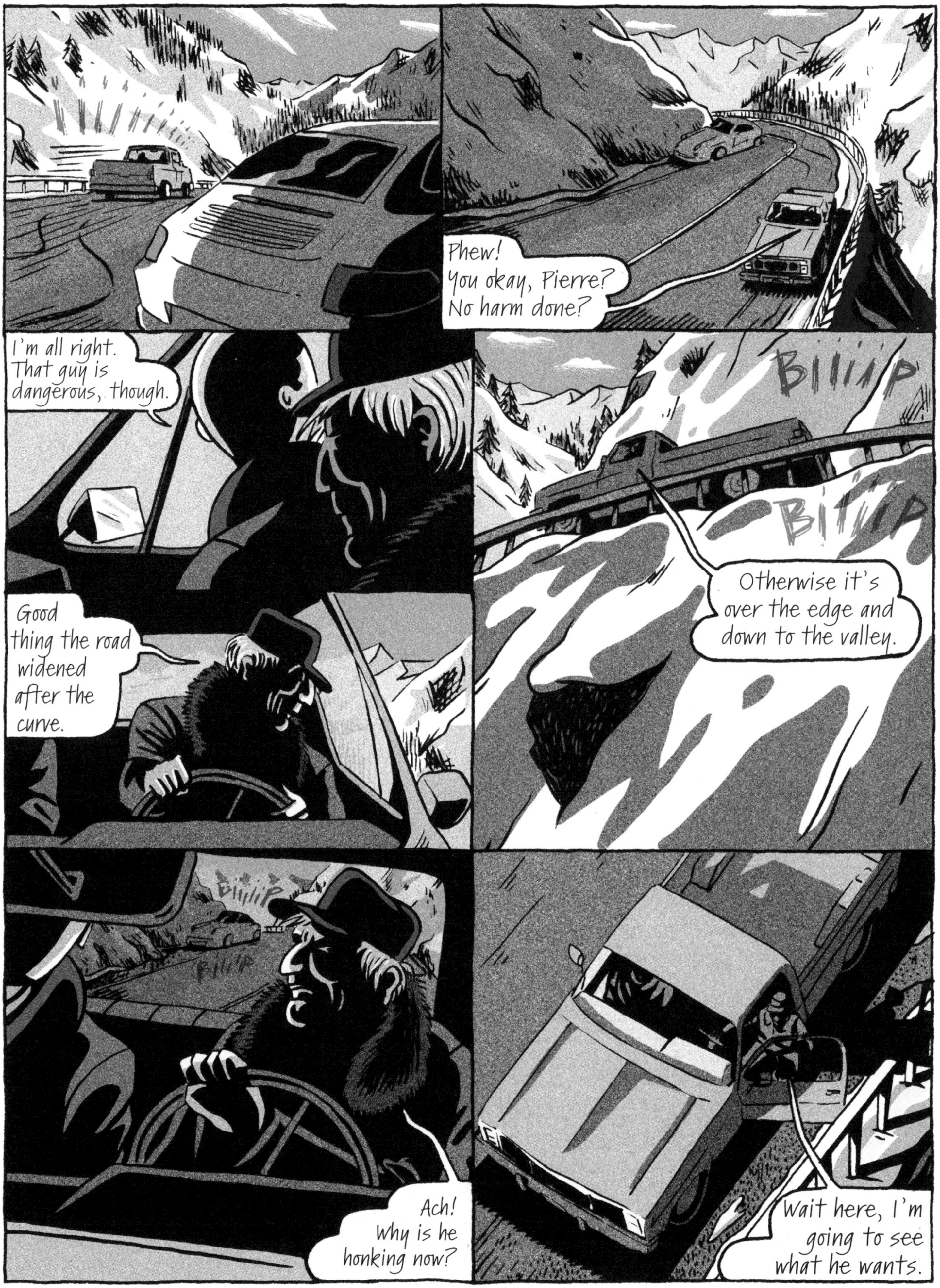

Phew!
You okay, Pierre?
No harm done?
I'm all right.
That guy is
dangerous, though.
BIIIIP
BIIIIP
Otherwise it's over the edge and down to the valley.
Good thing the road widened after the curve.
BIIIIP
BIIIP
Ach! Why is he honking now?
Wait here, I'm going to see what he wants.

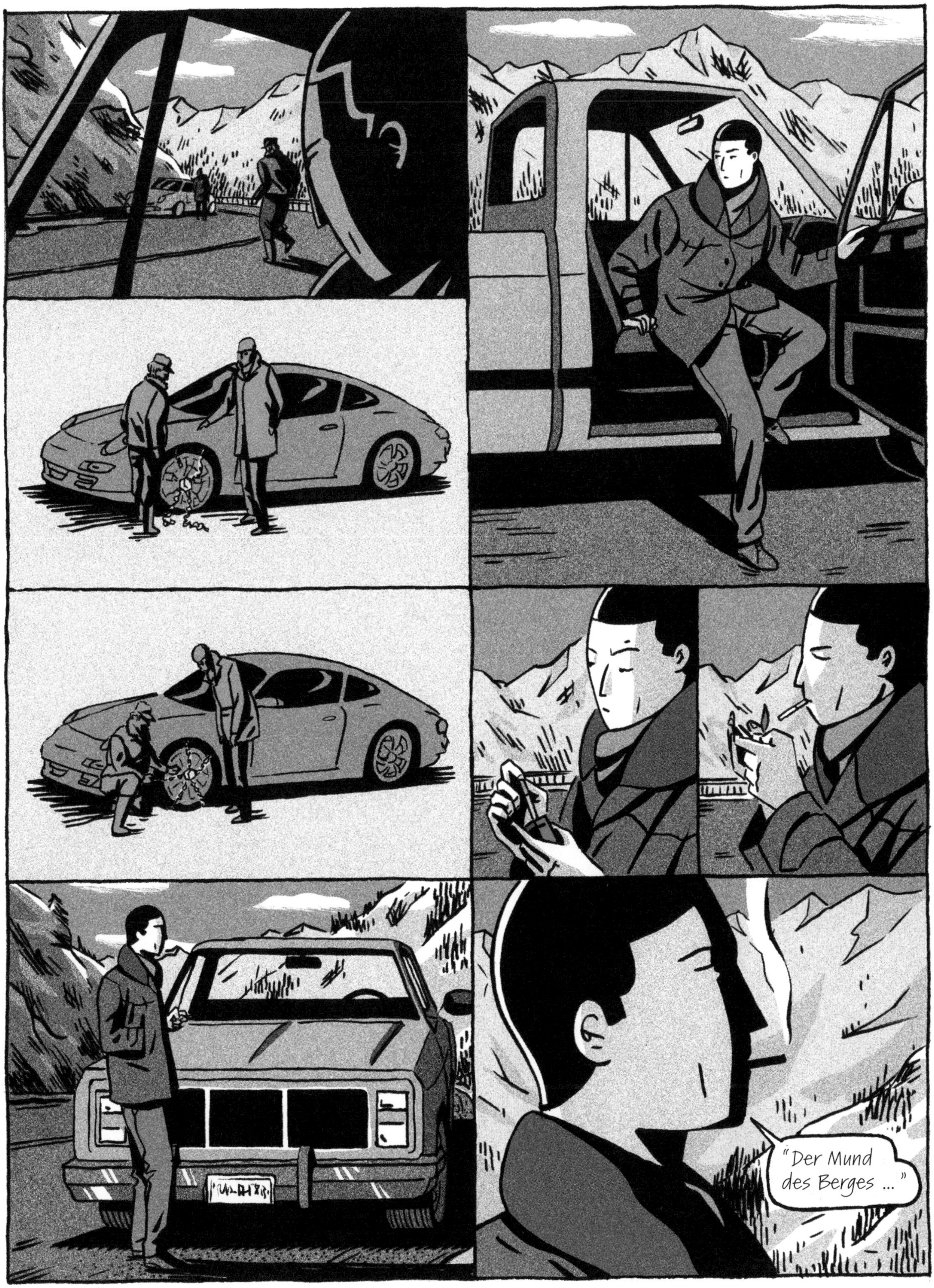
"Der Mund
des Berges ..."

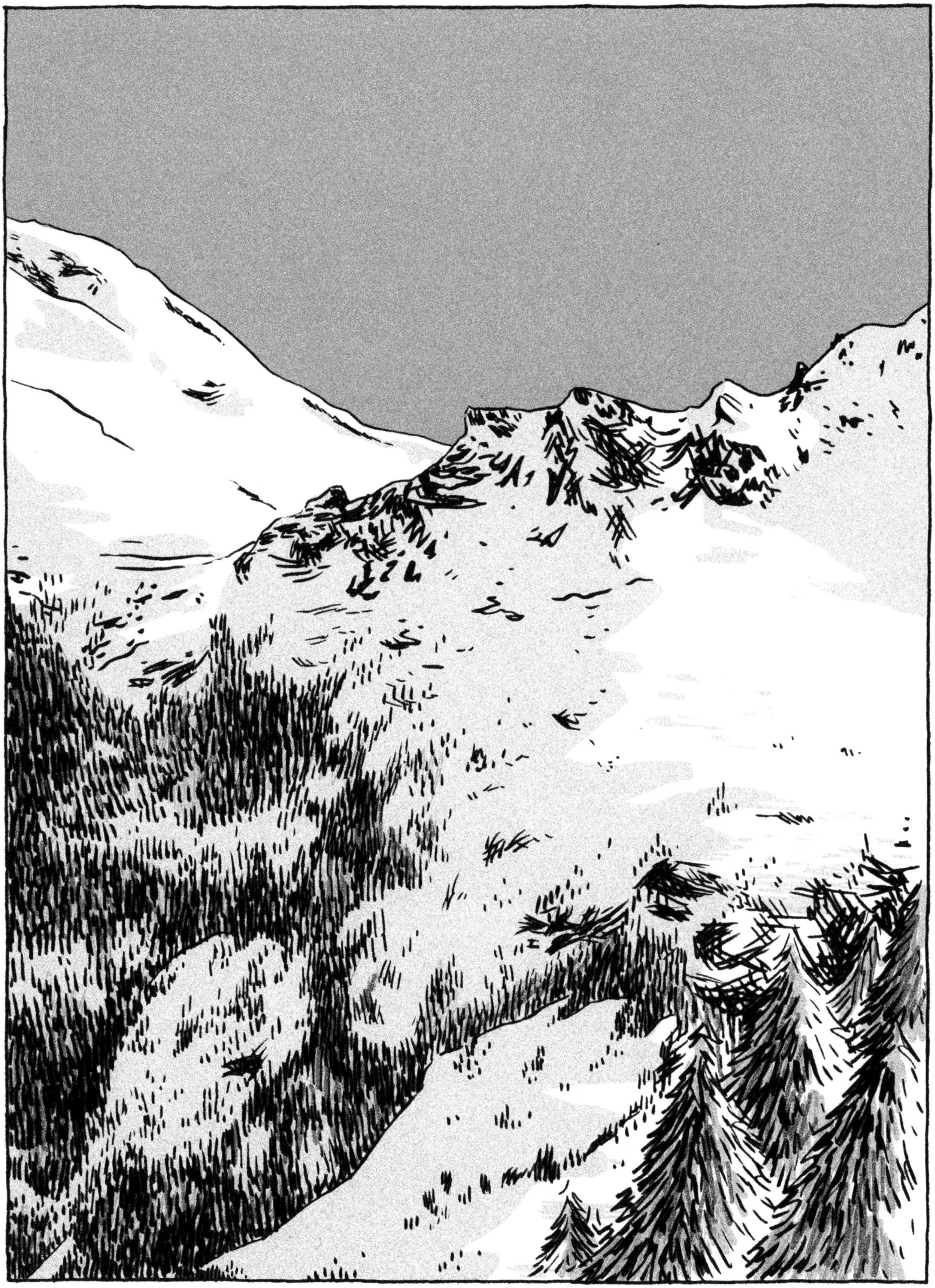

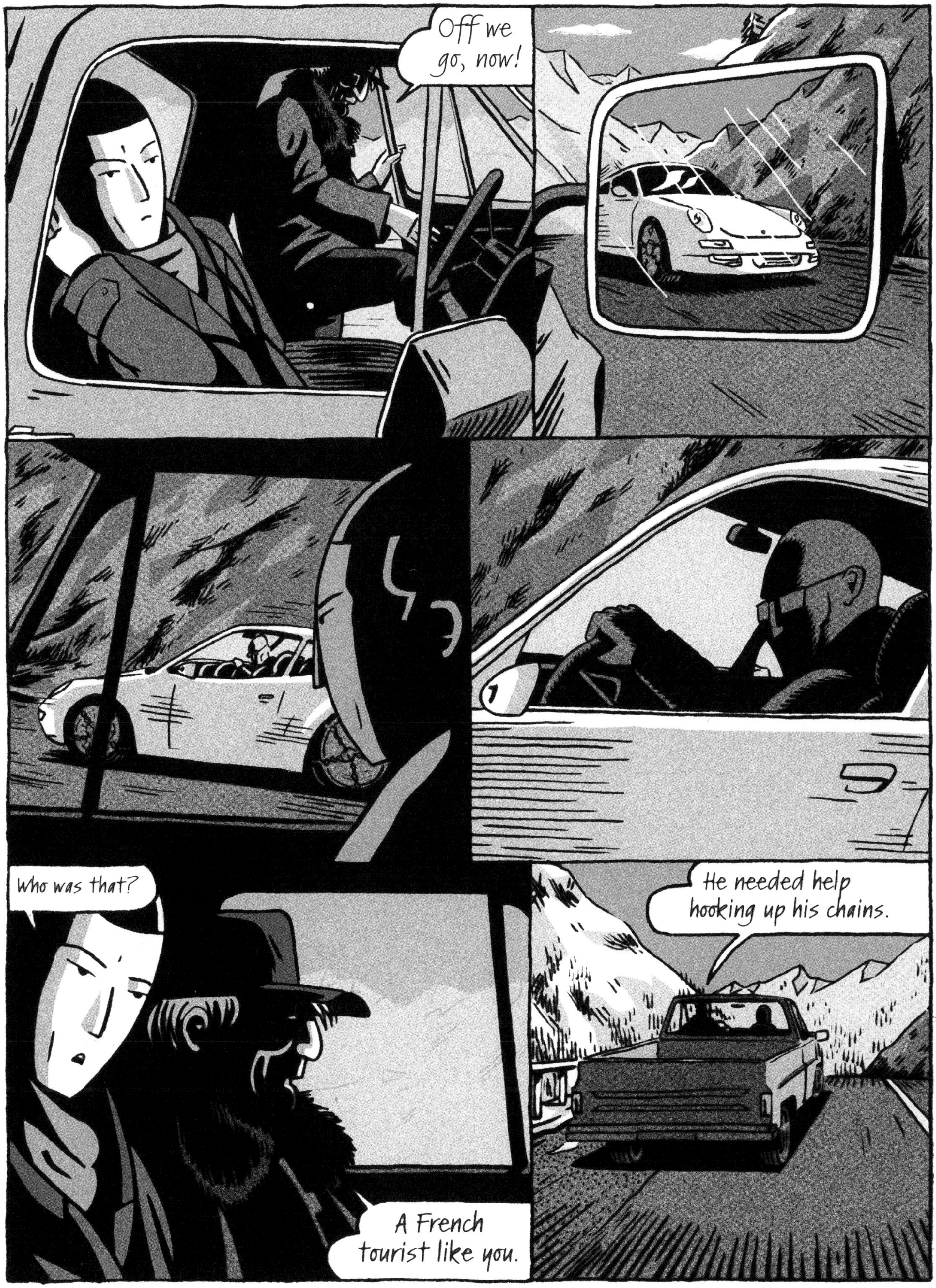
Off we go, now!
Who was that?
A French tourist like you.
He needed help hooking up his chains.

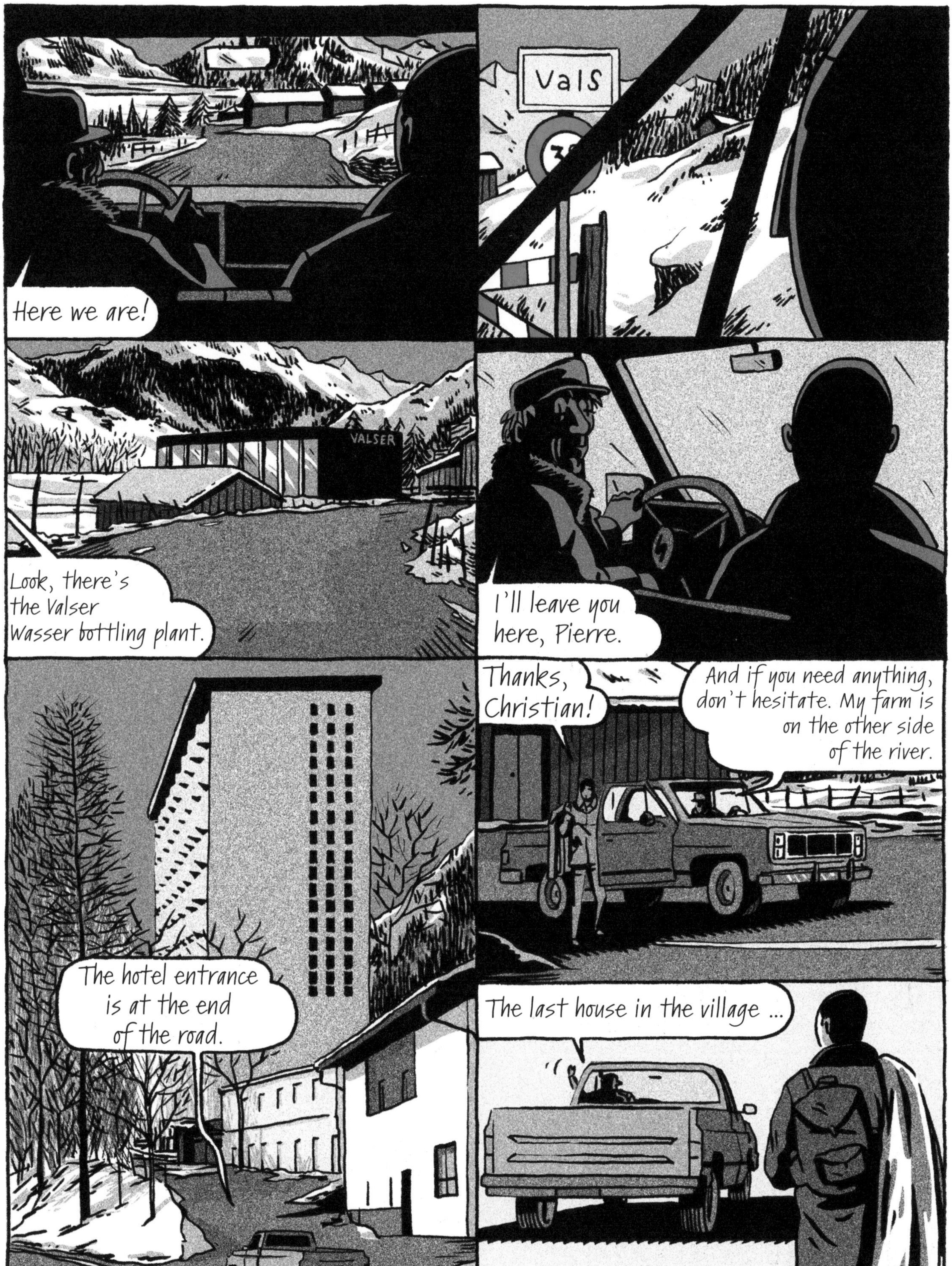
Here we are!
VaIS
VALSER
Look, there's the Valser Wasser bottling plant.
I'll leave you here, Pierre.
The hotel entrance is at the end of the road.
Thanks, Christian!
And if you need anything, don't hesitate. My farm is on the other side of the river.
The last house in the village ...

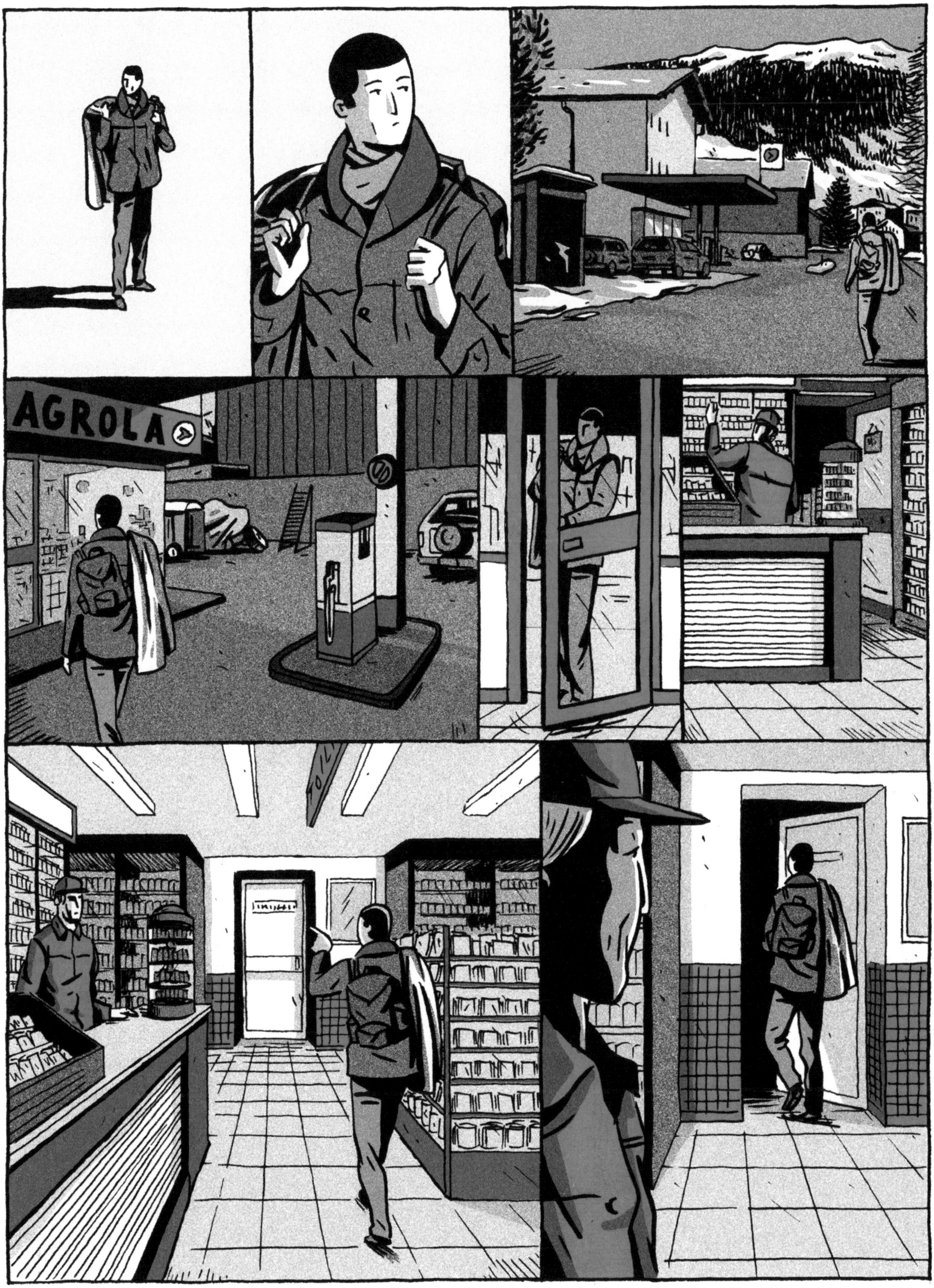
AGROLA

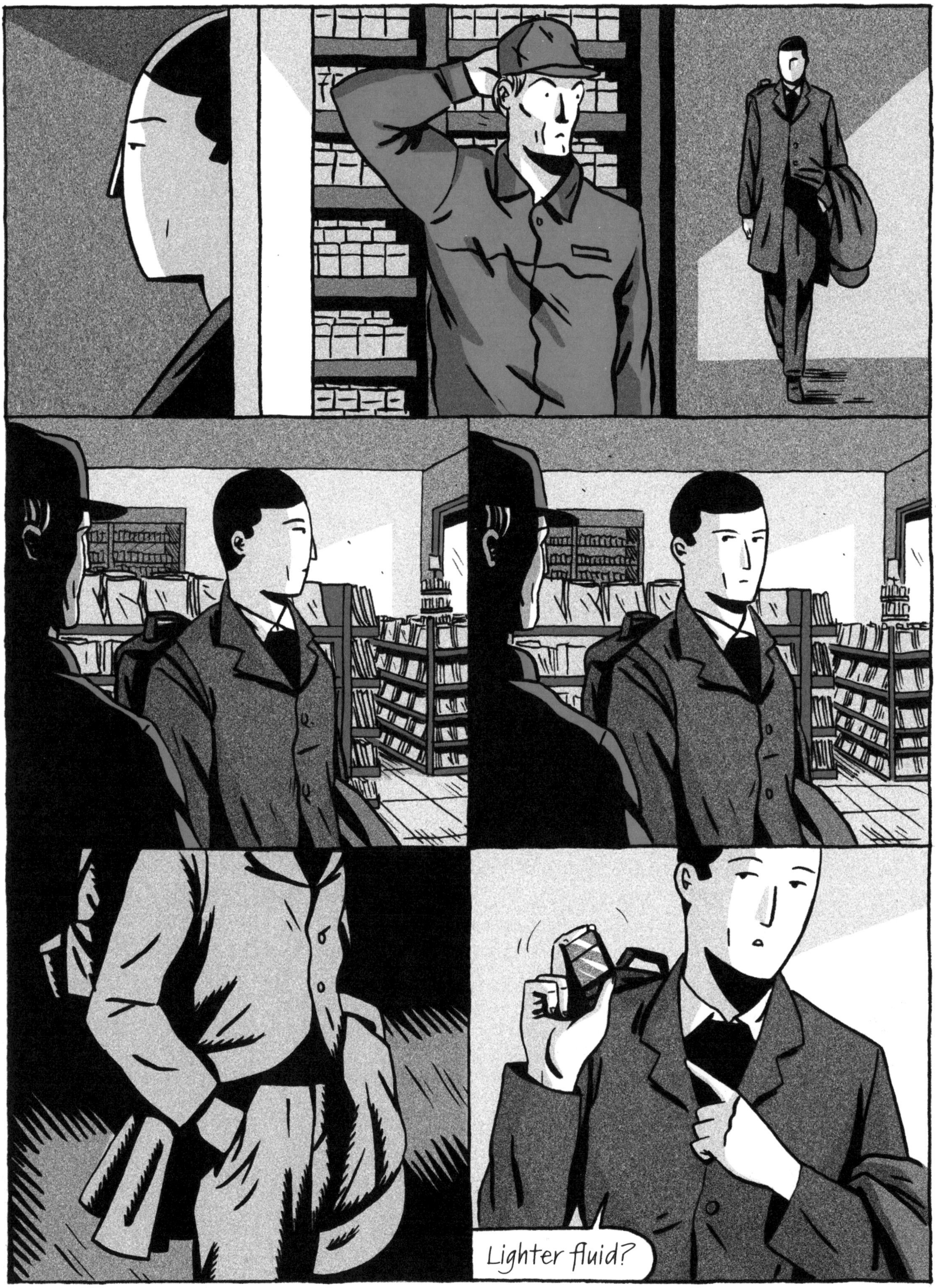
Lighter fluid?

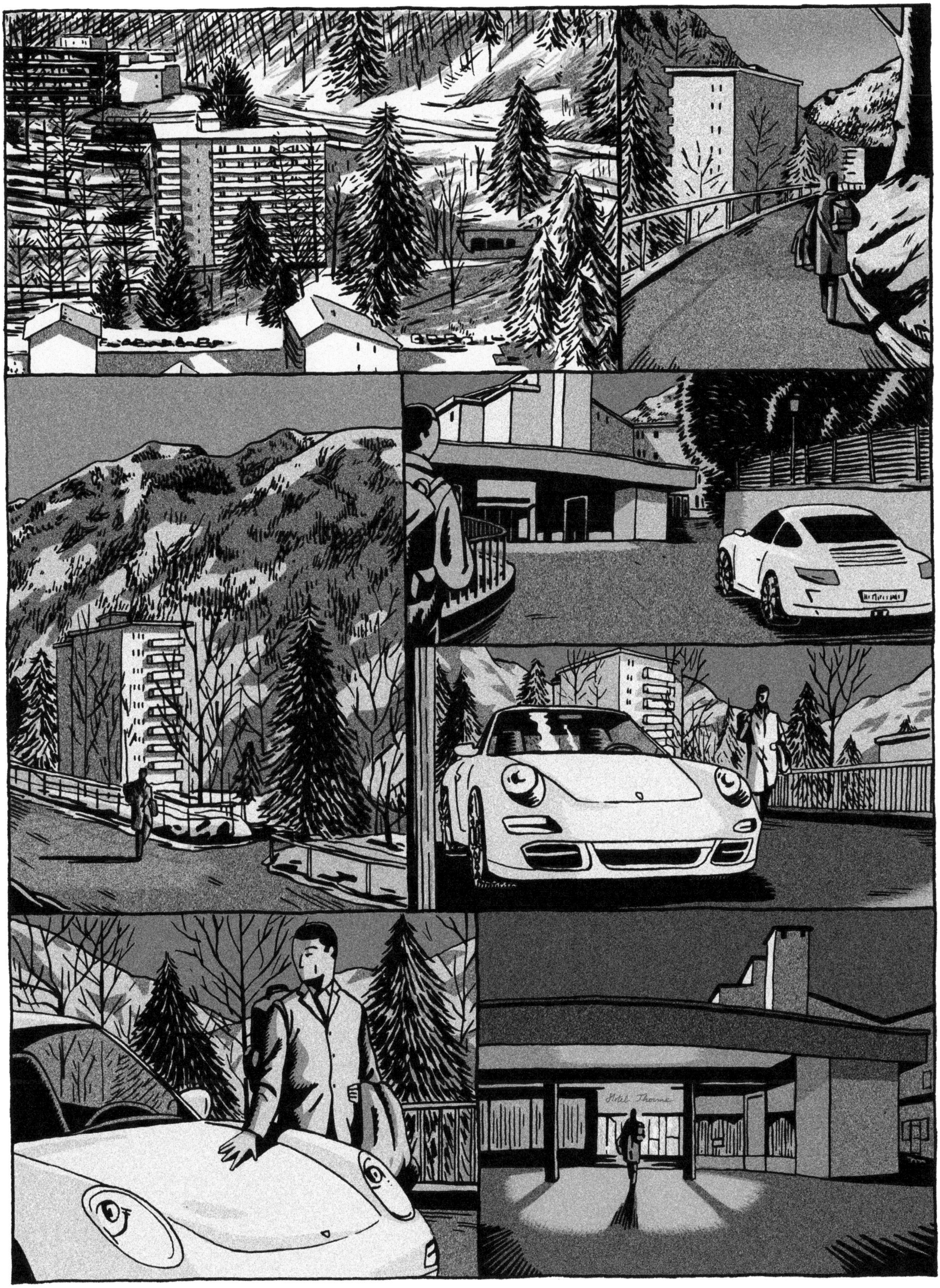
Hotel Thorne

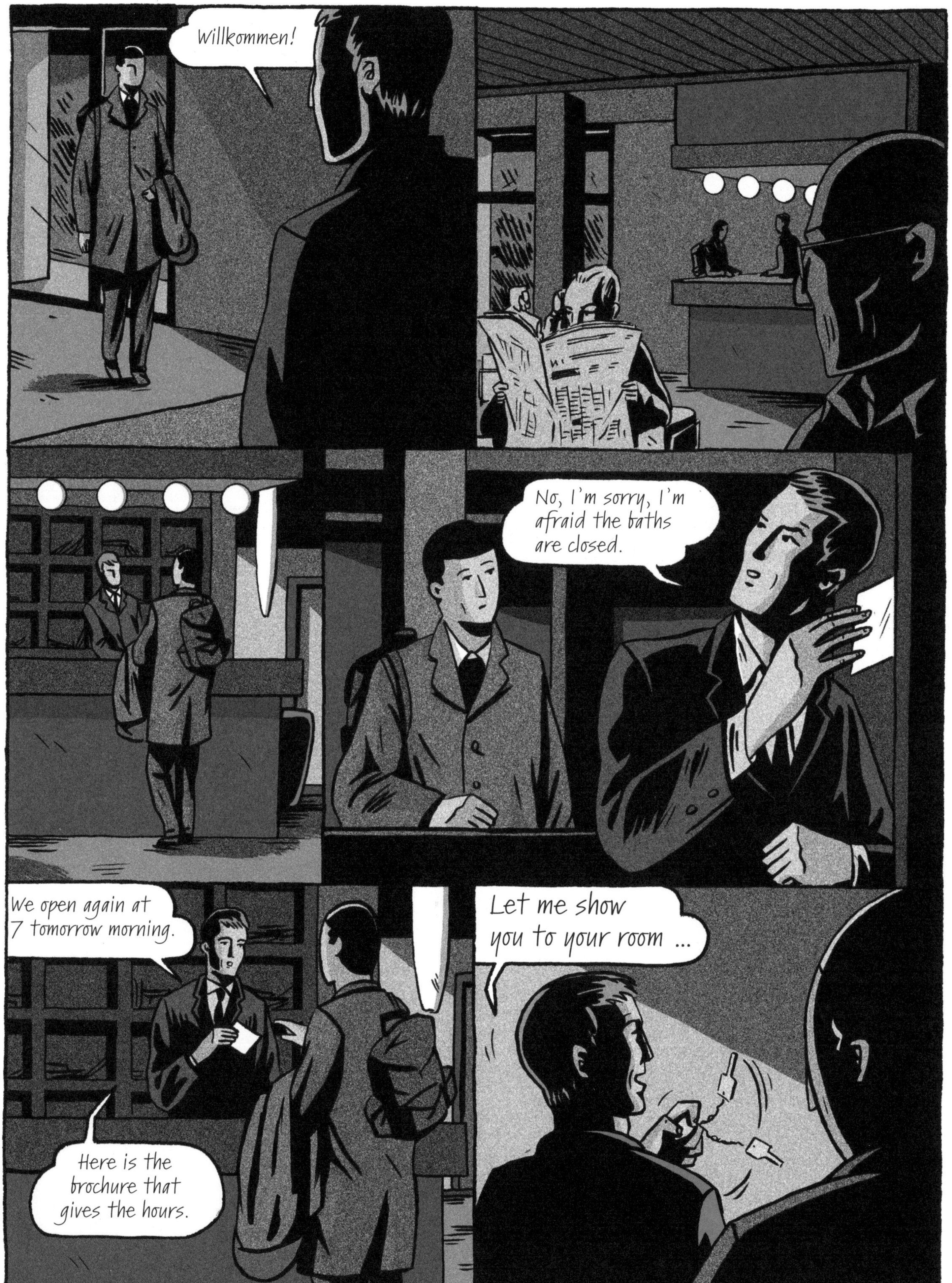
Willkommen!
No, I'm sorry, I'm afraid the baths are closed.
We open again at 7 tomorrow morning.
Here is the brochure that gives the hours.
Let me show you to your room ...

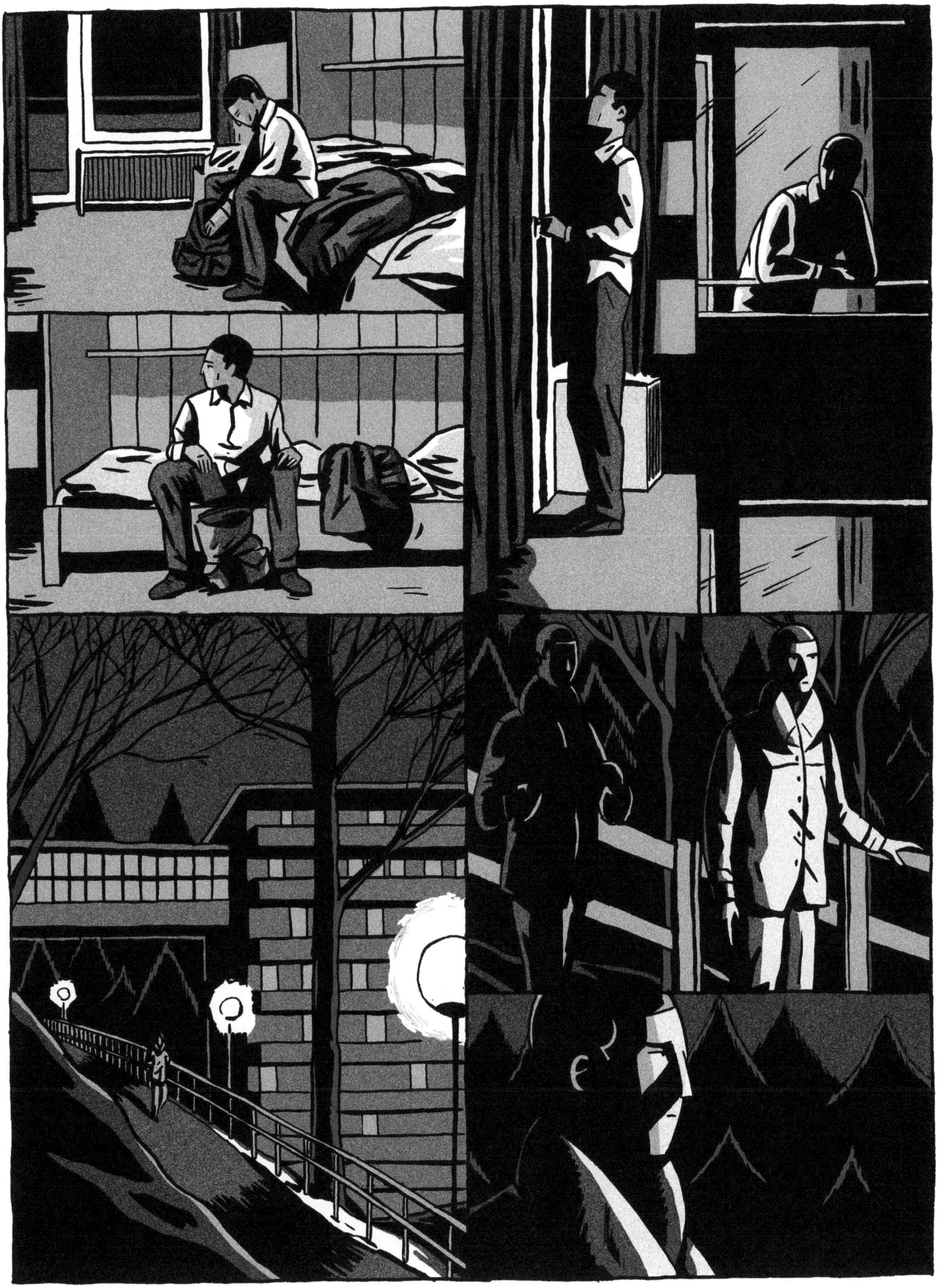

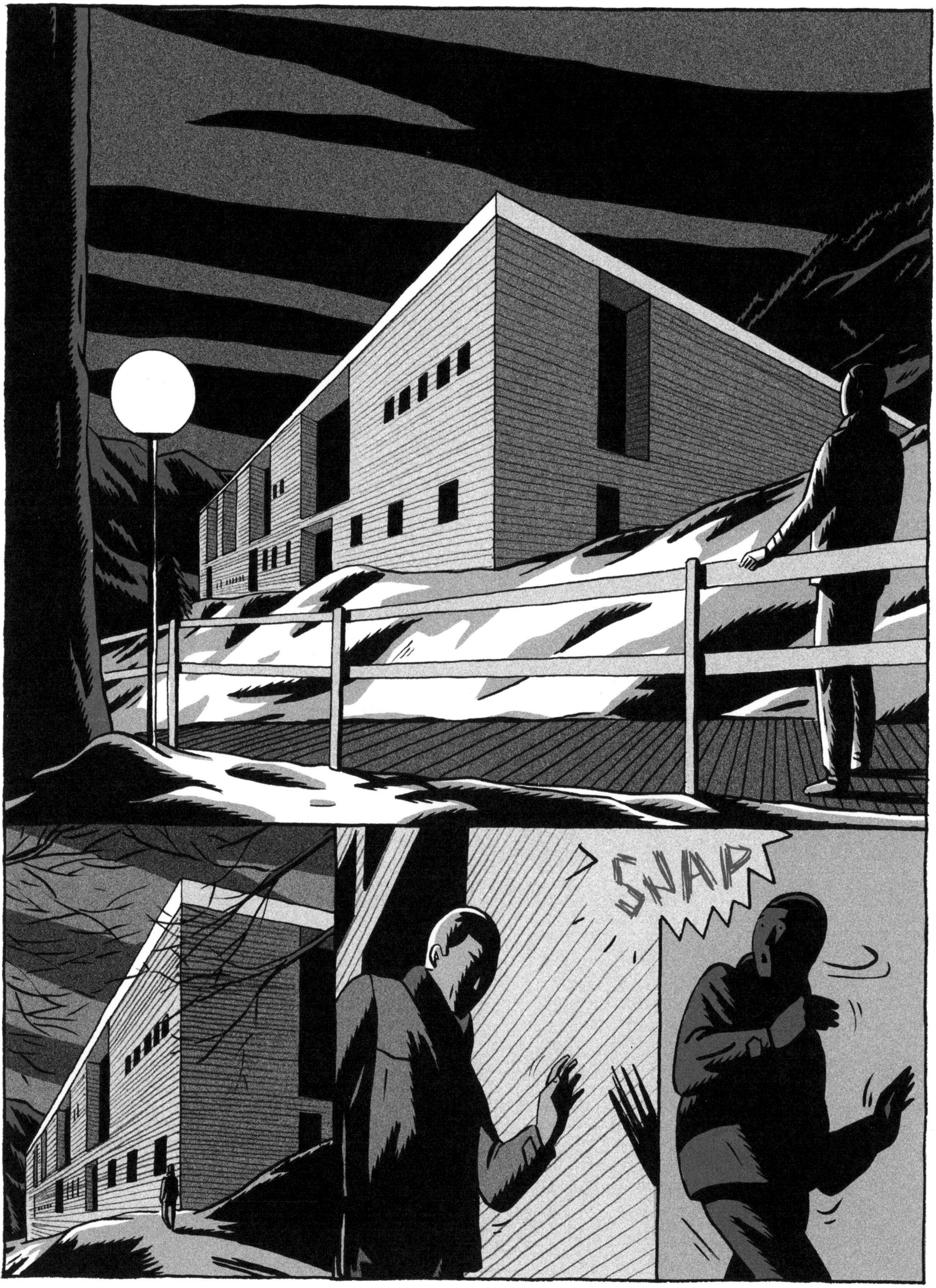
SNAP

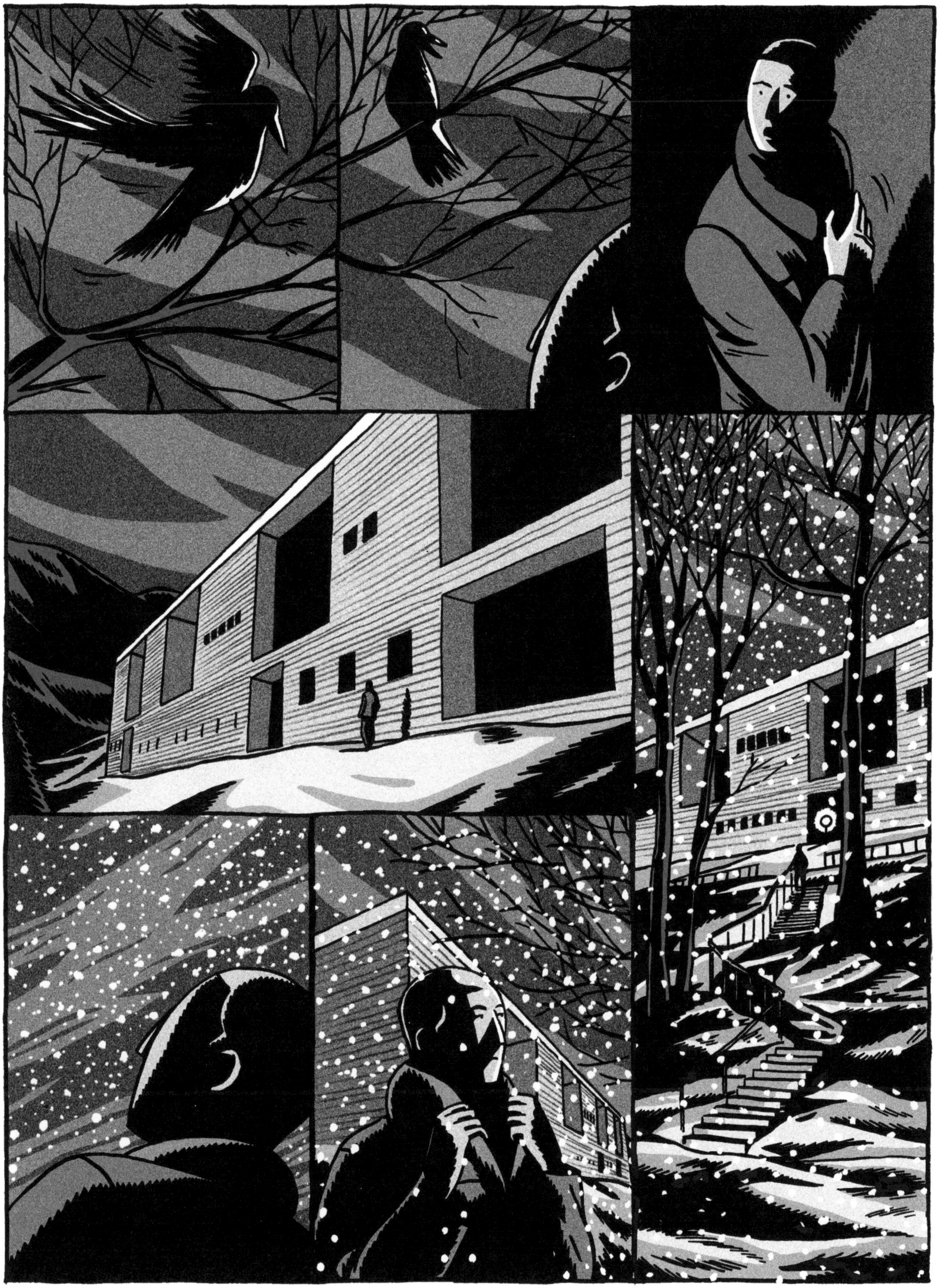

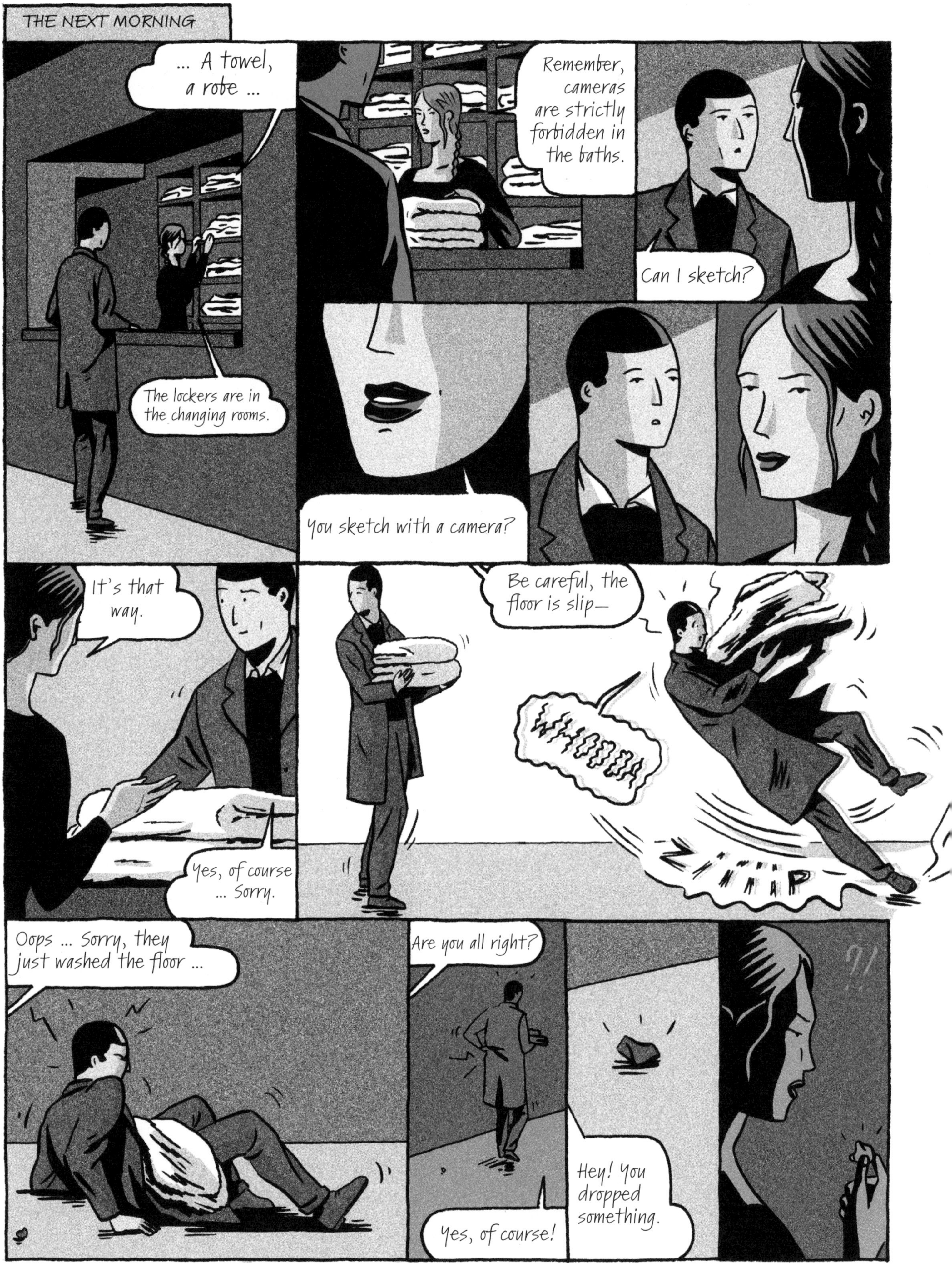

THE NEXT MORNING
... A towel, a robe ...
The lockers are in the changing rooms.
Remember, cameras are strictly forbidden in the baths.
Can I sketch?
You sketch with a camera?
It's that way.
Yes, of course ... Sorry.
Be careful, the floor is slip—
WHOOAA
ZIIIIP
Oops ... Sorry, they just washed the floor ...
Are you all right?
Yes, of course!
Hey! You dropped something.
?!

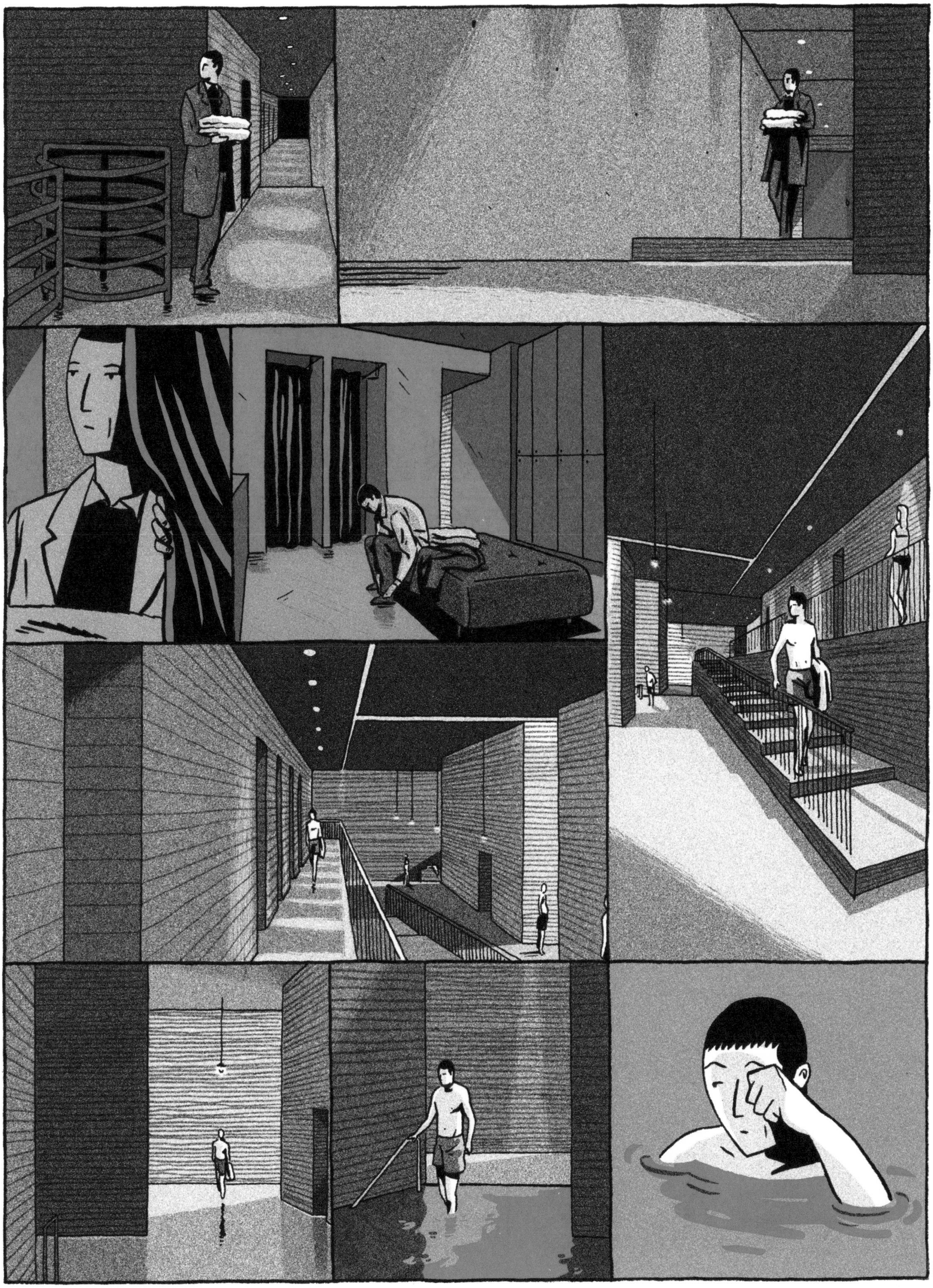

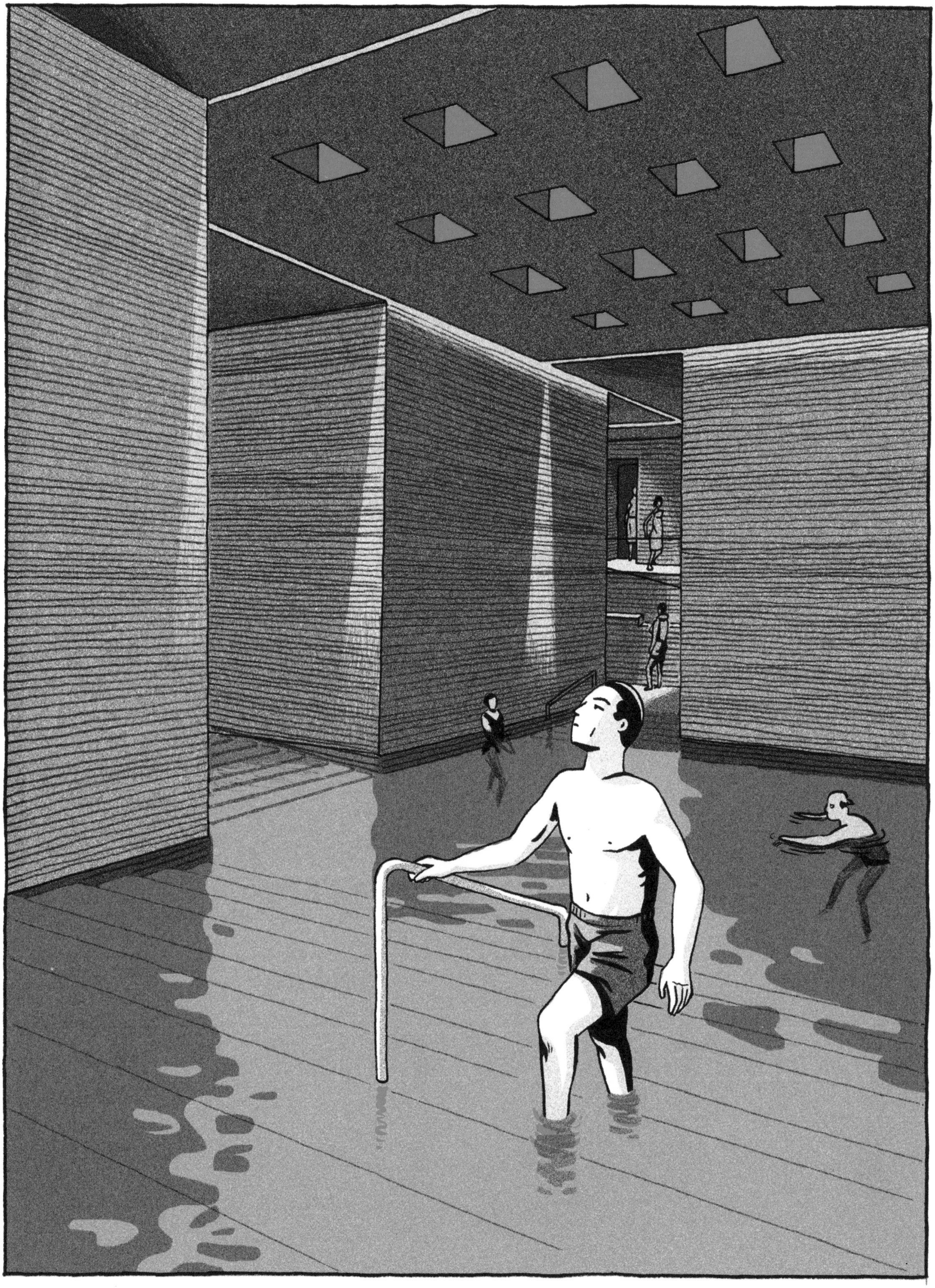

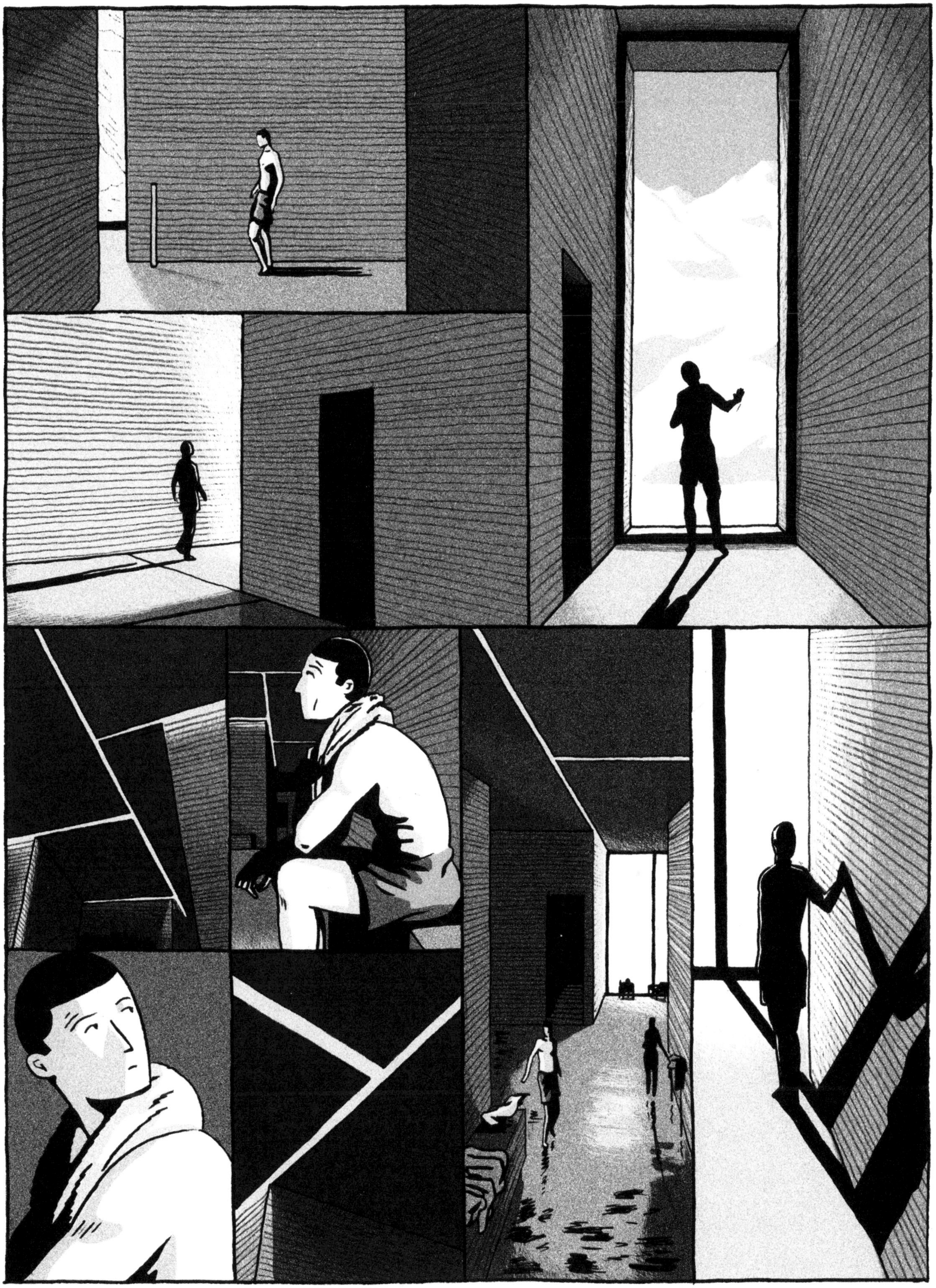

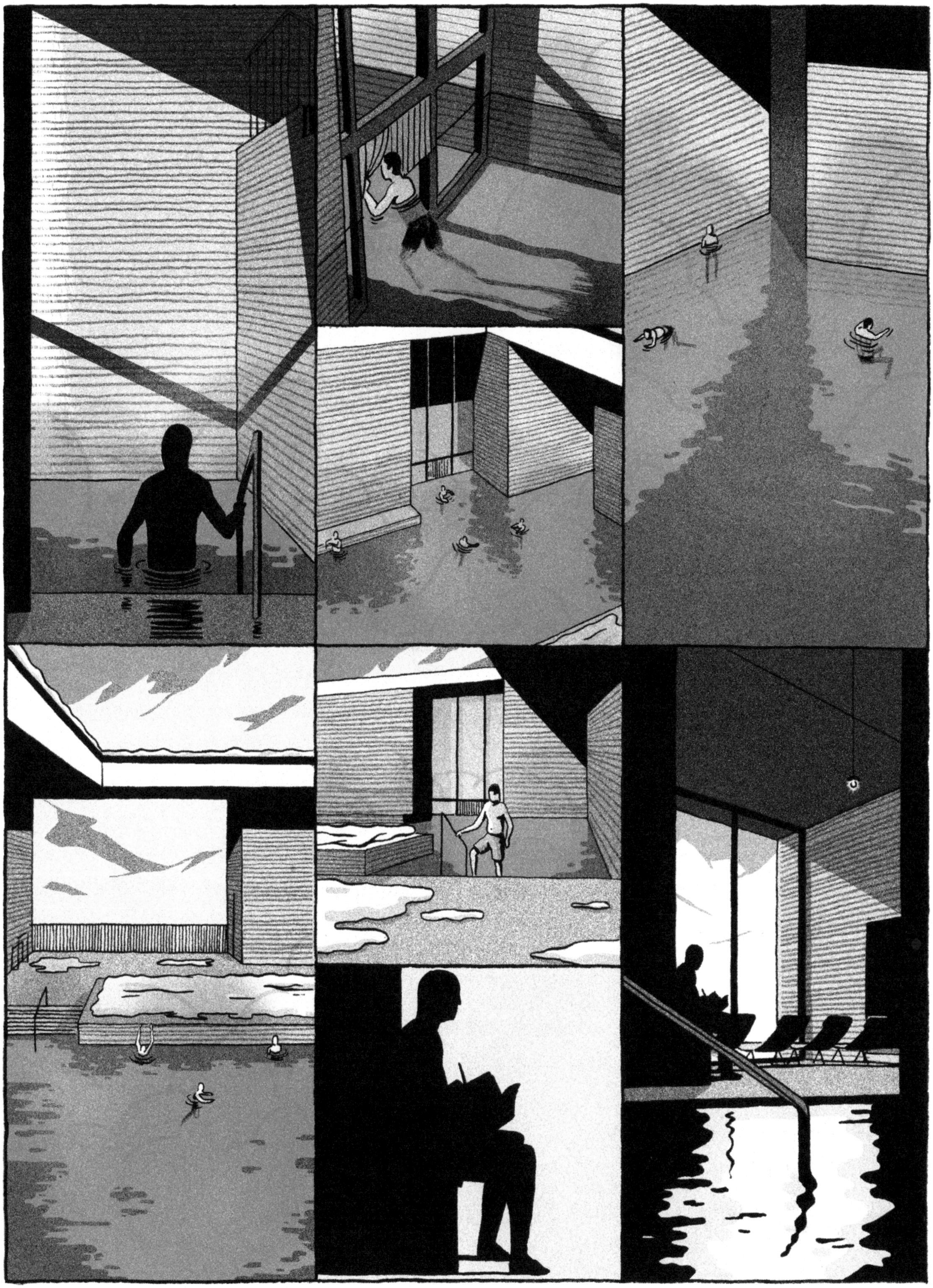

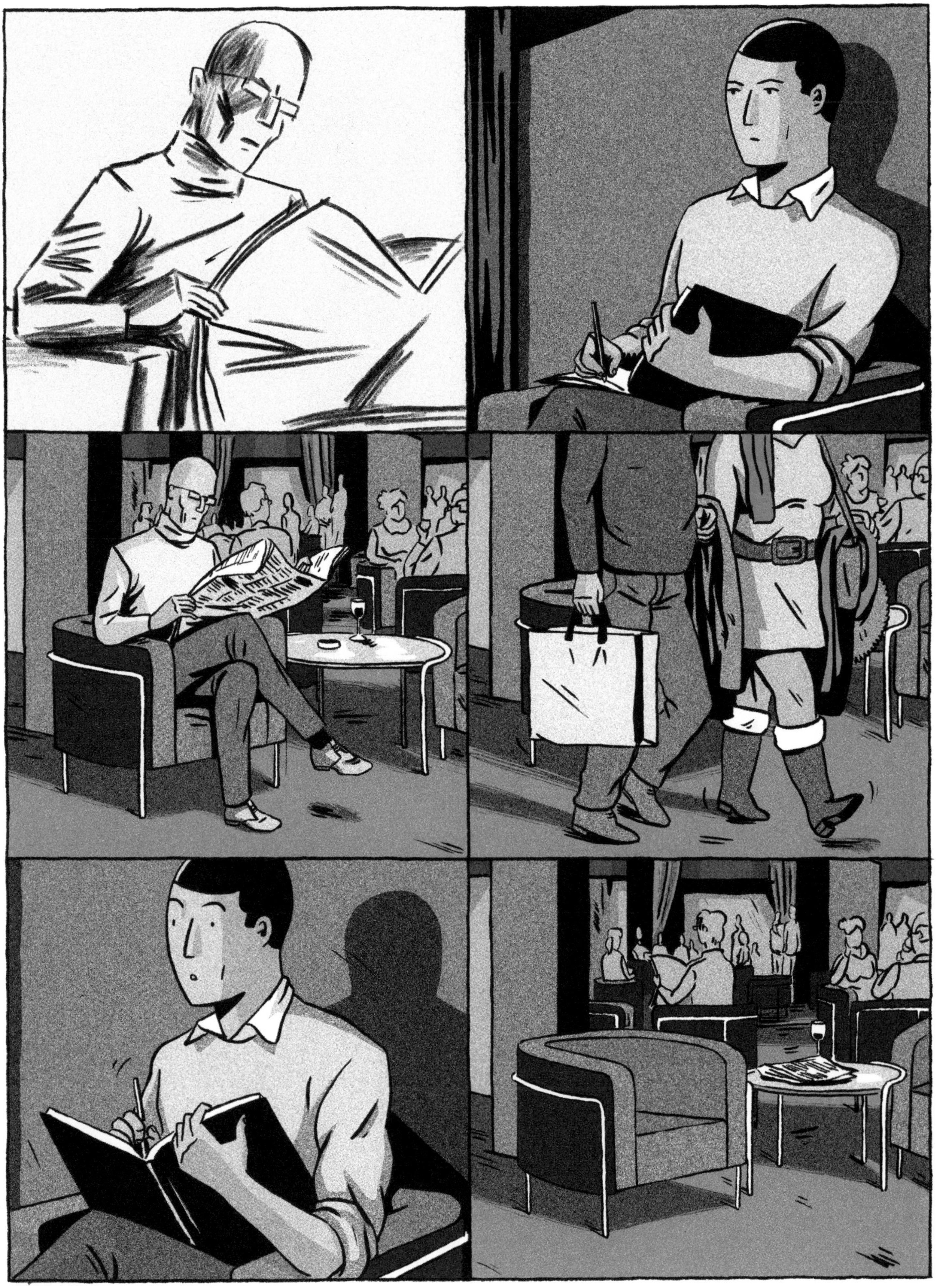

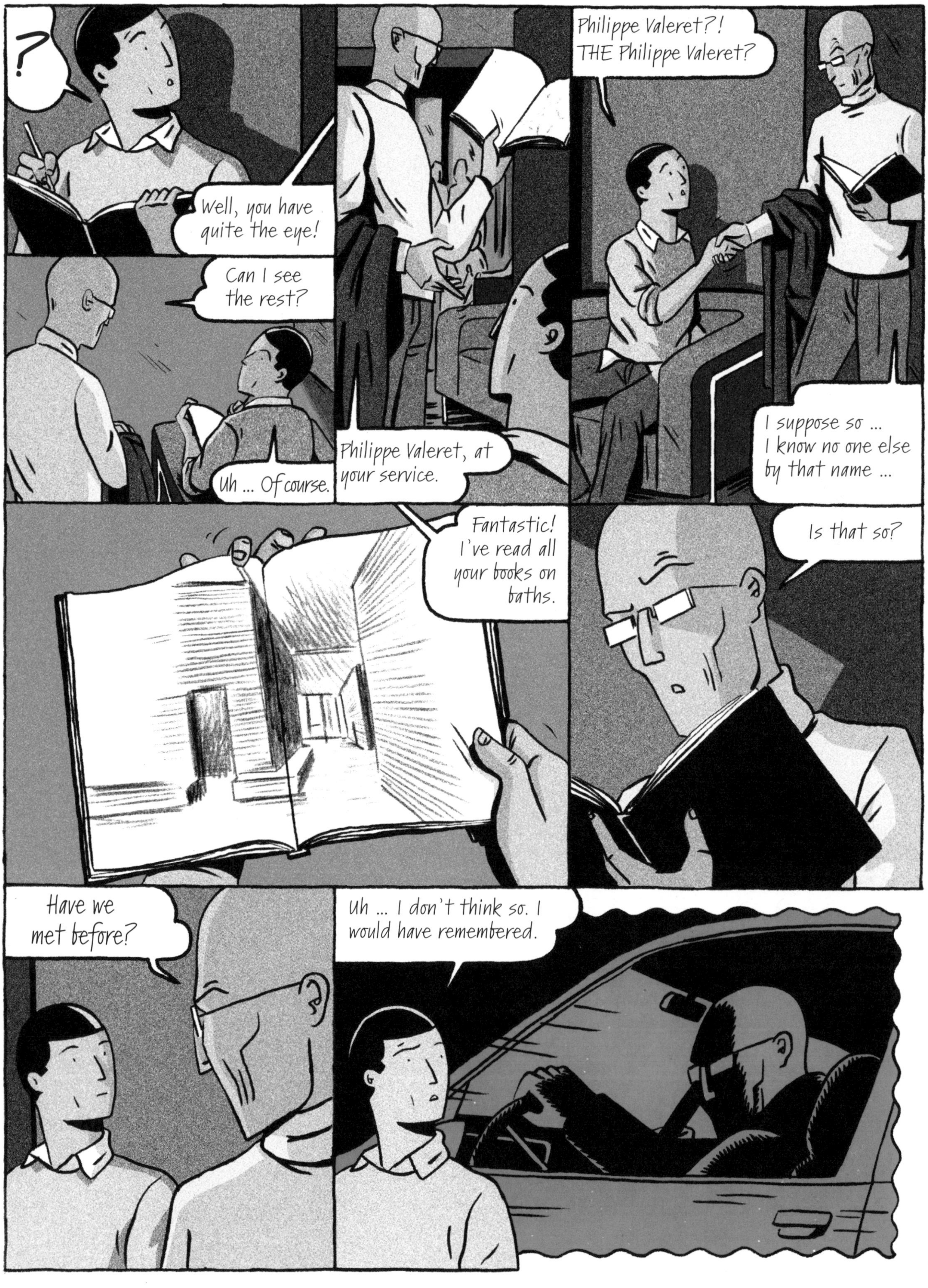
?
Well, you have quite the eye!
Can I see the rest?
Uh ... Of course.
Philippe Valeret, at your service.
Philippe Valeret?! THE Philippe Valeret?
I suppose so ... I know no one else by that name ...
Fantastic! I've read all your books on baths.
Is that so?
Have we met before?
Uh ... I don't think so. I would have remembered.

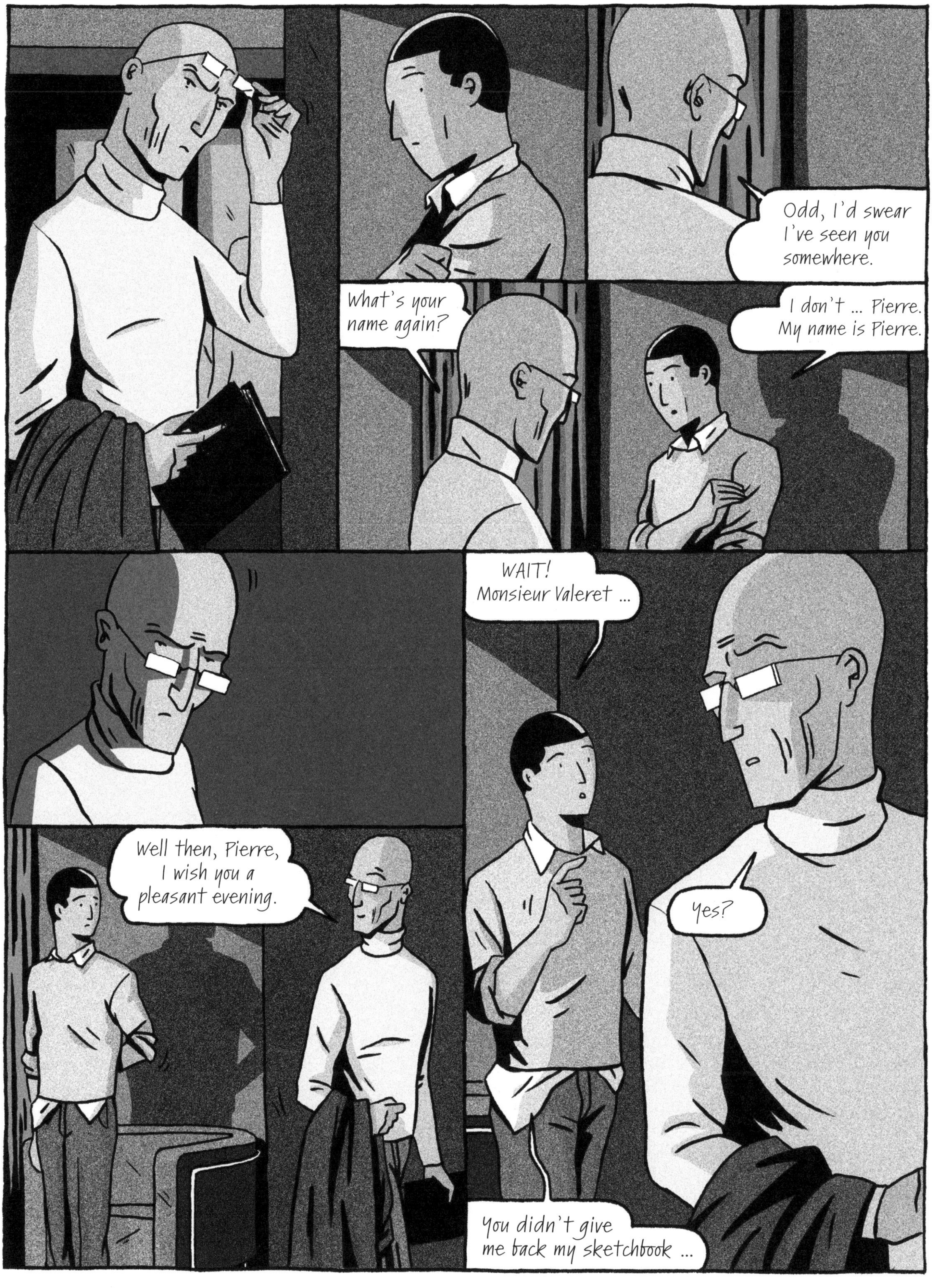
Odd, I'd swear I've seen you somewhere.
What's your name again?
I don't ... Pierre. My name is Pierre.
Well then, Pierre, I wish you a pleasant evening.
WAIT! Monsieur Valeret ...
Yes?
You didn't give me back my sketchbook ...

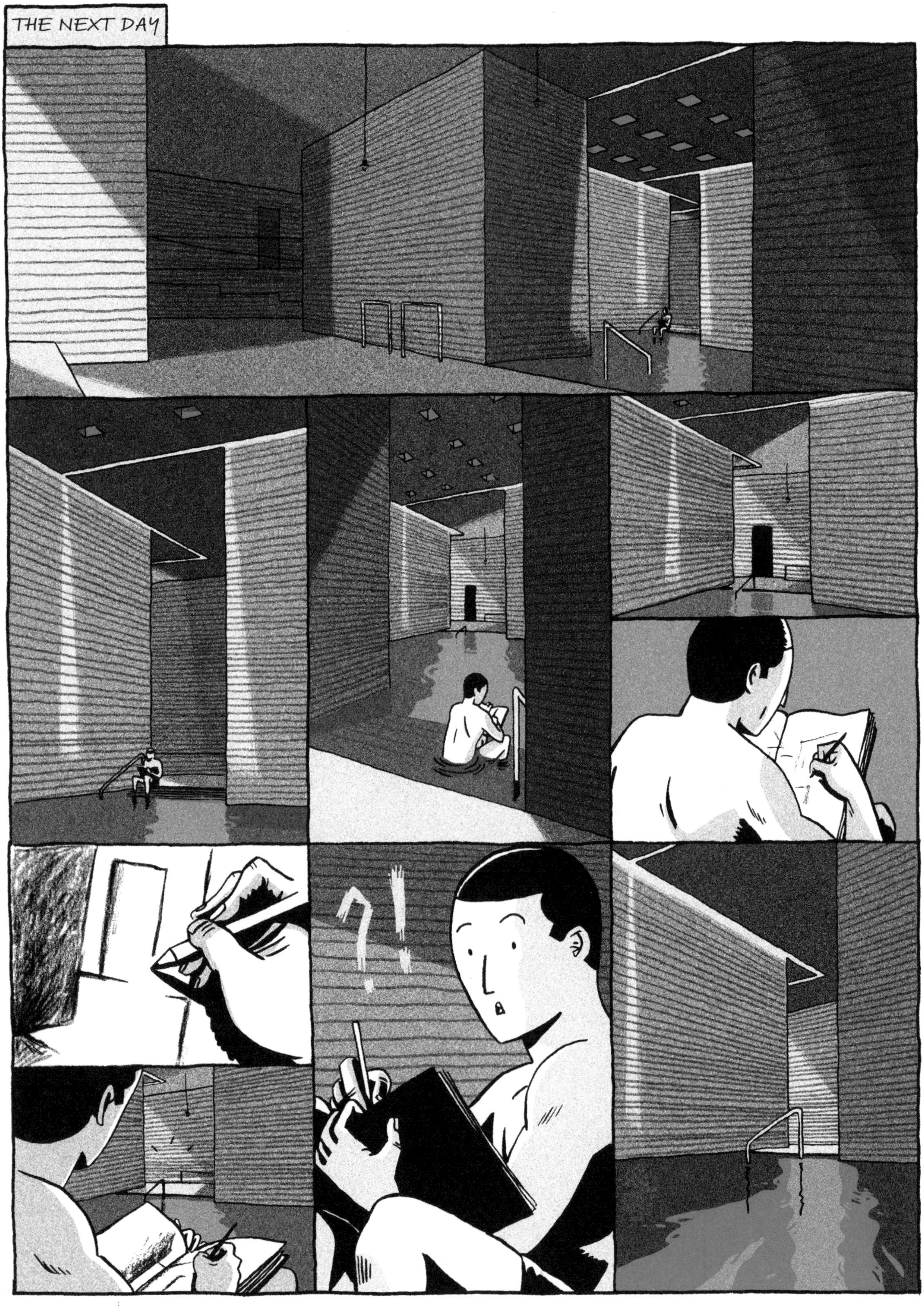
THE NEXT DAY
?!

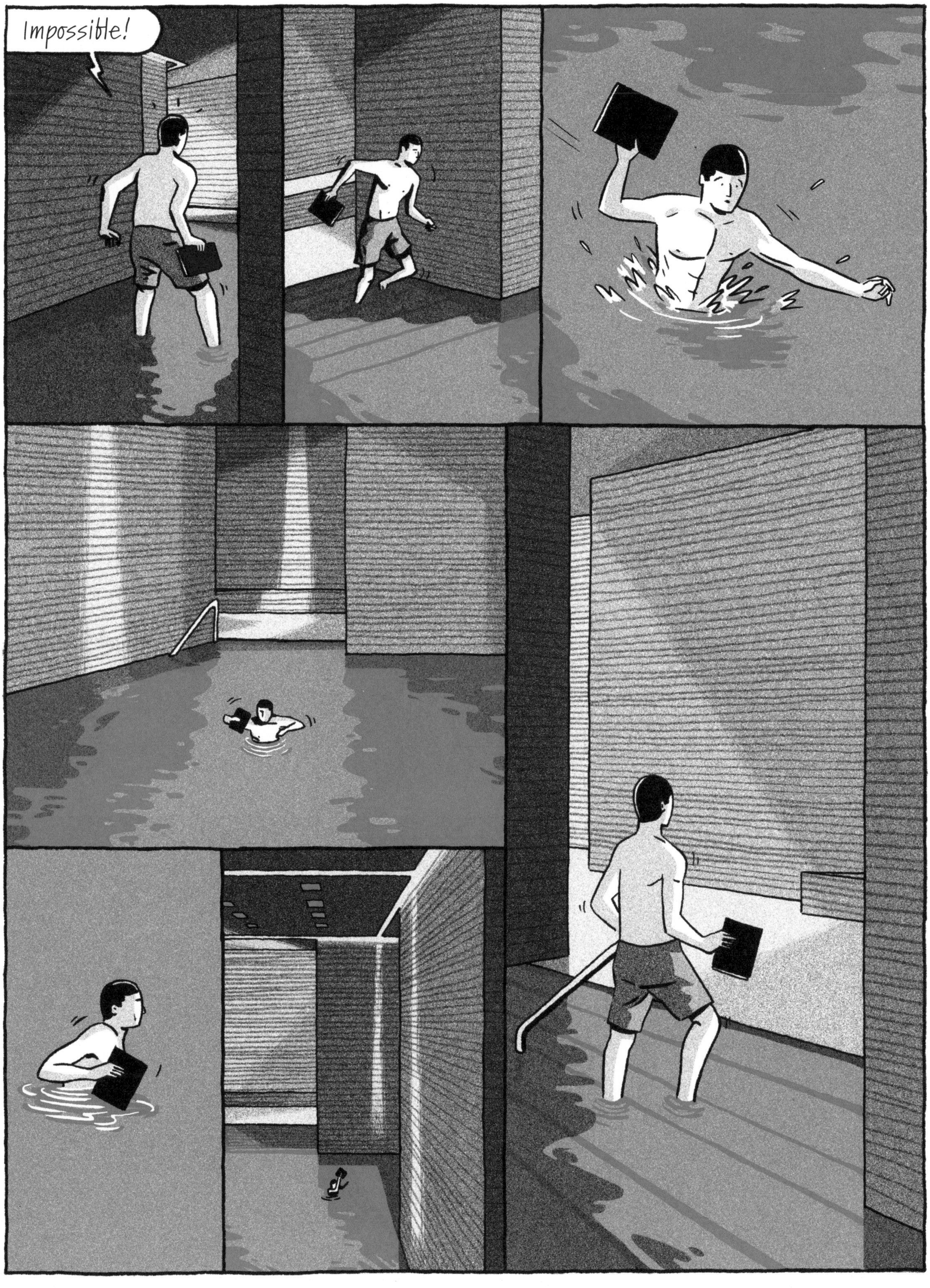
Impossible!

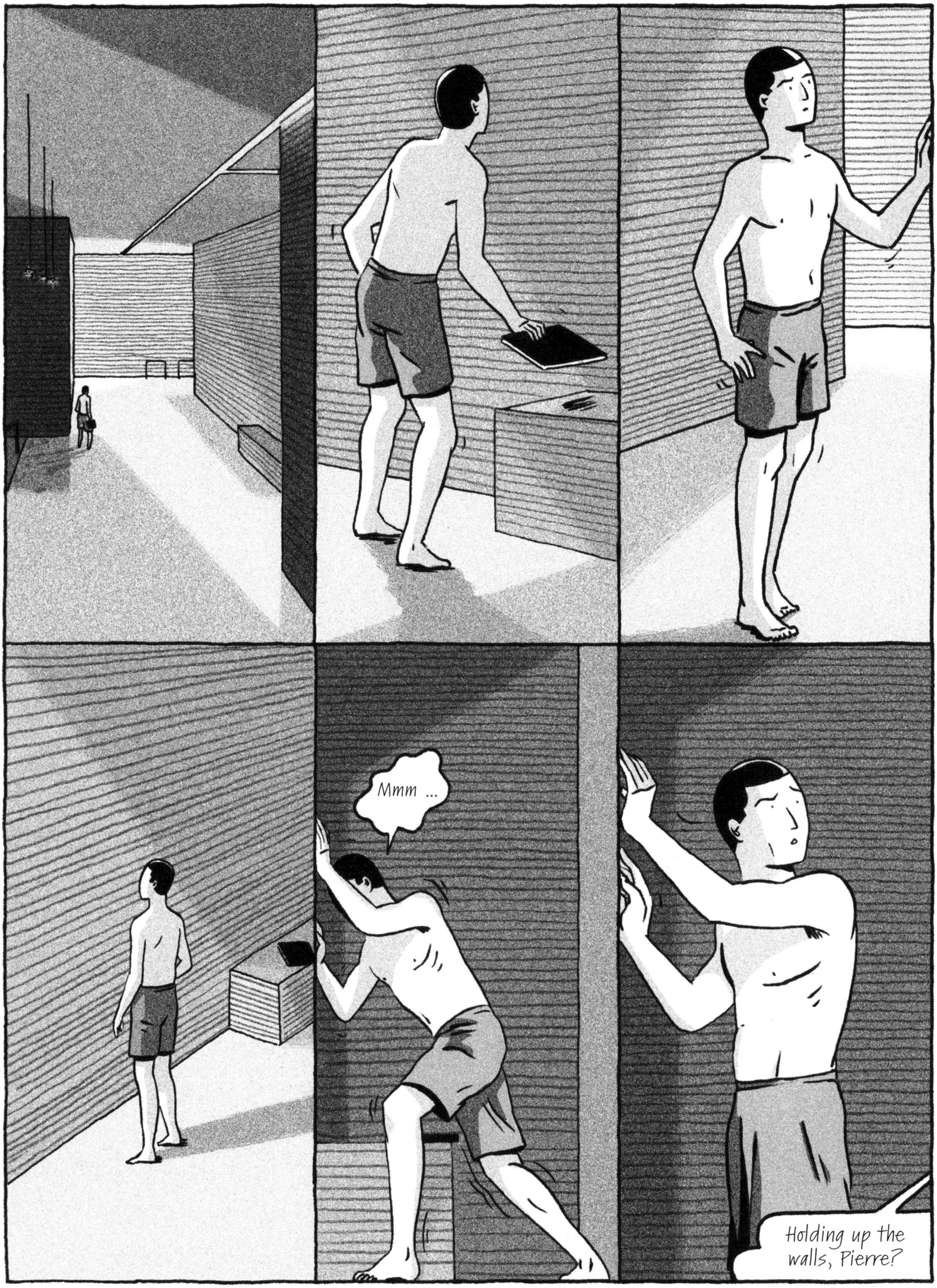
Mmm ...
Holding up the walls, Pierre?

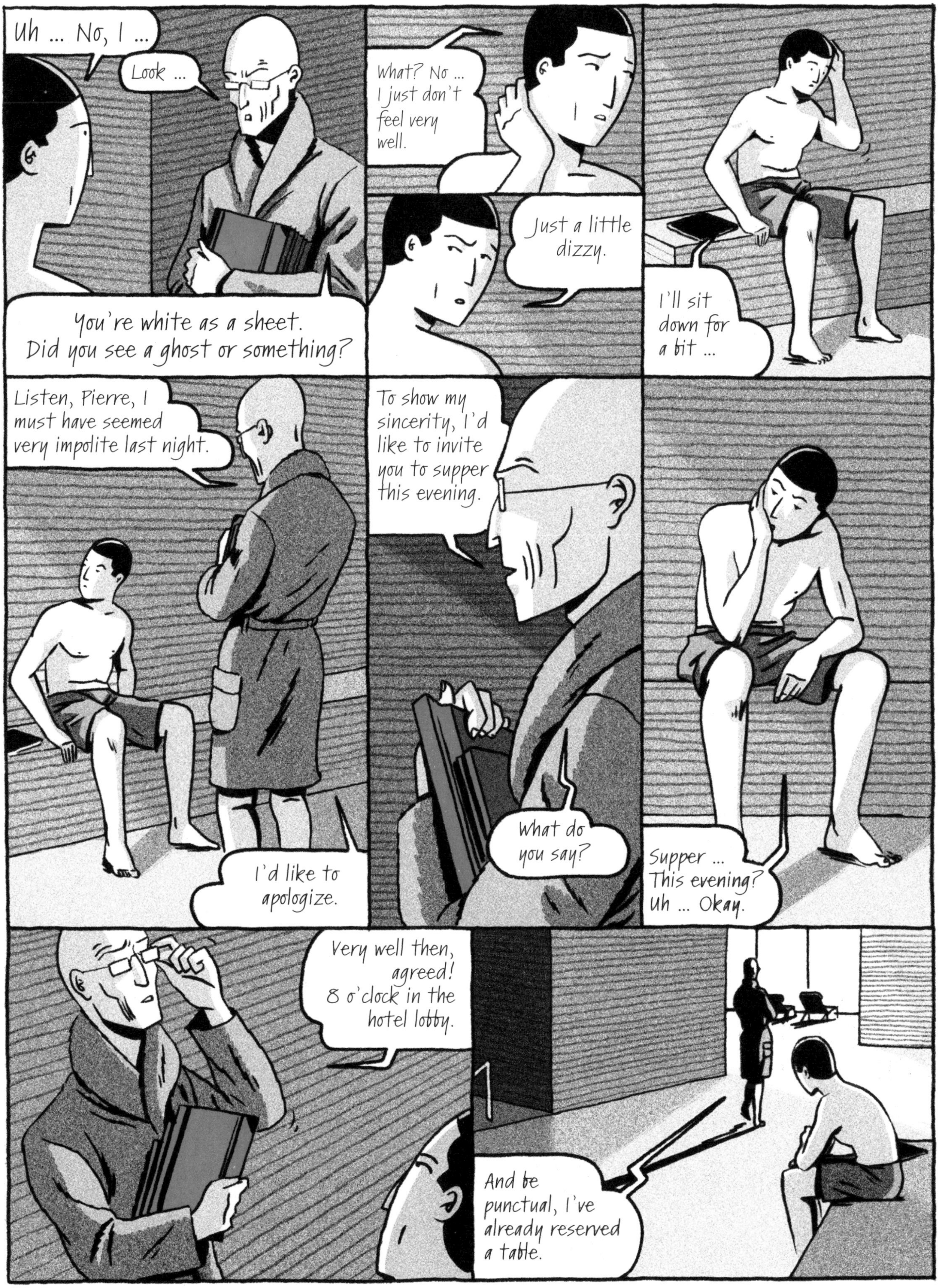
Uh ... No, I ...
Look ...
You're white as a sheet. Did you see a ghost or something?
What? No ... I just don't feel very well.
Just a little dizzy.
I'll sit down for a bit ...
Listen, Pierre, I must have seemed very impolite last night.
I'd like to apologize.
To show my sincerity, I'd like to invite you to supper this evening.
What do you say?
Supper ... This evening? Uh ... Okay.
Very well then, agreed! 8 o'clock in the hotel lobby.
And be punctual, I've already reserved a table.

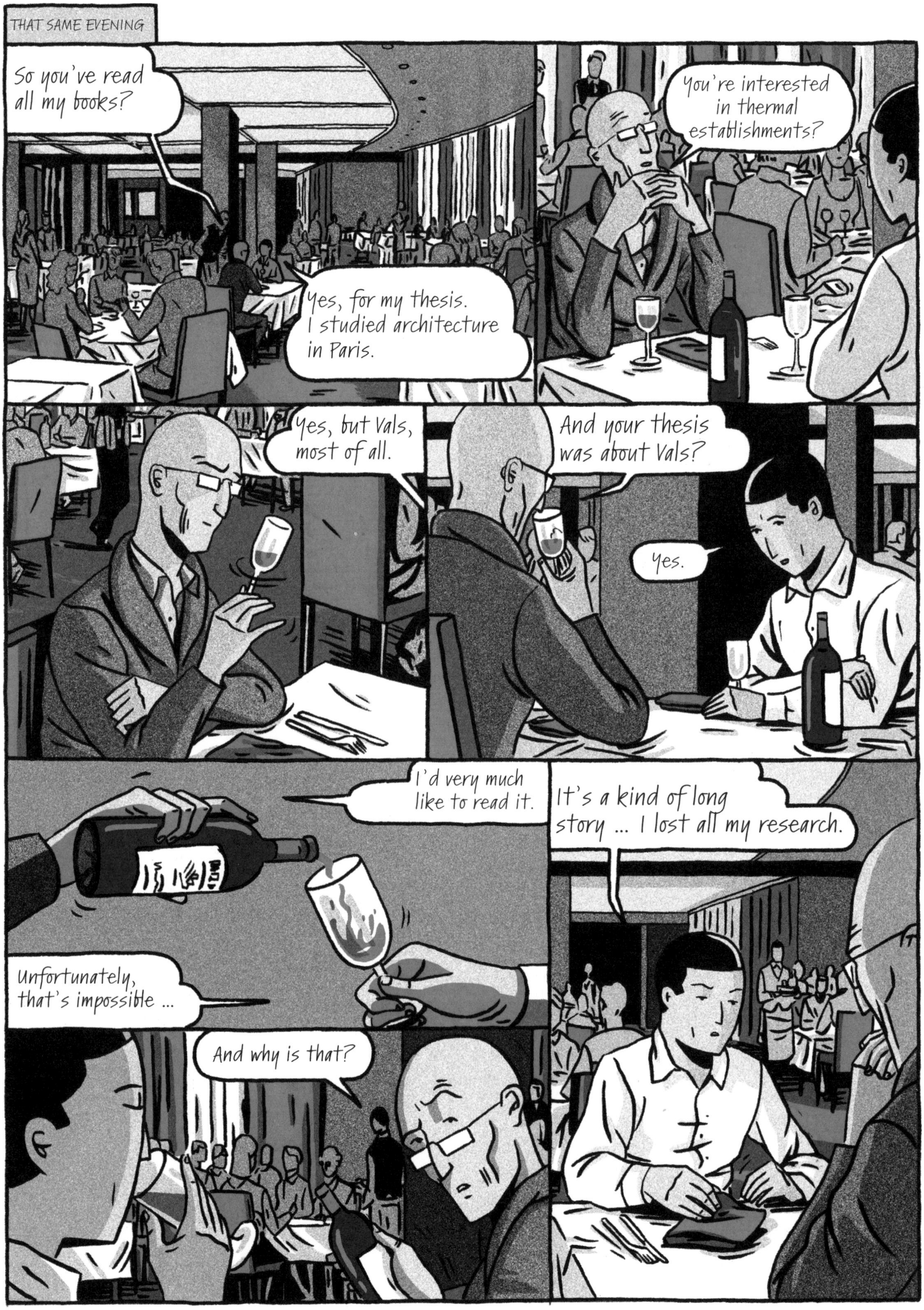
THAT SAME EVENING
So you've read all my books?
Yes, for my thesis. I studied architecture in Paris.
You're interested in thermal establishments?
Yes, but Vals, most of all.
And your thesis was about Vals?
Yes.
I'd very much like to read it.
Unfortunately, that's impossible ...
And why is that?
It's a kind of long story ... I lost all my research.

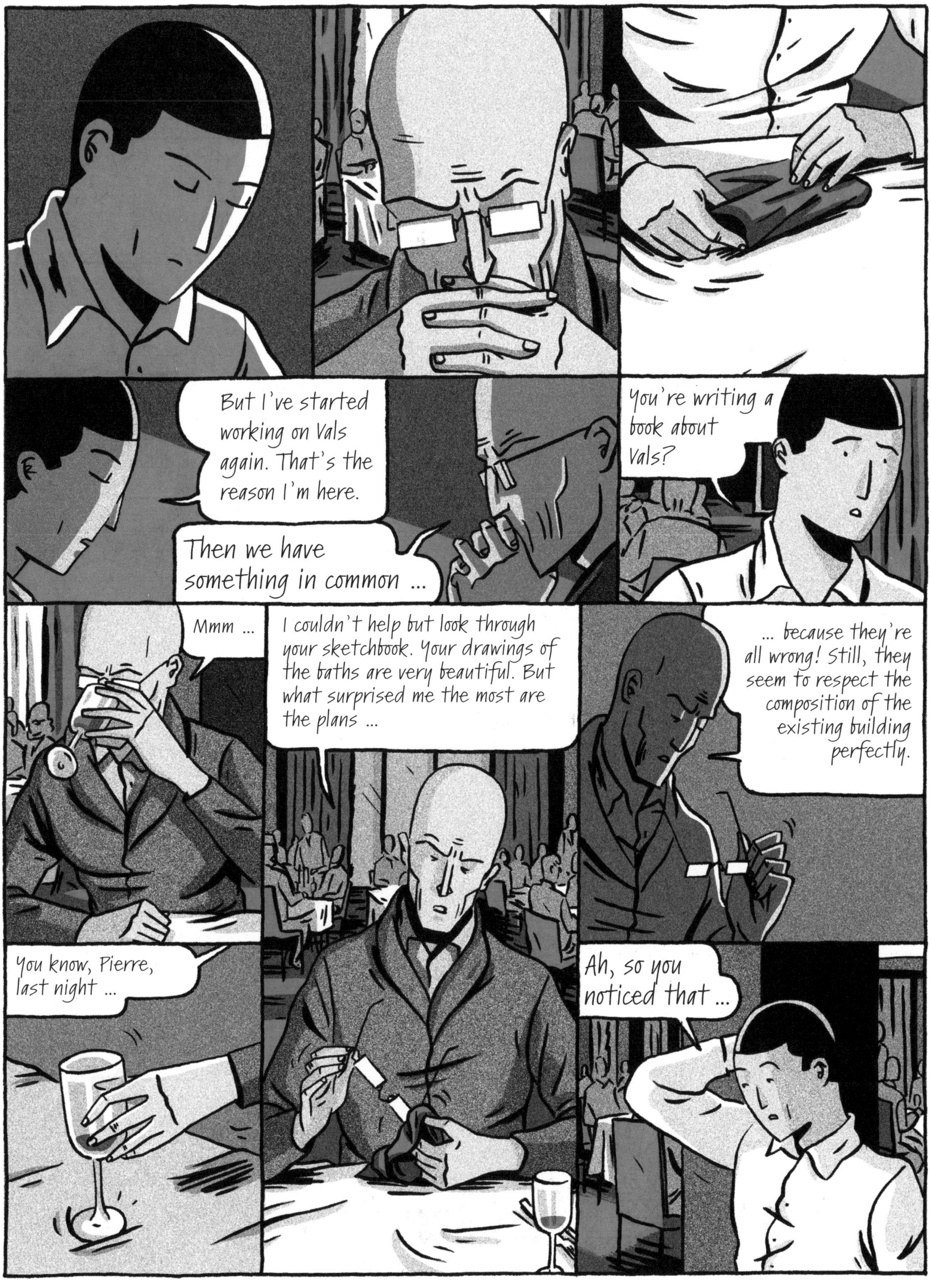
But I've started working on Vals again. That's the reason I'm here.
Then we have something in common ...
You're writing a book about Vals?
Mmm ...
I couldn't help but look through your sketchbook. Your drawings of the baths are very beautiful. But what surprised me the most are the plans ...
... because they're all wrong! Still, they seem to respect the composition of the existing building perfectly.
You know, Pierre, last night ...
Ah, so you noticed that ...

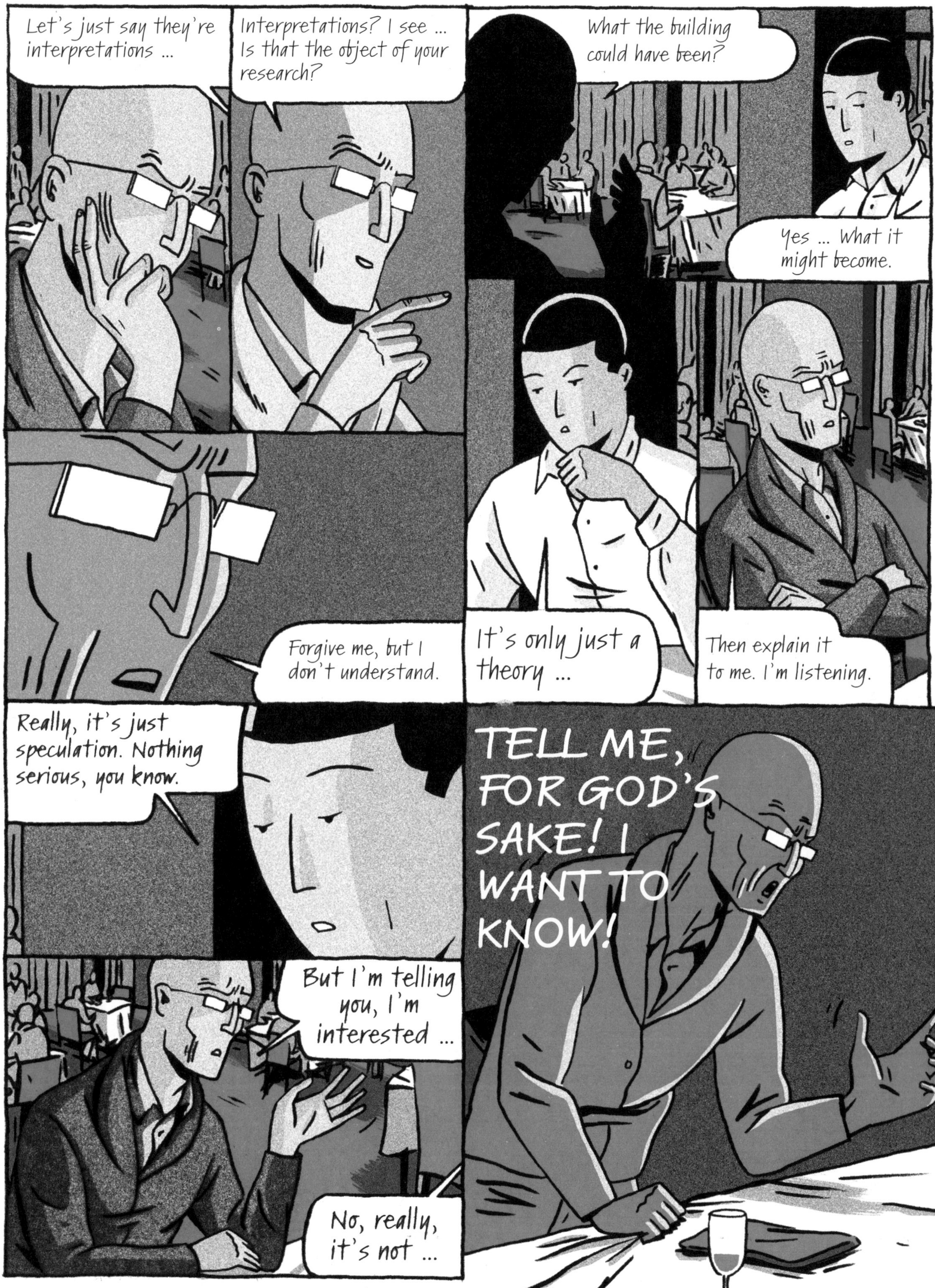
Let's just say they're interpretations ...
Interpretations? I see ... Is that the object of your research?
What the building could have been?
Yes ... What it might become.
Forgive me, but I don't understand.
It's only just a theory ...
Then explain it to me. I'm listening.
Really, it's just speculation. Nothing serious, you know.
TELL ME, FOR GOD'S SAKE! I WANT TO KNOW!
But I'm telling you, I'm interested ...
No, really, it's not ...

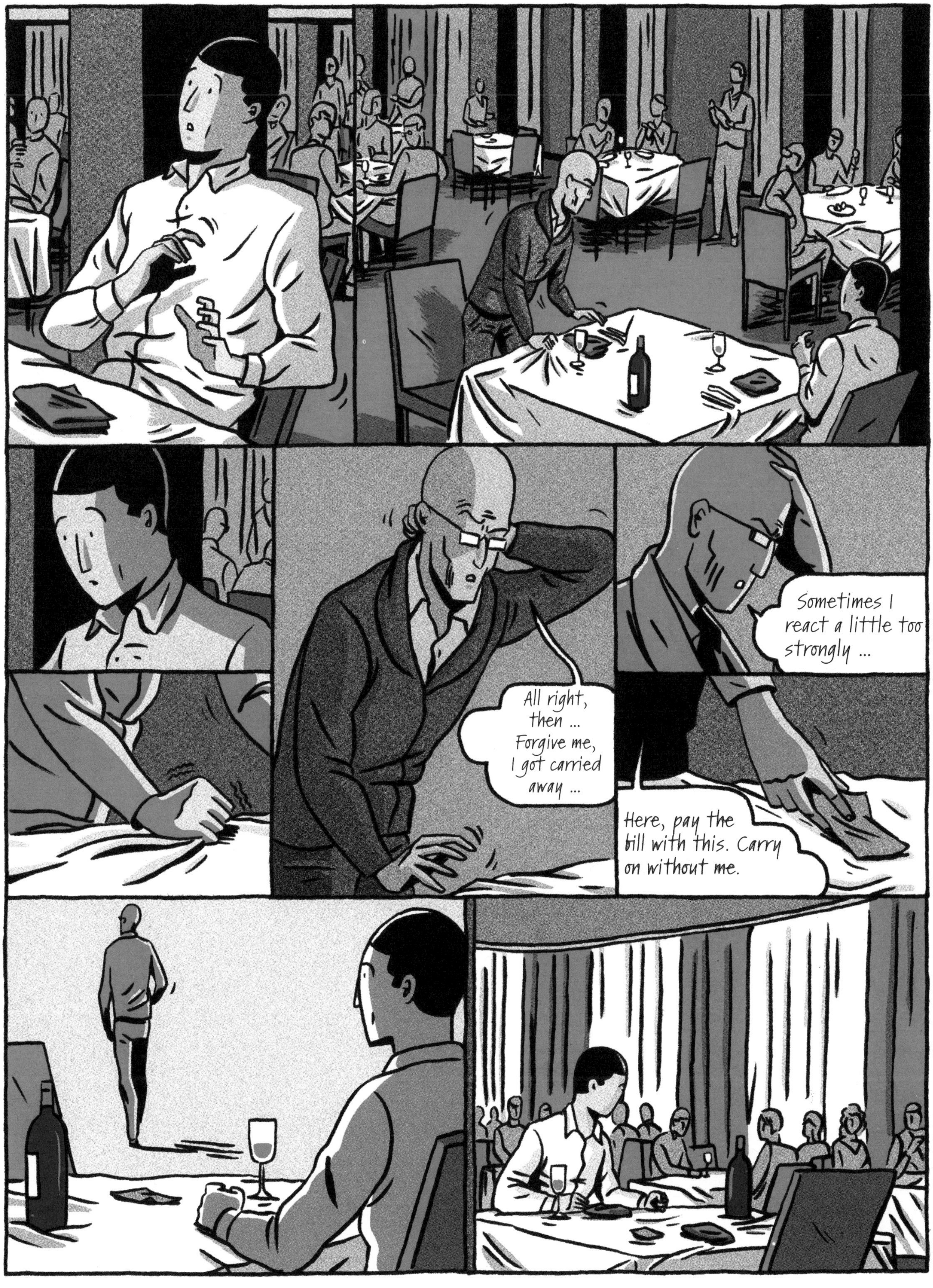
All right, then ... Forgive me, I got carried away ...
Sometimes I react a little too strongly ...
Here, pay the bill with this. Carry on without me.

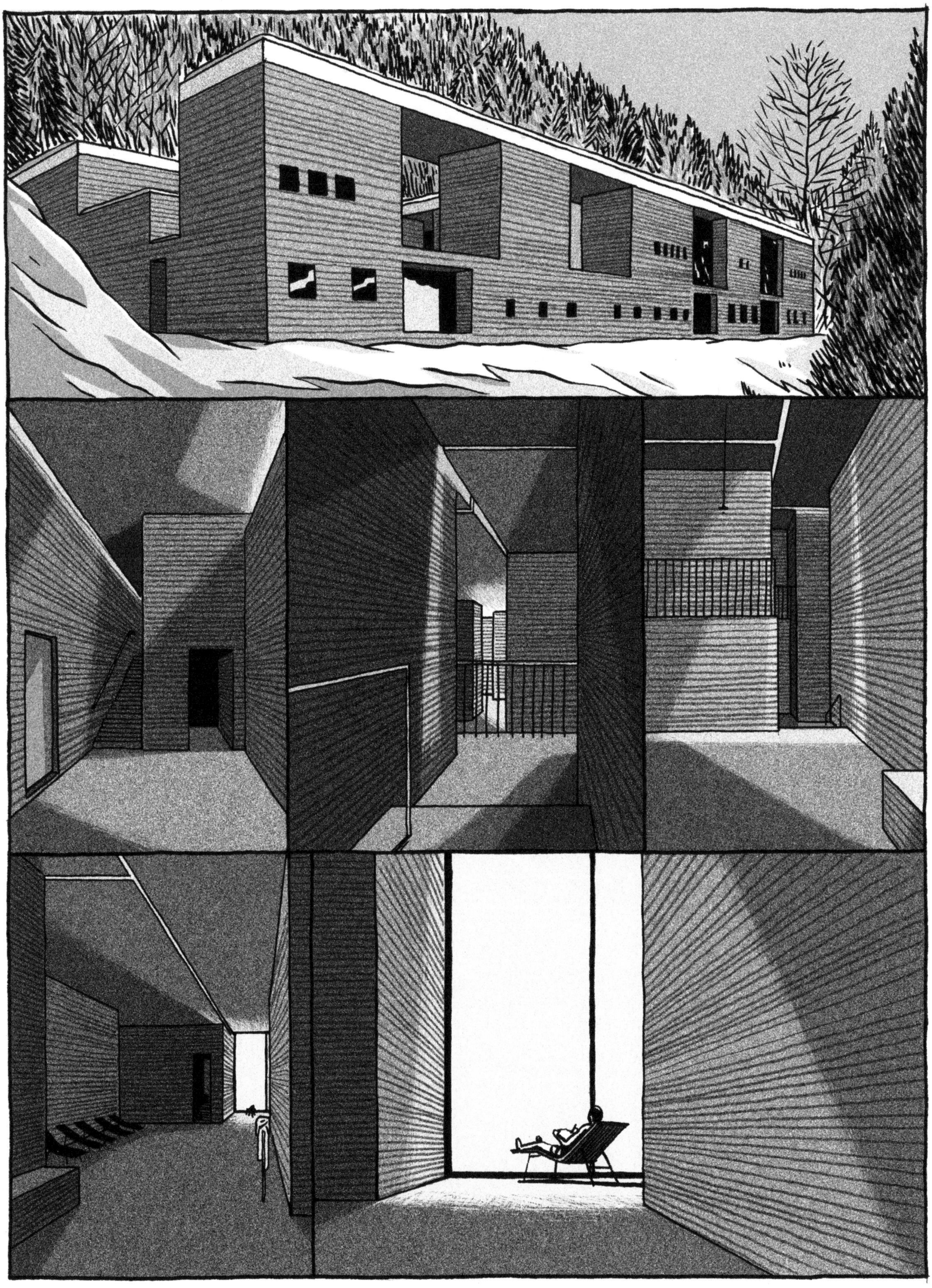

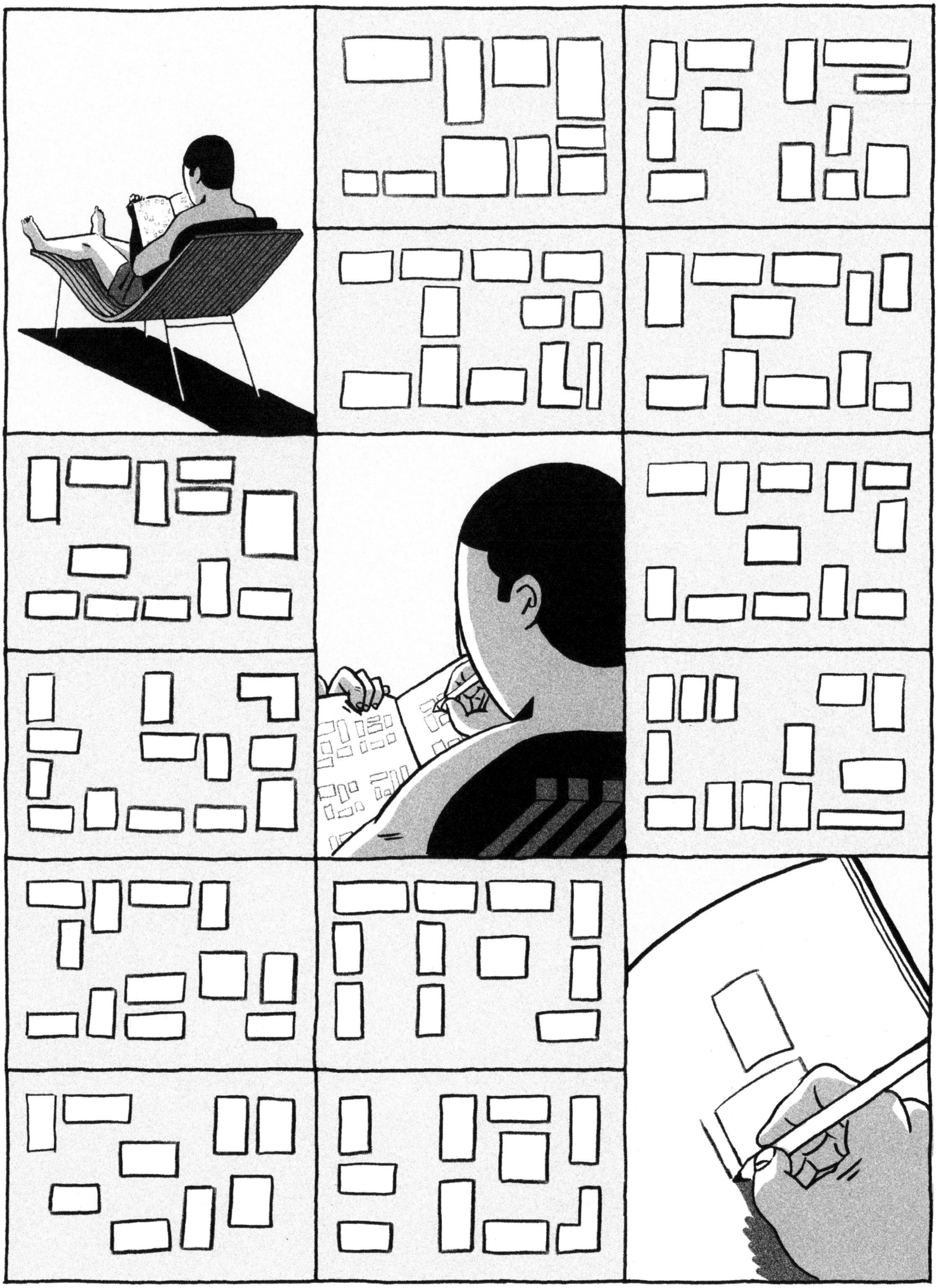

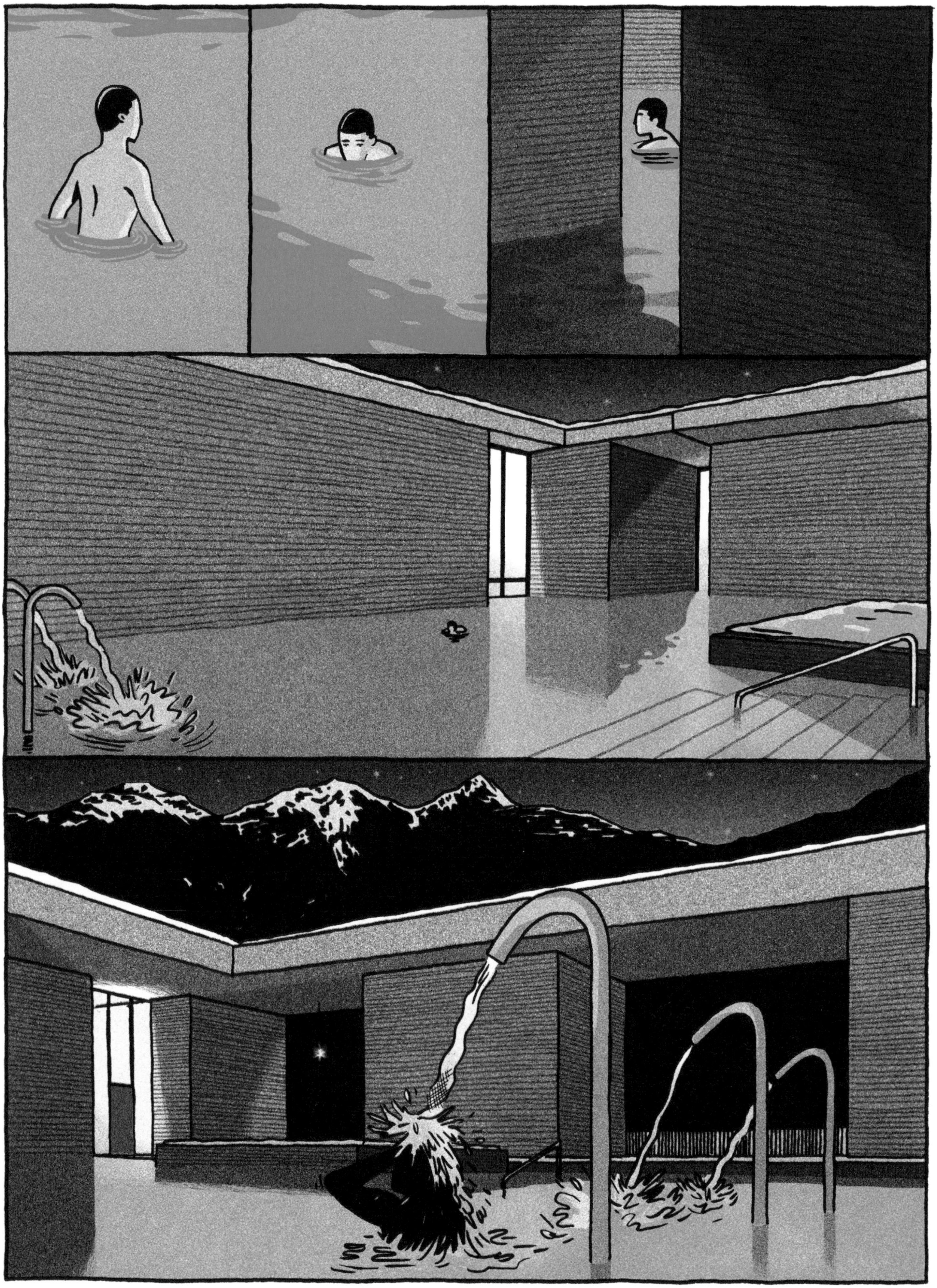

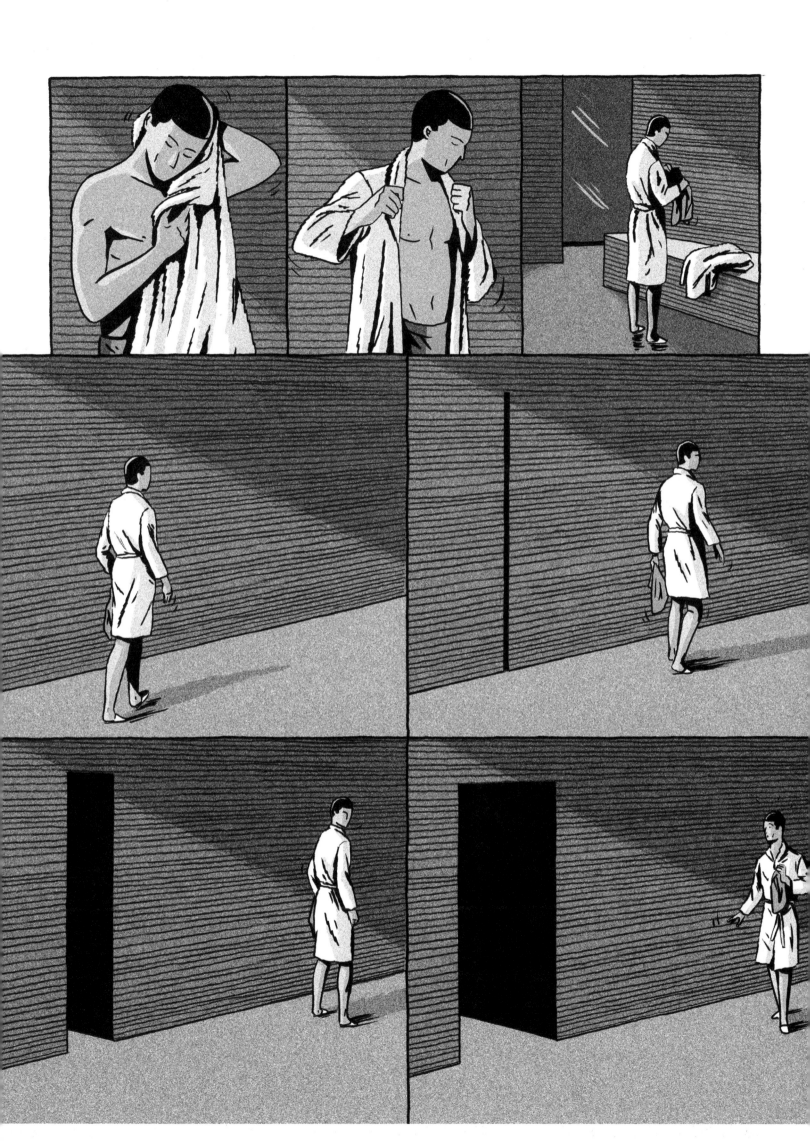

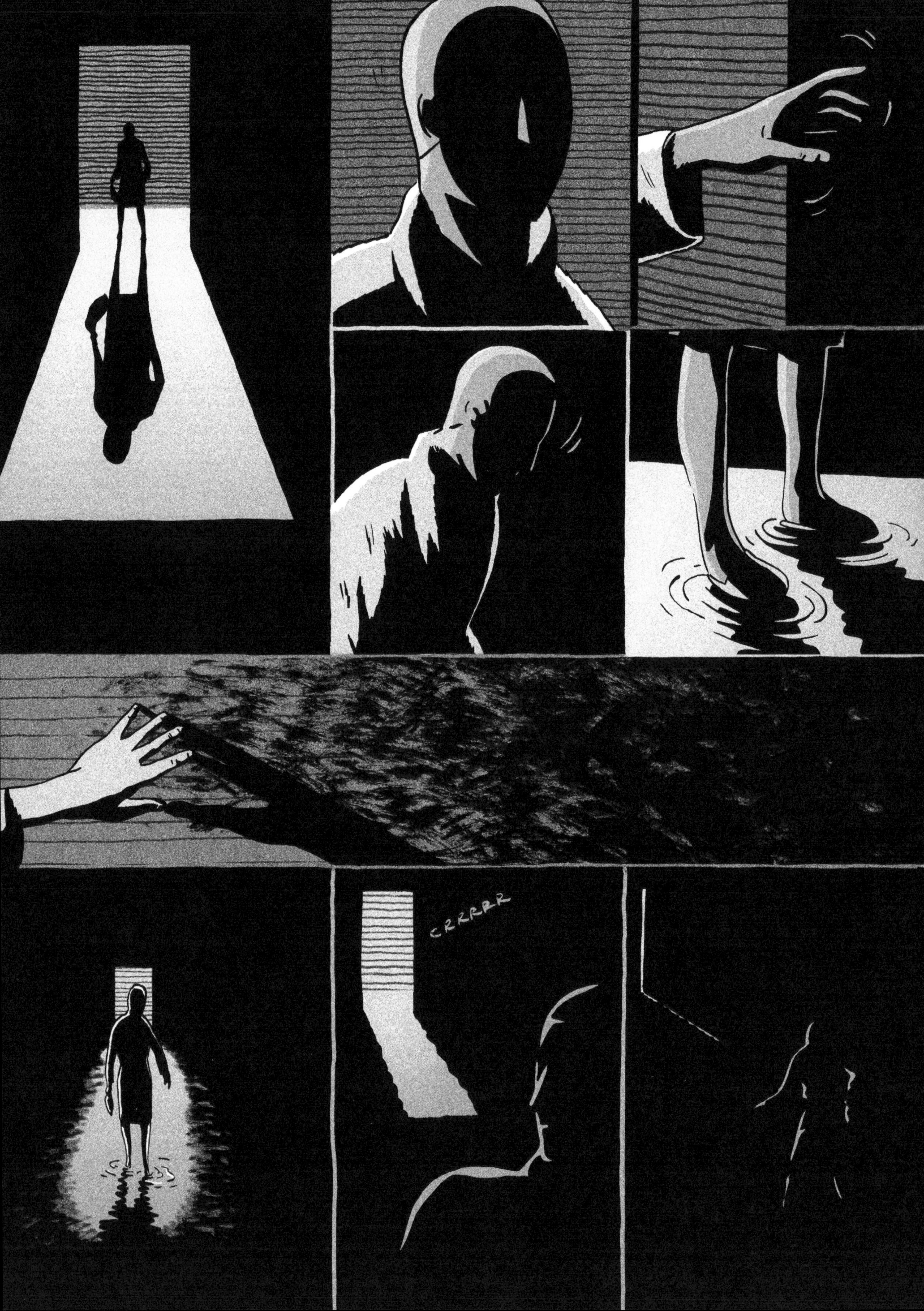
CRRRRR

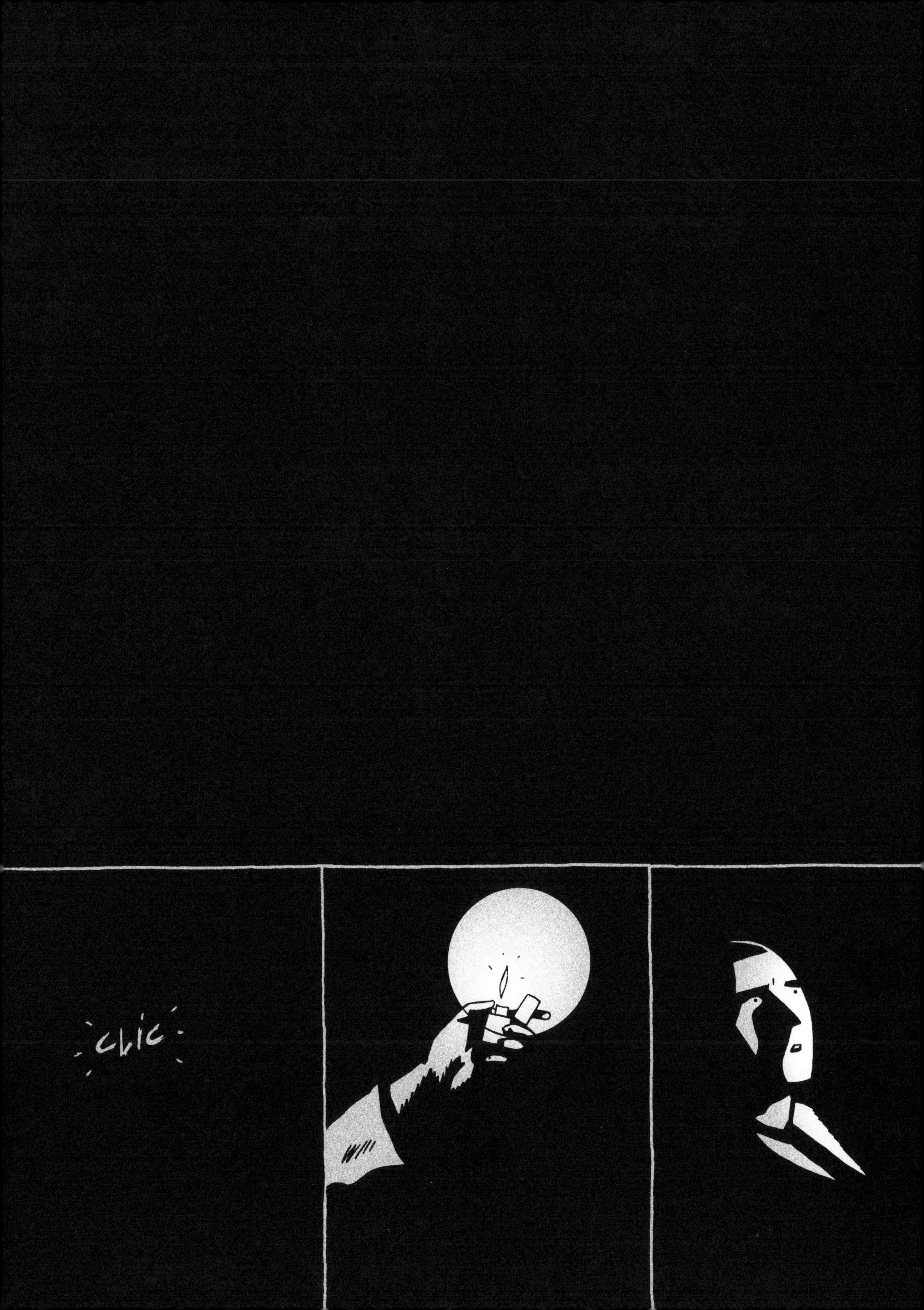
CLIC

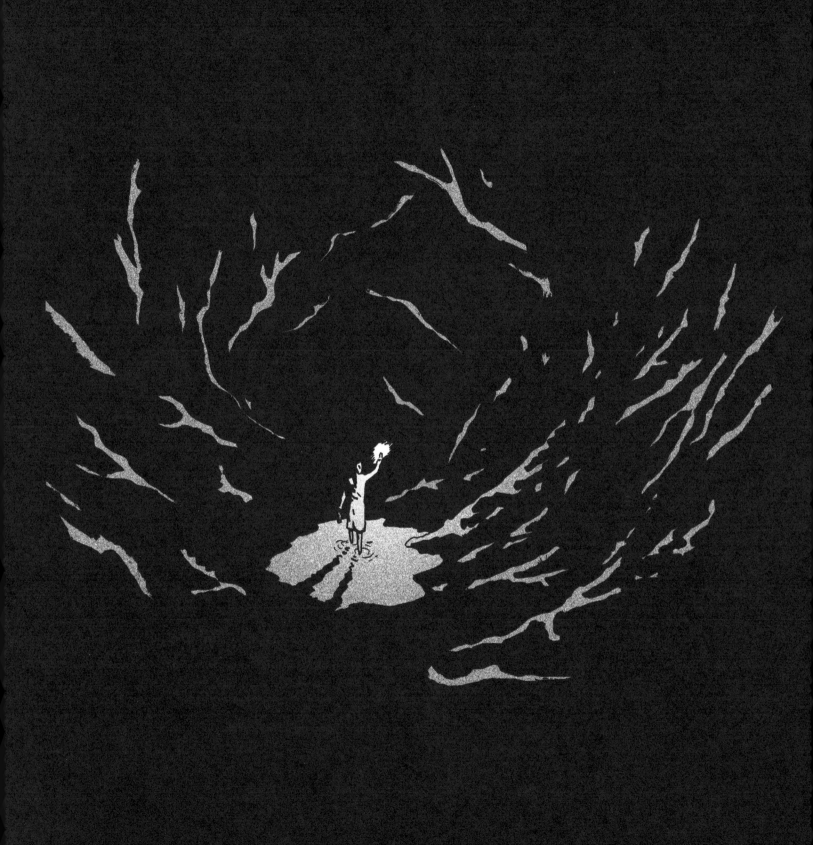

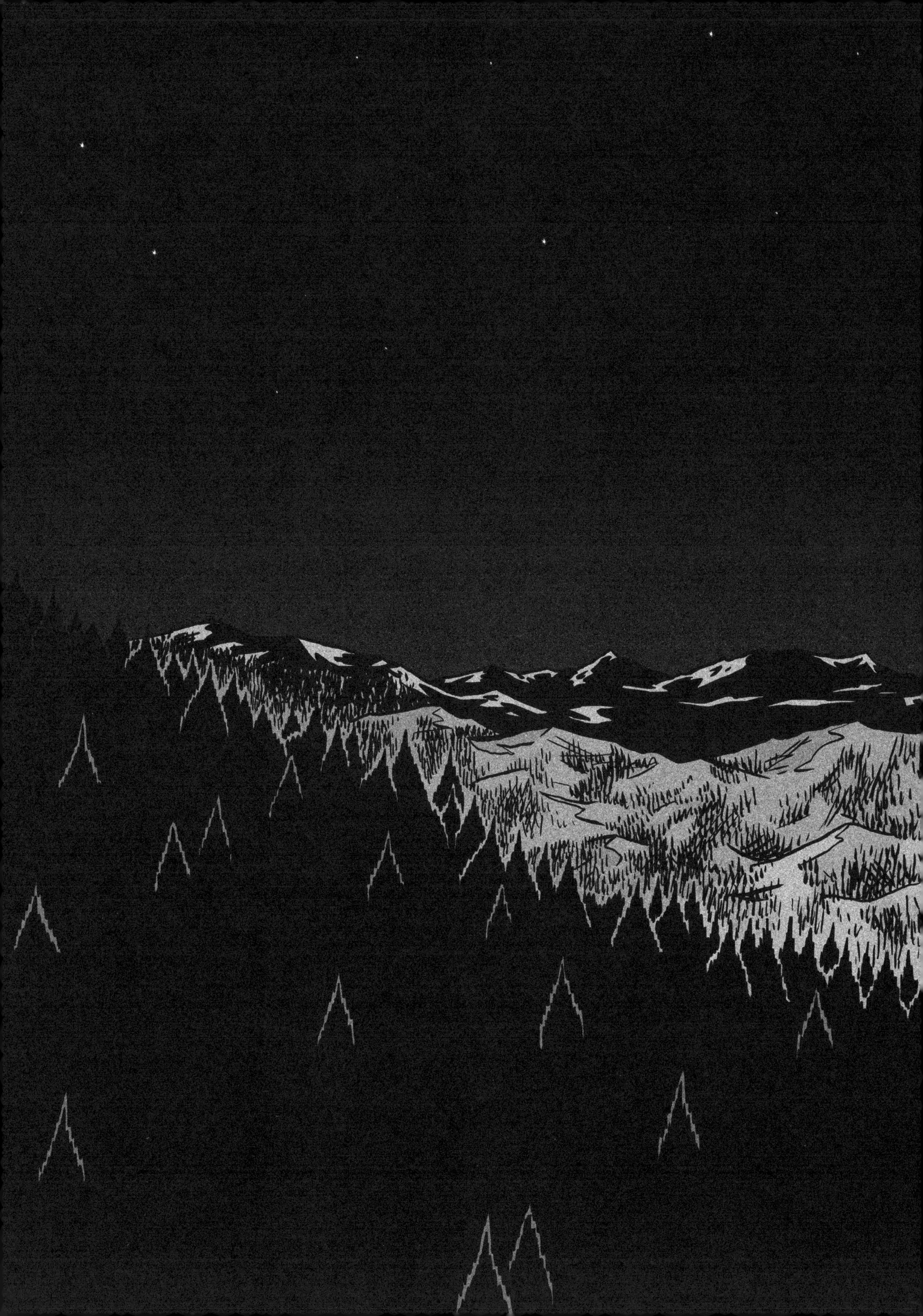

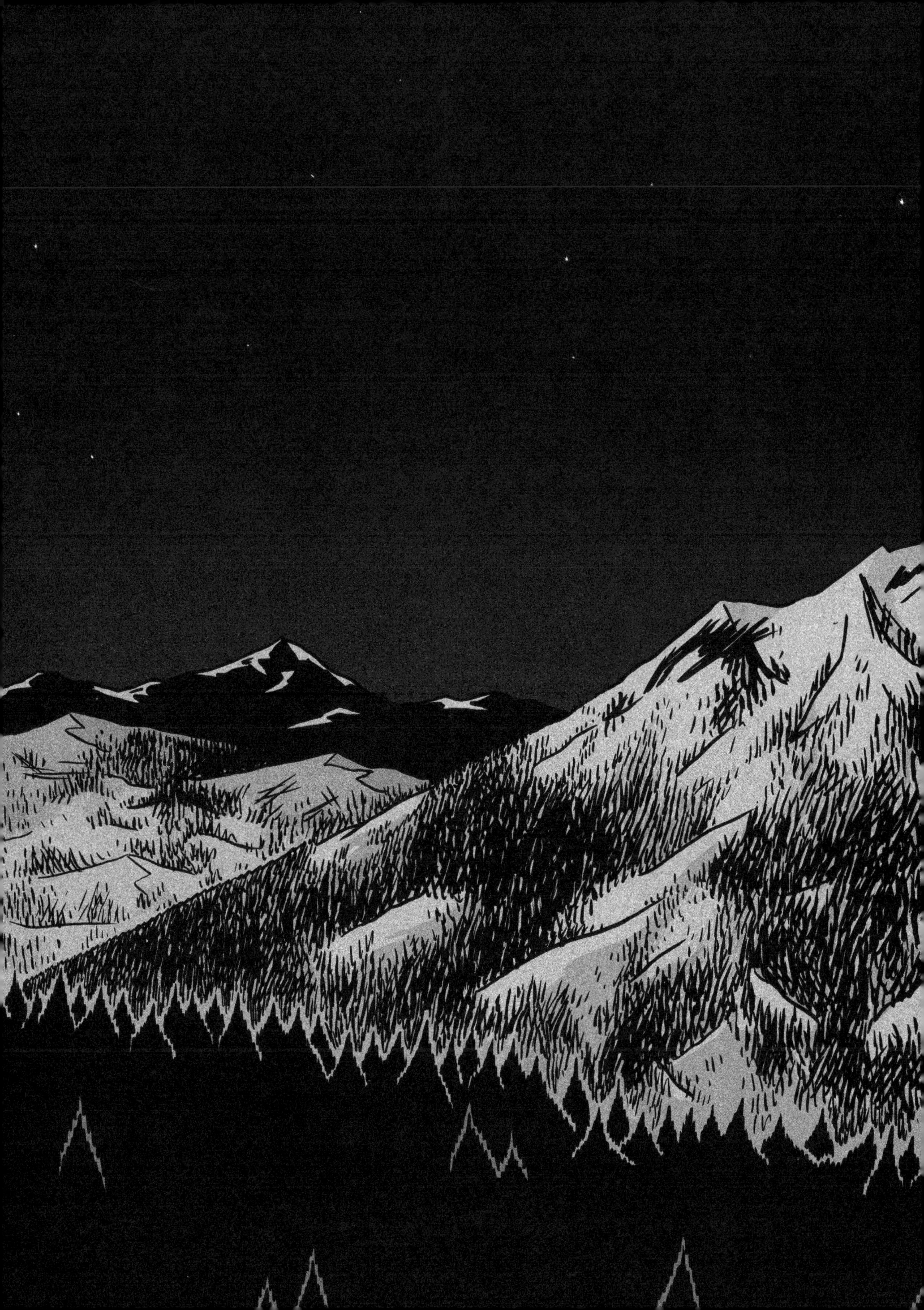

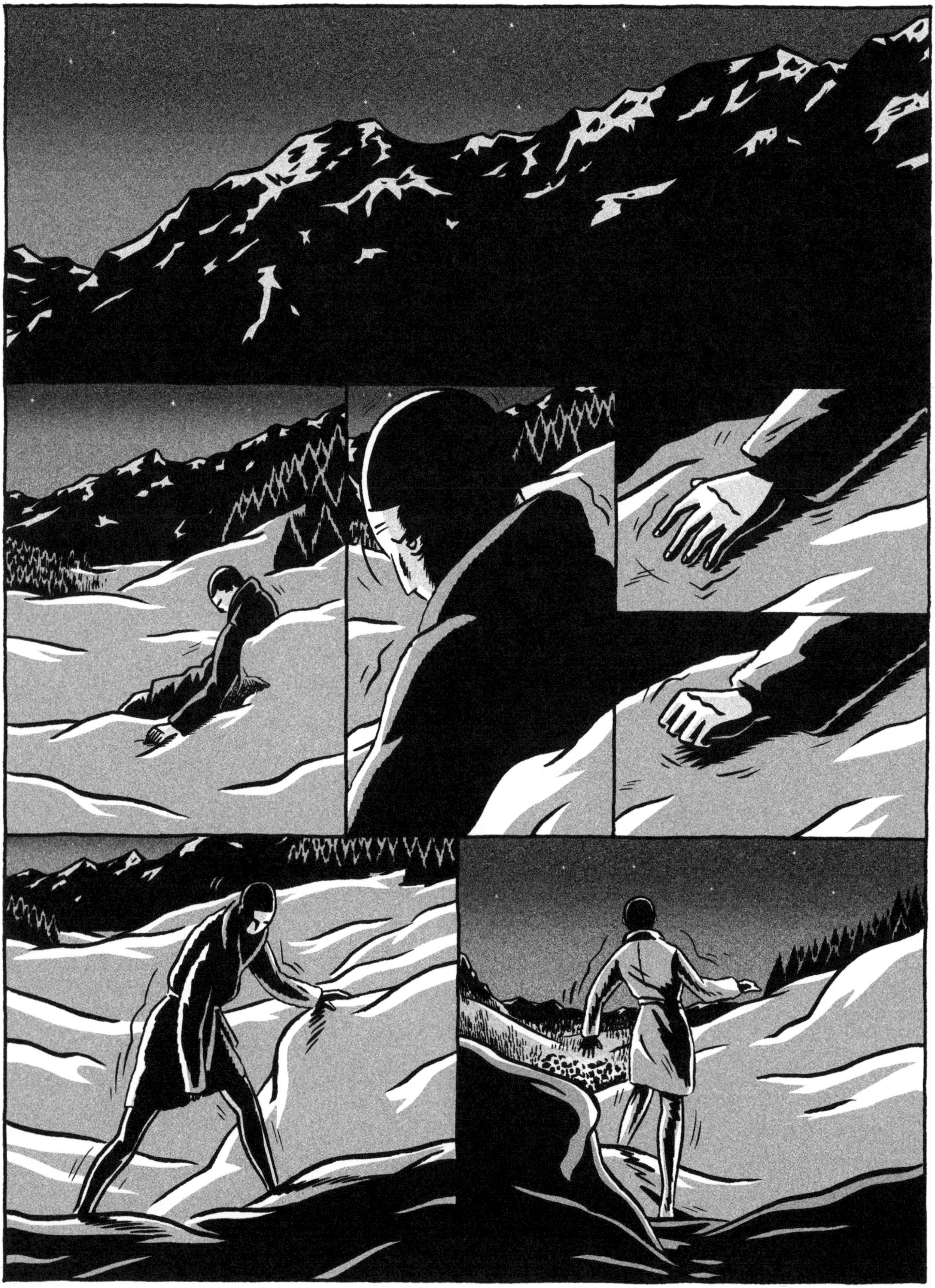

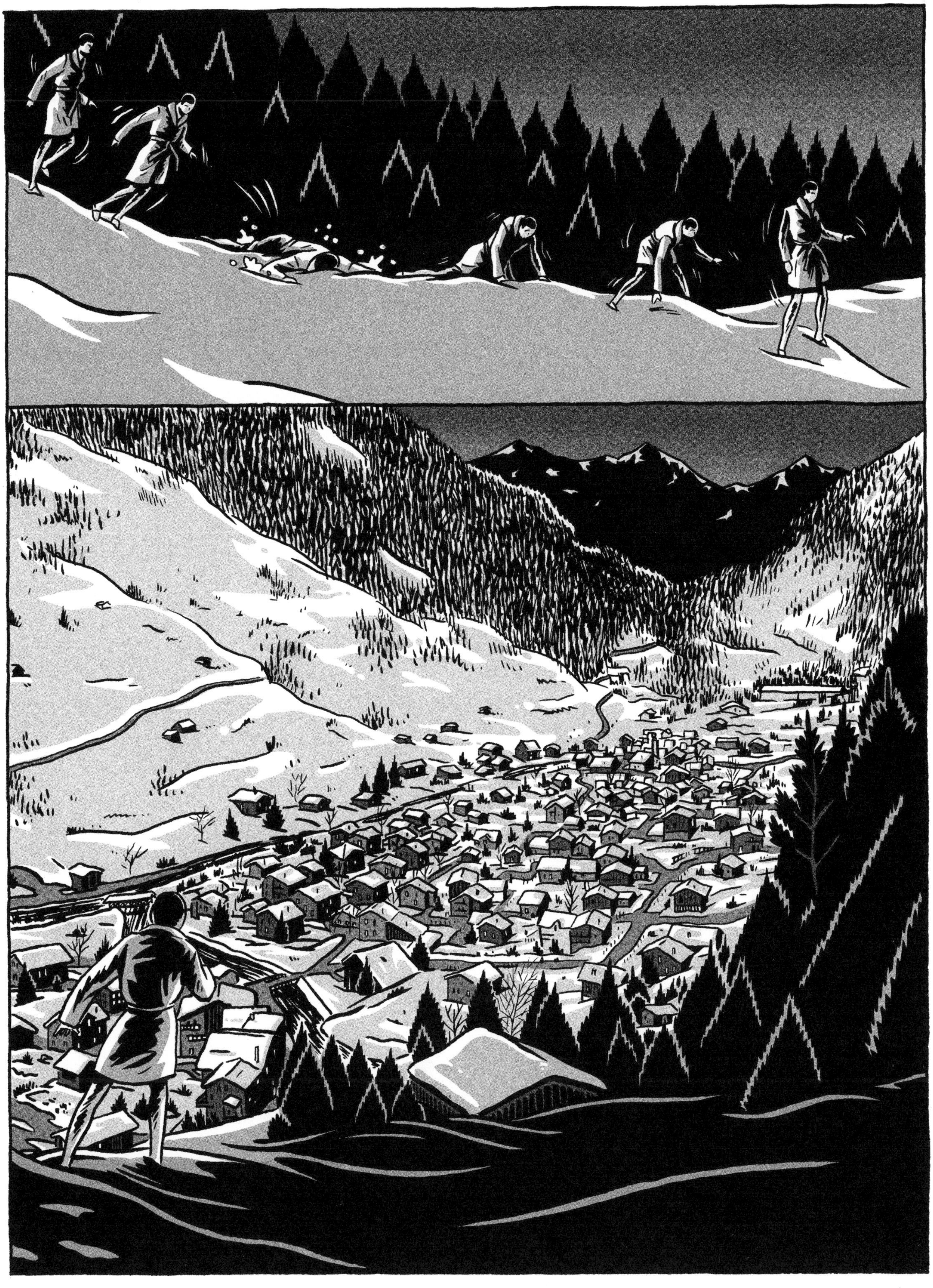

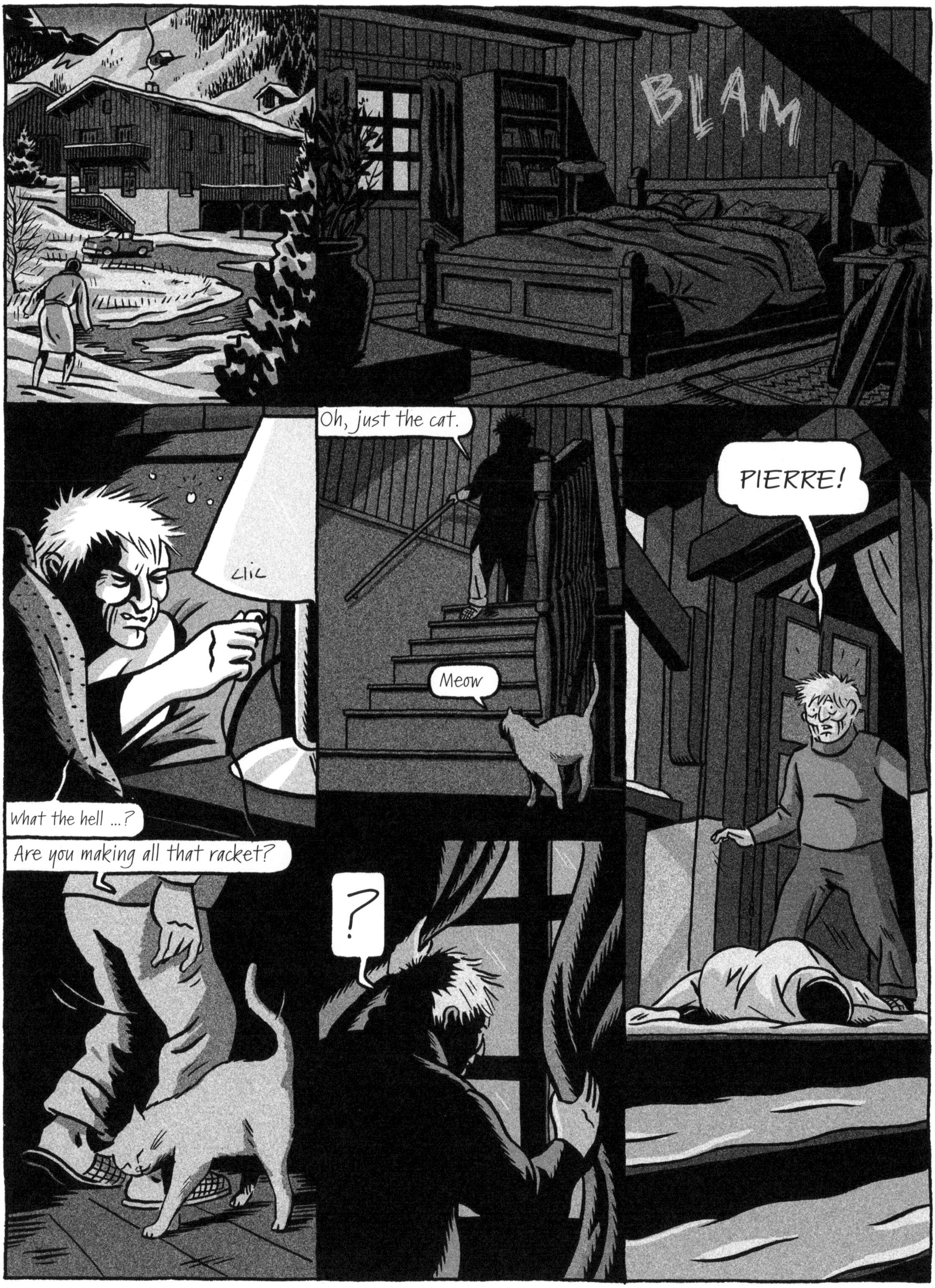
BLAM
CLIC
What the hell ...?
Oh, just the cat.
Meow
PIERRE!
Are you making all that racket?
?

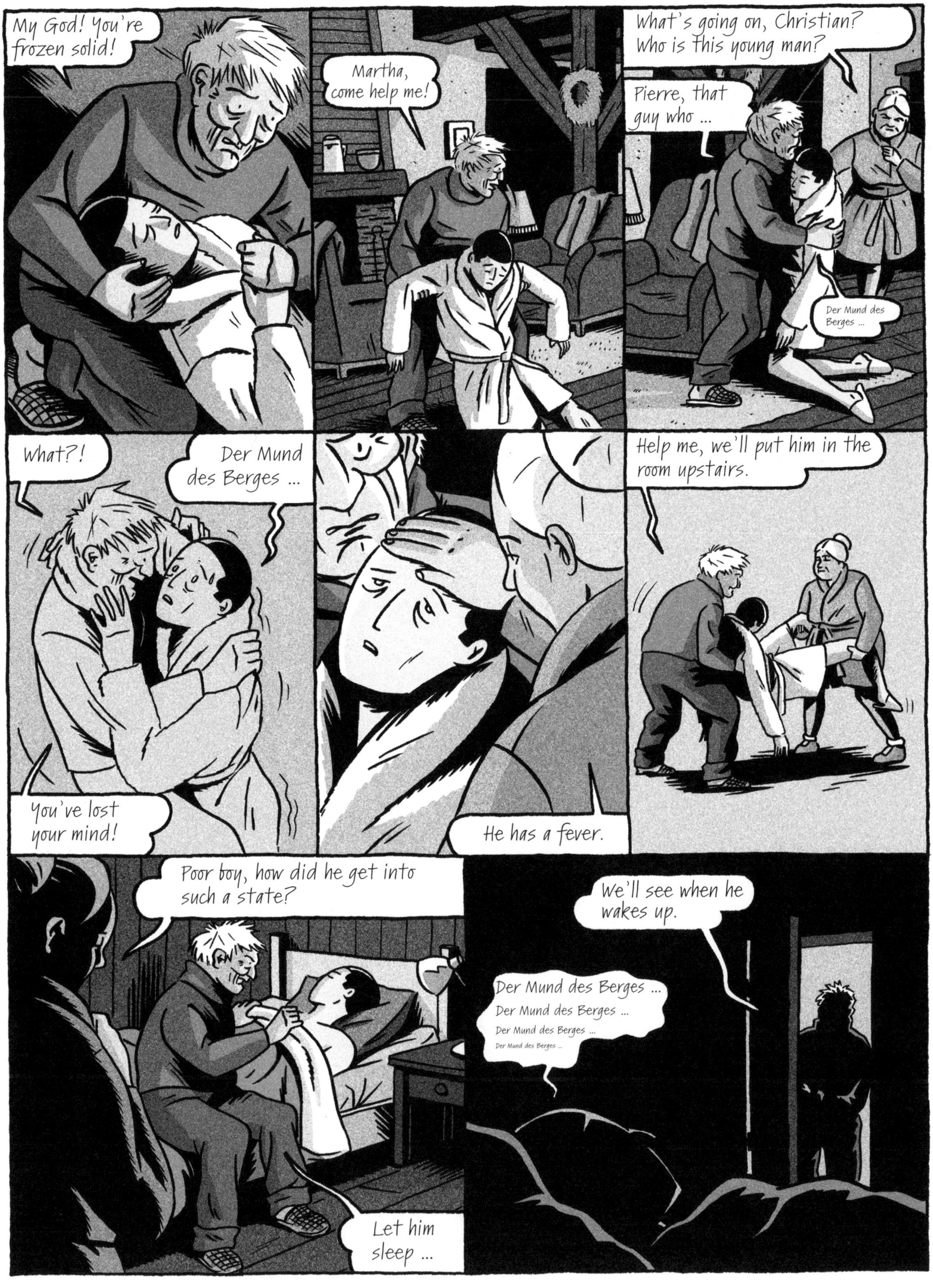
My God! You're frozen solid!
Martha, come help me!
What's going on, Christian? Who is this young man?
Pierre, that guy who ...
Der Mund des Berges ...
What?!
Der Mund des Berges ...
You've lost your mind!
He has a fever.
Help me, we'll put him in the room upstairs.
Poor boy, how did he get into such a state?
Let him sleep ...
We'll see when he wakes up.
Der Mund des Berges ...
Der Mund des Berges ...
Der Mund des Berges ...
Der Mund des Berges ...

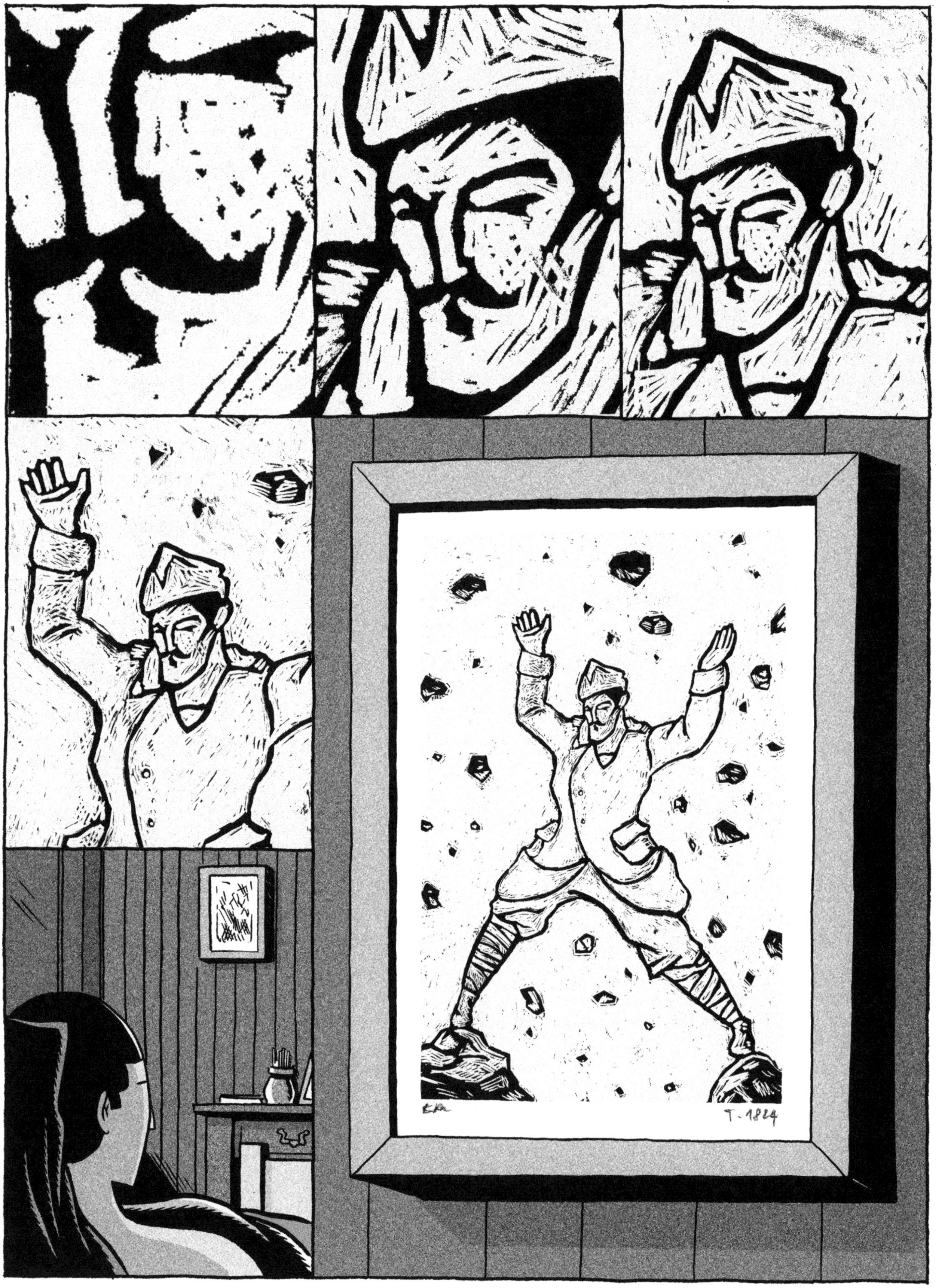
T-1824

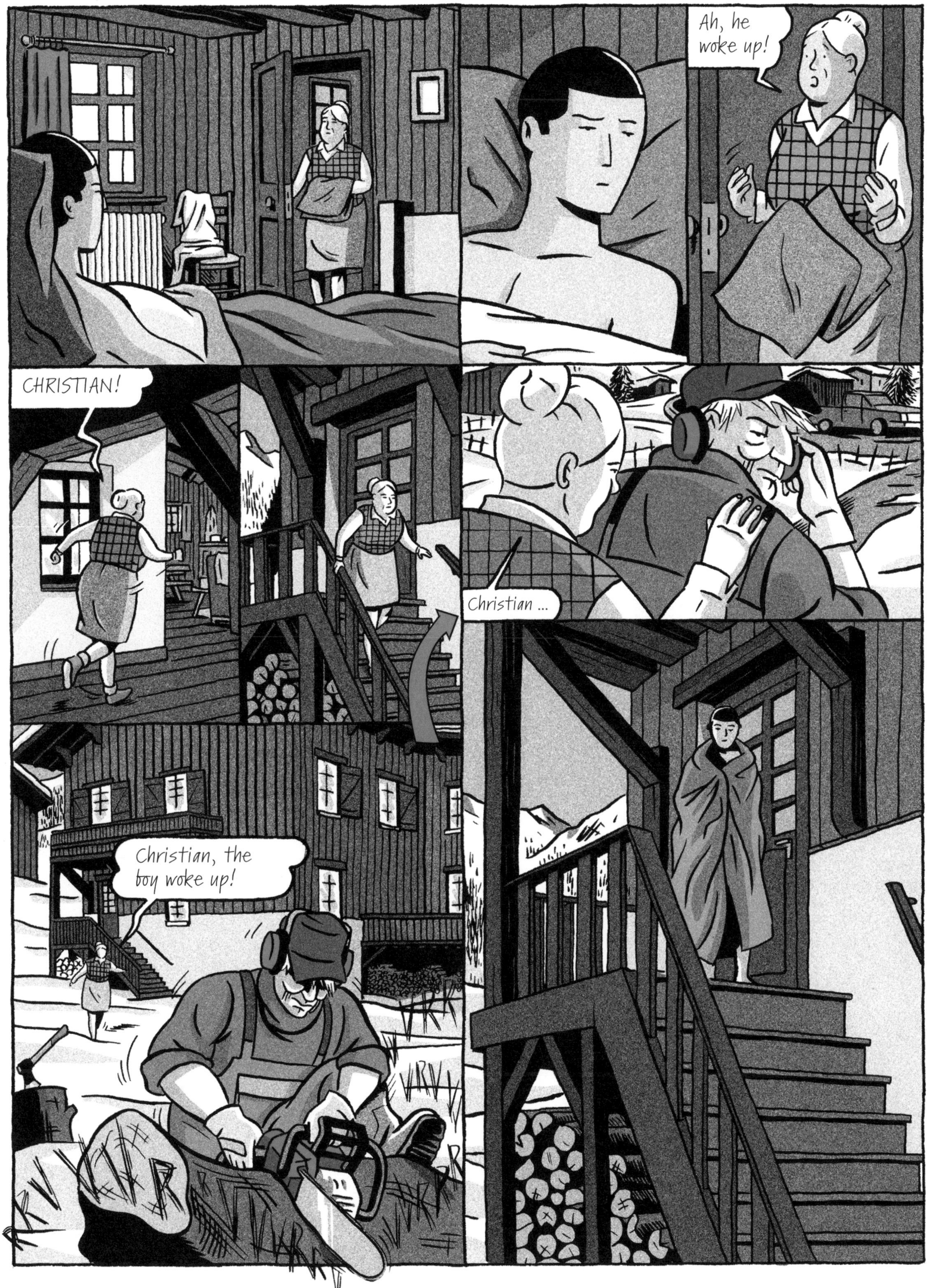
Ah, he woke up!
CHRISTIAN!
Christian ...
Christian, the boy woke up!

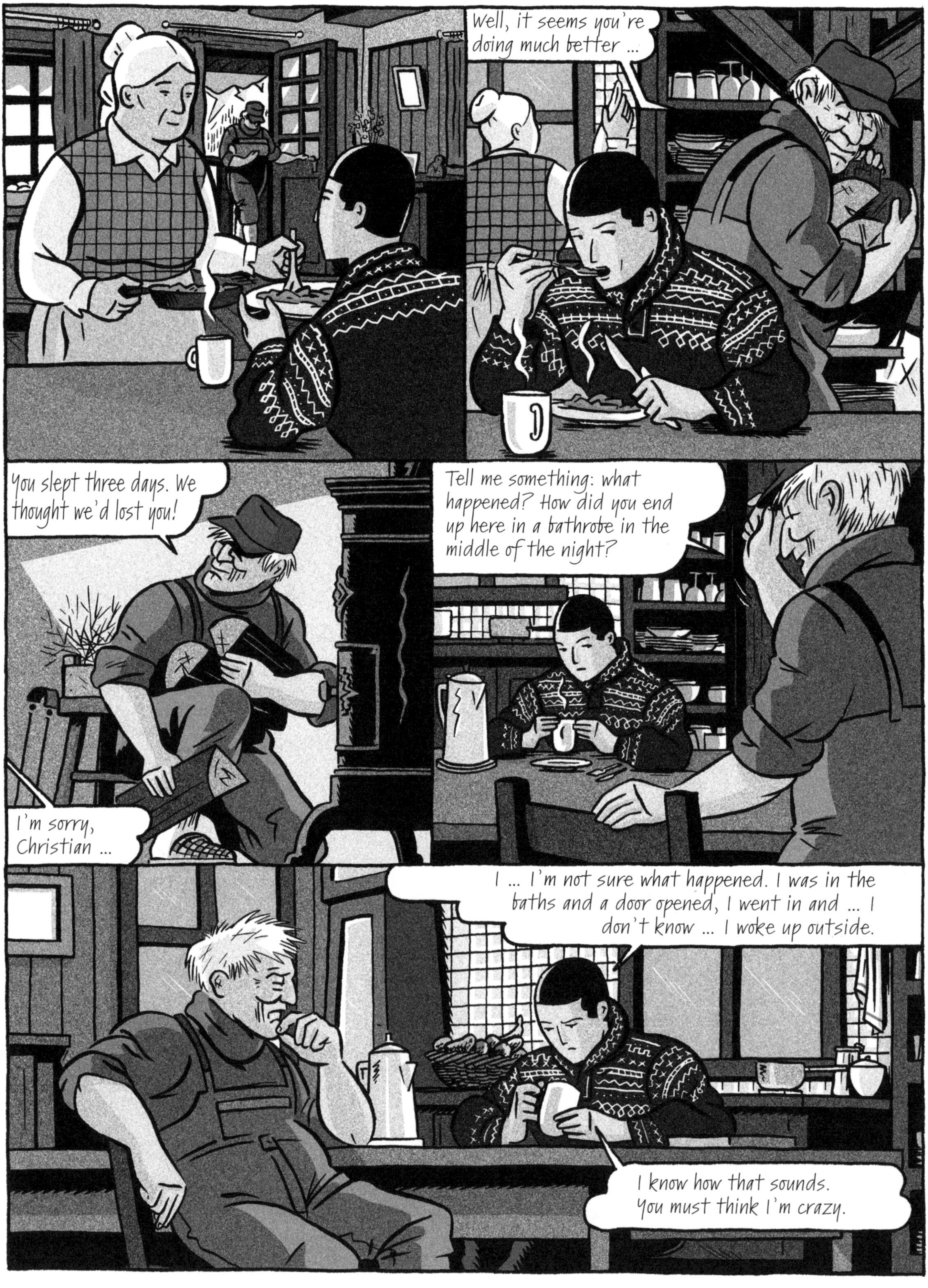
Well, it seems you're doing much better ...
You slept three days. We thought we'd lost you!
I'm sorry, Christian ...
Tell me something: what happened? How did you end up here in a bathrobe in the middle of the night?
I ... I'm not sure what happened. I was in the baths and a door opened, I went in and ... I don't know ... I woke up outside.
I know how that sounds. You must think I'm crazy.

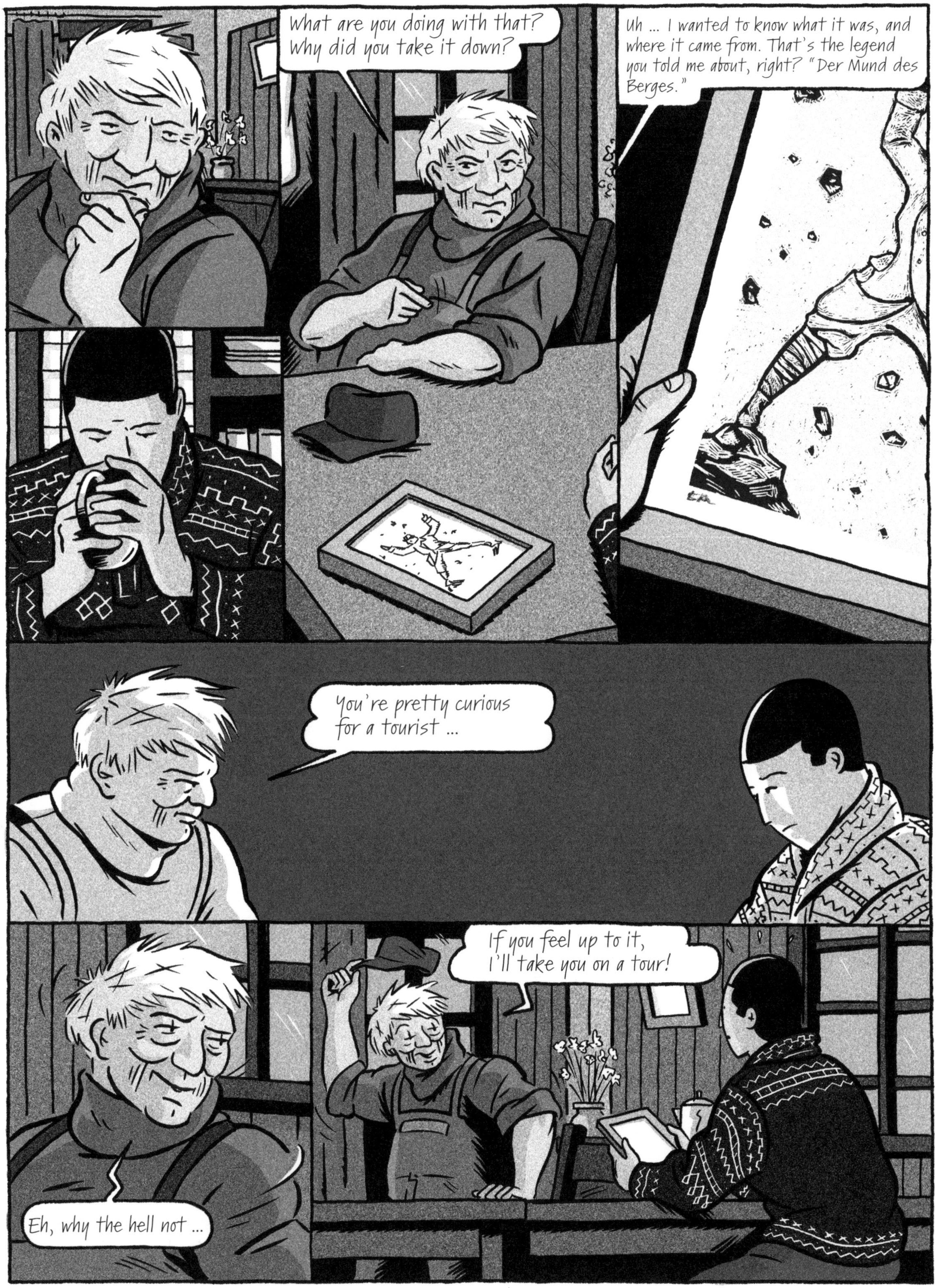
What are you doing with that? Why did you take it down?
Uh ... I wanted to know what it was, and where it came from. That's the legend you told me about, right? "Der Mund des Berges."
You're pretty curious for a tourist ...
Eh, why the hell not ...
If you feel up to it, I'll take you on a tour!

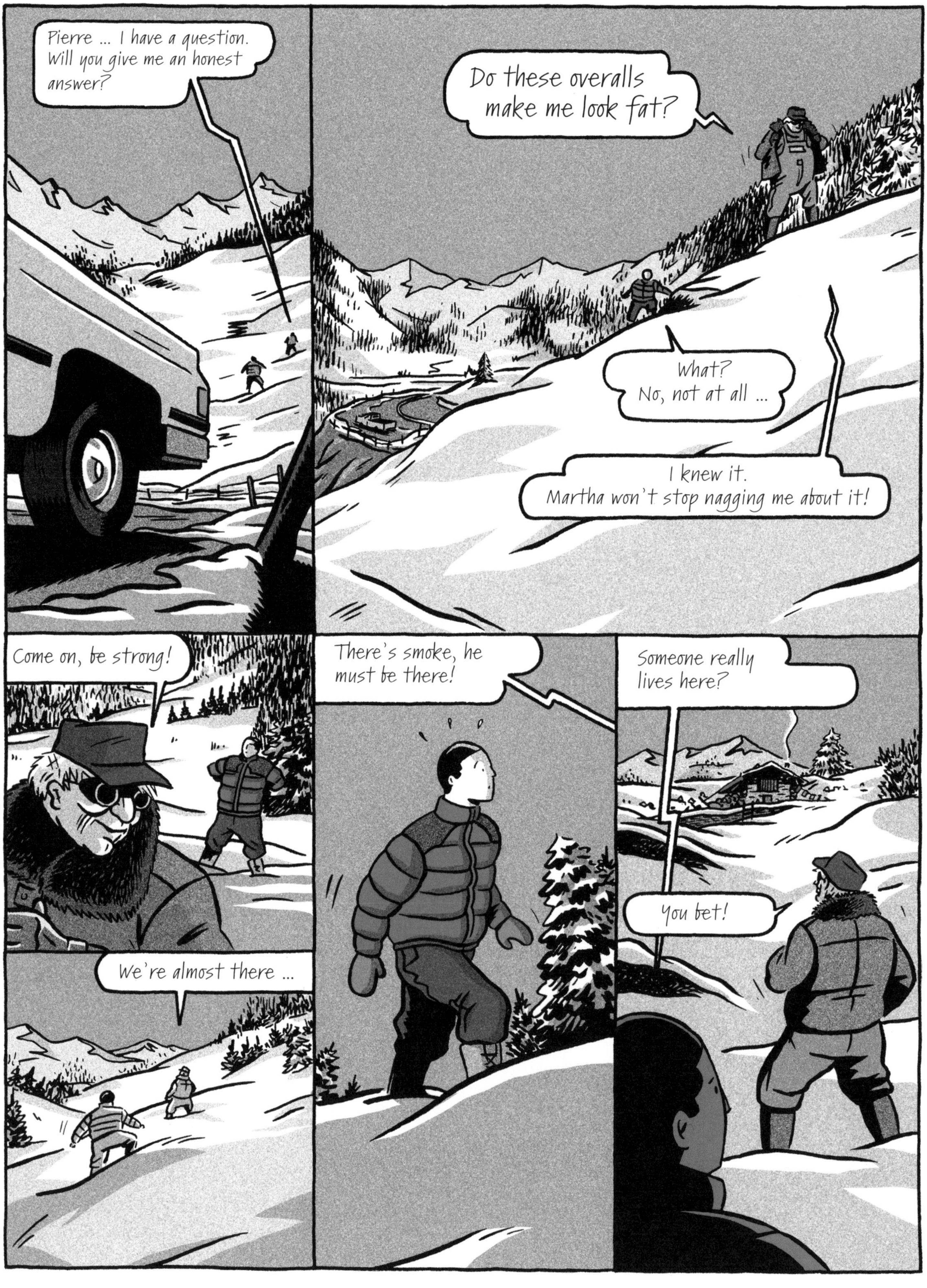
Pierre ... I have a question. Will you give me an honest answer?
Do these overalls make me look fat?
What? No, not at all ...
I knew it. Martha won't stop nagging me about it!
Come on, be strong!
We're almost there ...
There's smoke, he must be there!
Someone really lives here?
You bet!

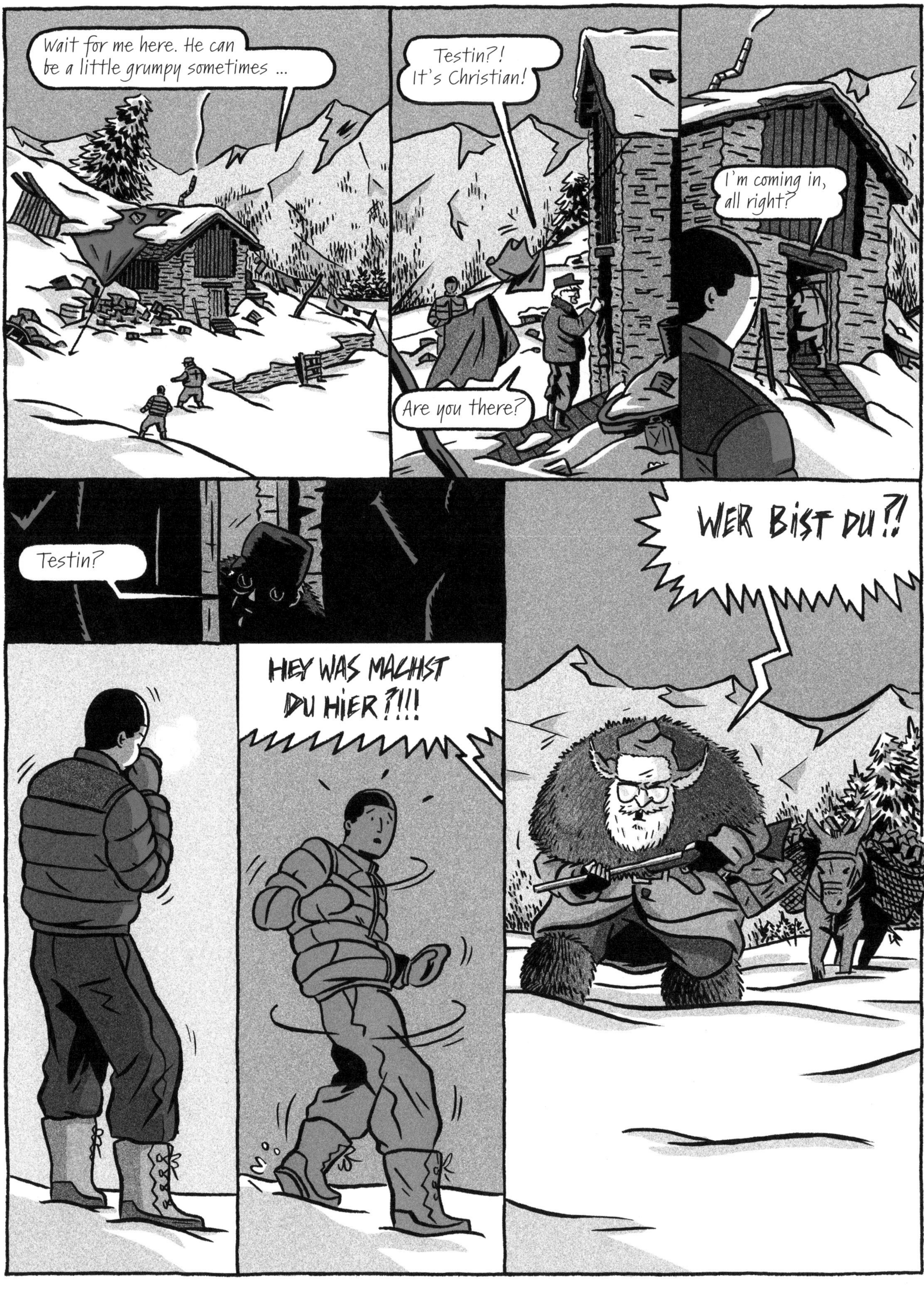
Wait for me here. He can be a little grumpy sometimes ...
Testin?! It's Christian!
Are you there?
I'm coming in, all right?
Testin?
WER BIST DU?!
HEY WAS MACHST DU HIER?!!!

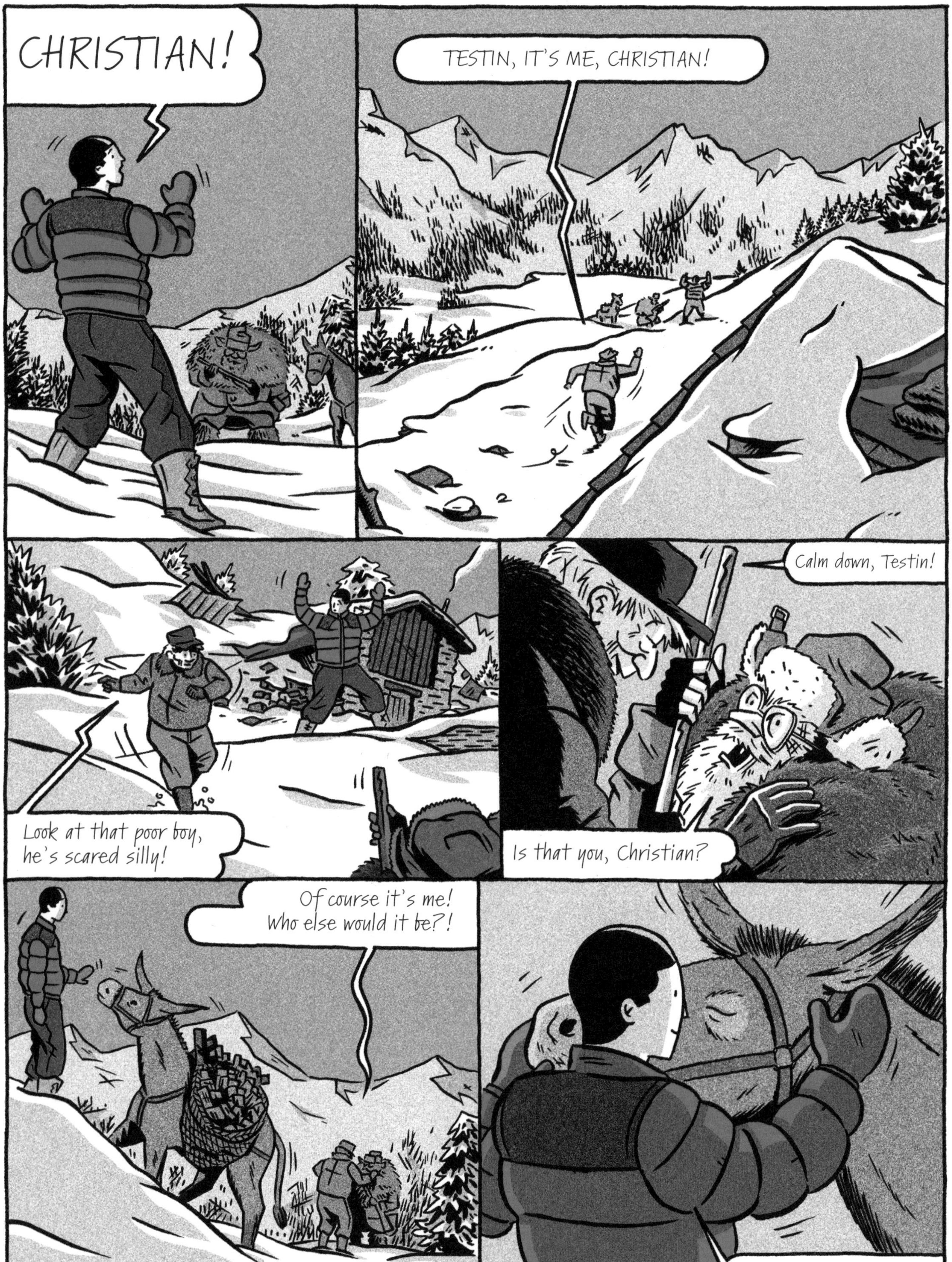
CHRISTIAN!
TESTIN, IT'S ME, CHRISTIAN!
Look at that poor boy, he's scared silly!
Calm down, Testin!
Is that you, Christian?
Of course it's me! Who else would it be?!
Nice and easy now ...

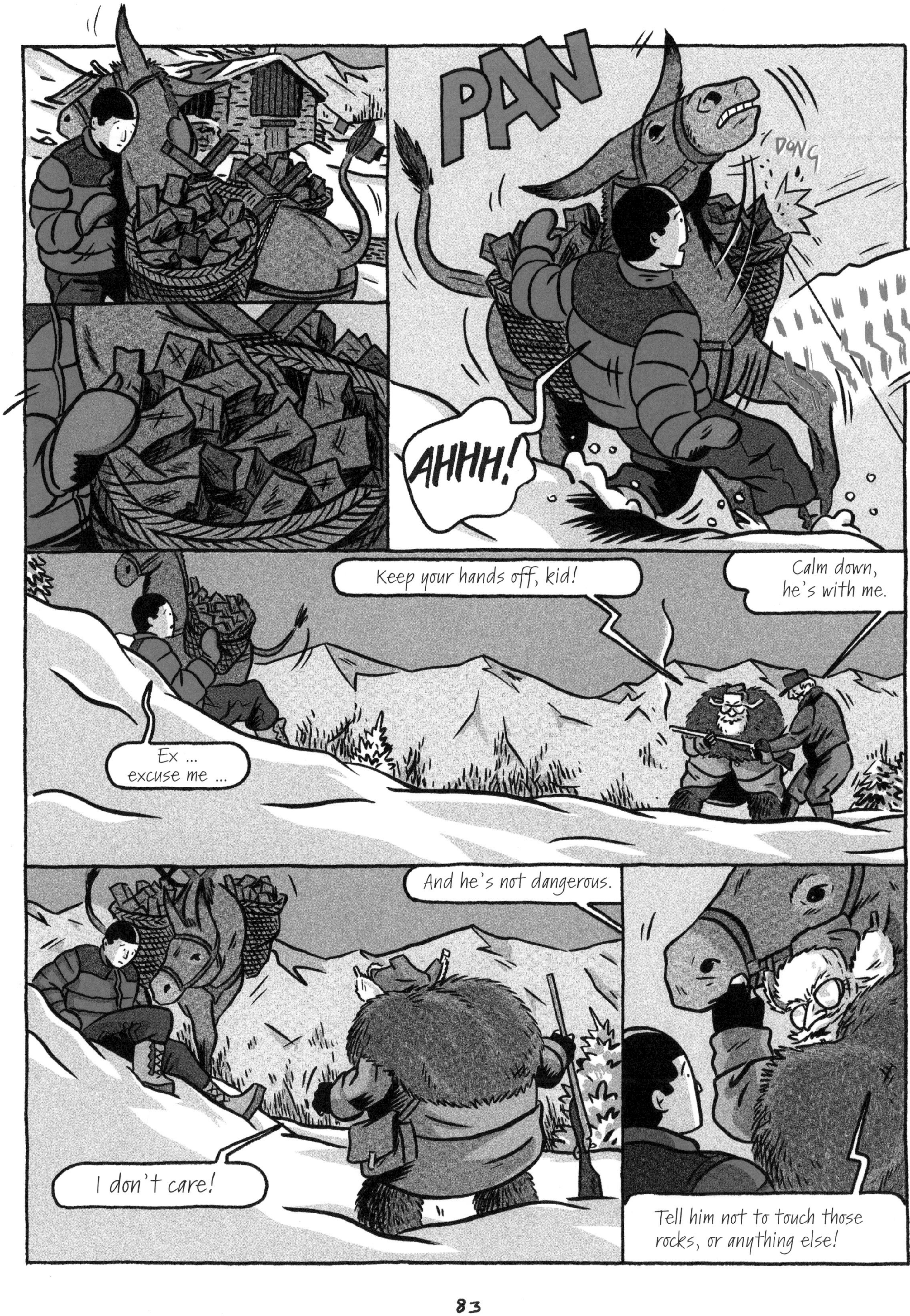
PAN
DONG
AHHH!
Keep your hands off, kid!
Calm down, he's with me.
Ex ... excuse me ...
And he's not dangerous.
I don't care!
Tell him not to touch those rocks, or anything else!

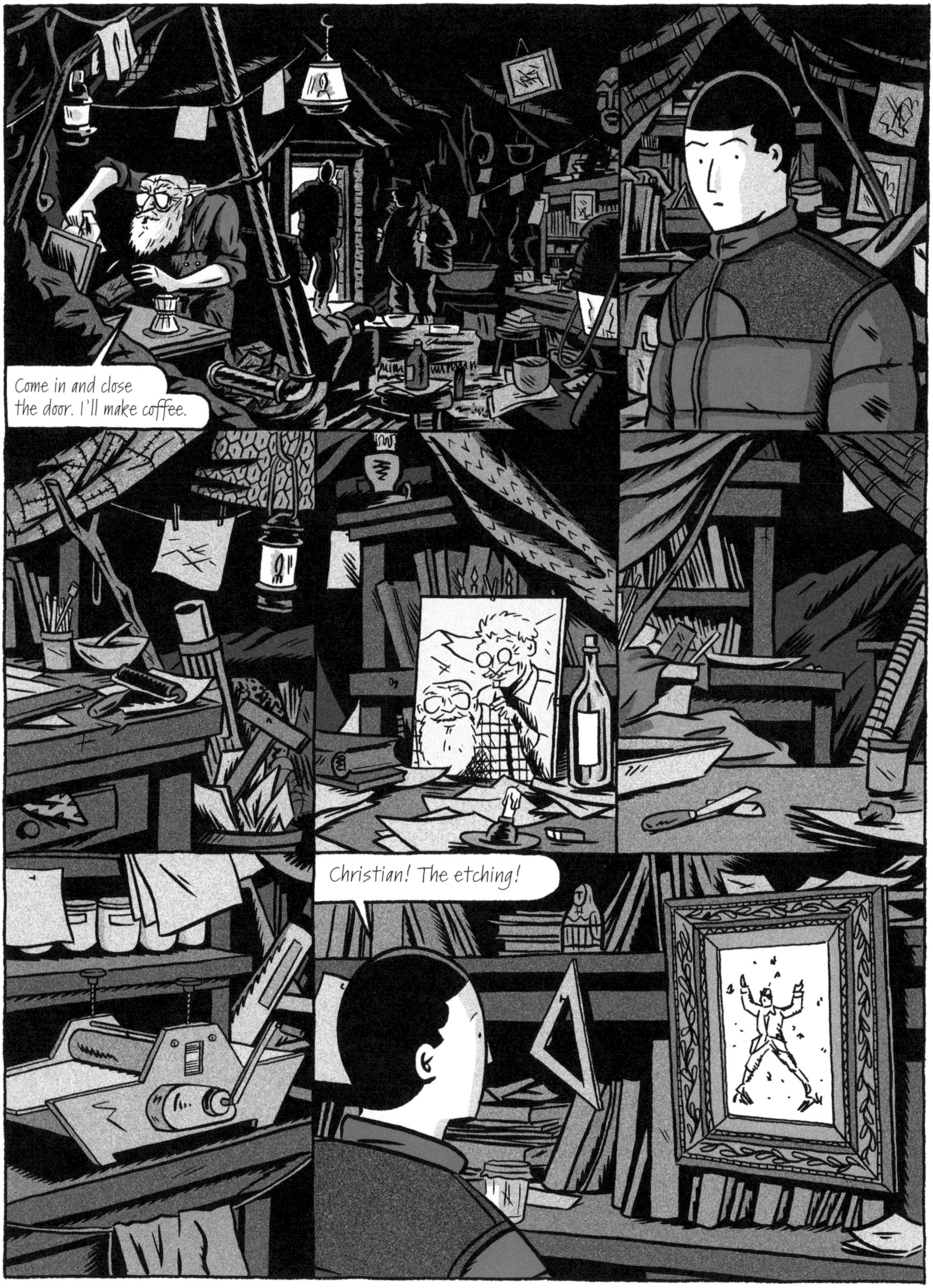
Come in and close the door. I'll make coffee.
Christian! The etching!

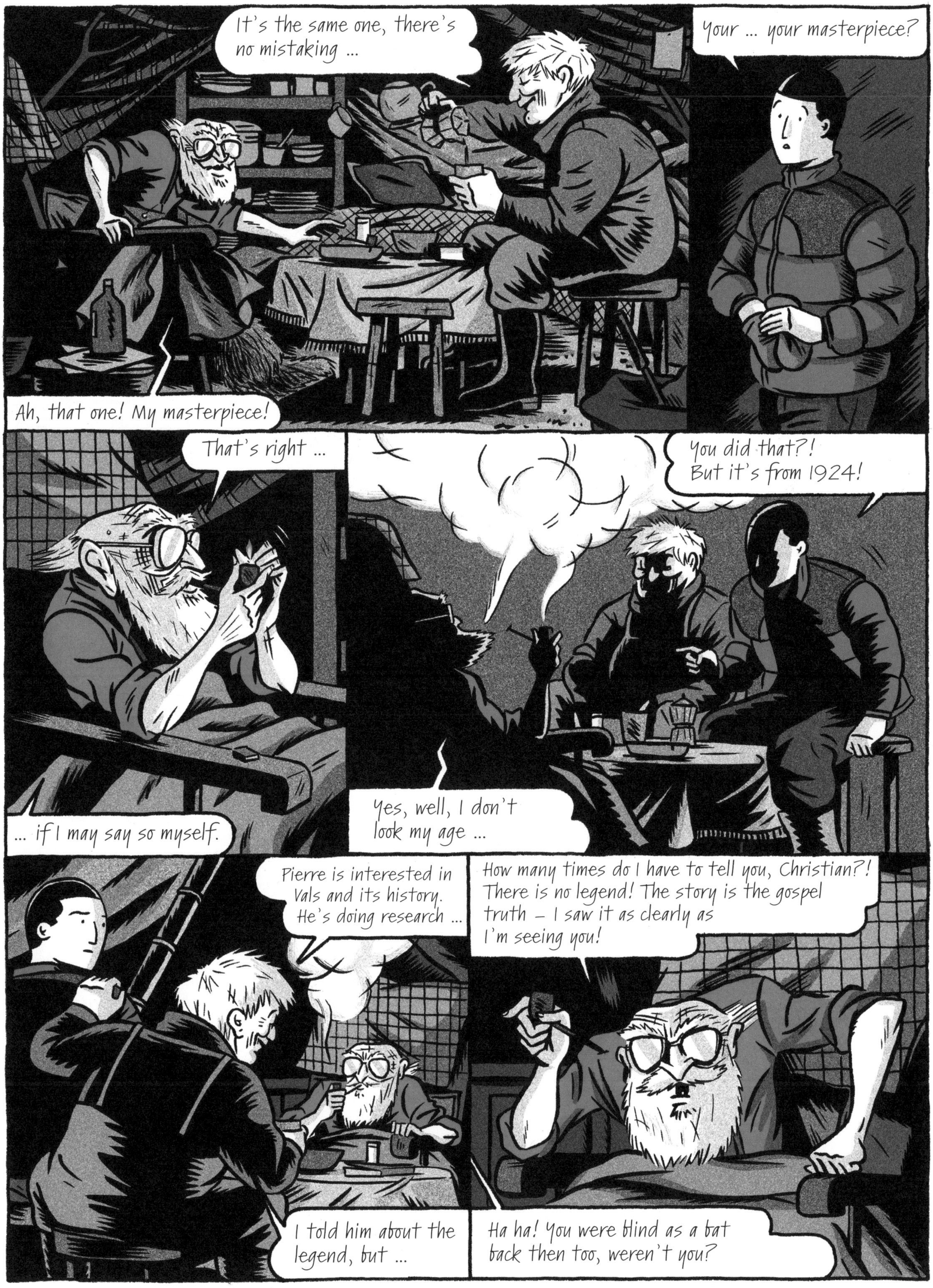

It's the same one, there's no mistaking ...
Ah, that one! My masterpiece!
Your ... your masterpiece?
That's right ...
... if I may say so myself.
You did that?! But it's from 1924!
Yes, well, I don't look my age ...
Pierre is interested in Vals and its history. He's doing research ...
I told him about the legend, but ...
How many times do I have to tell you, Christian?! There is no legend! The story is the gospel truth – I saw it as clearly as I'm seeing you!
Ha ha! You were blind as a bat back then too, weren't you?

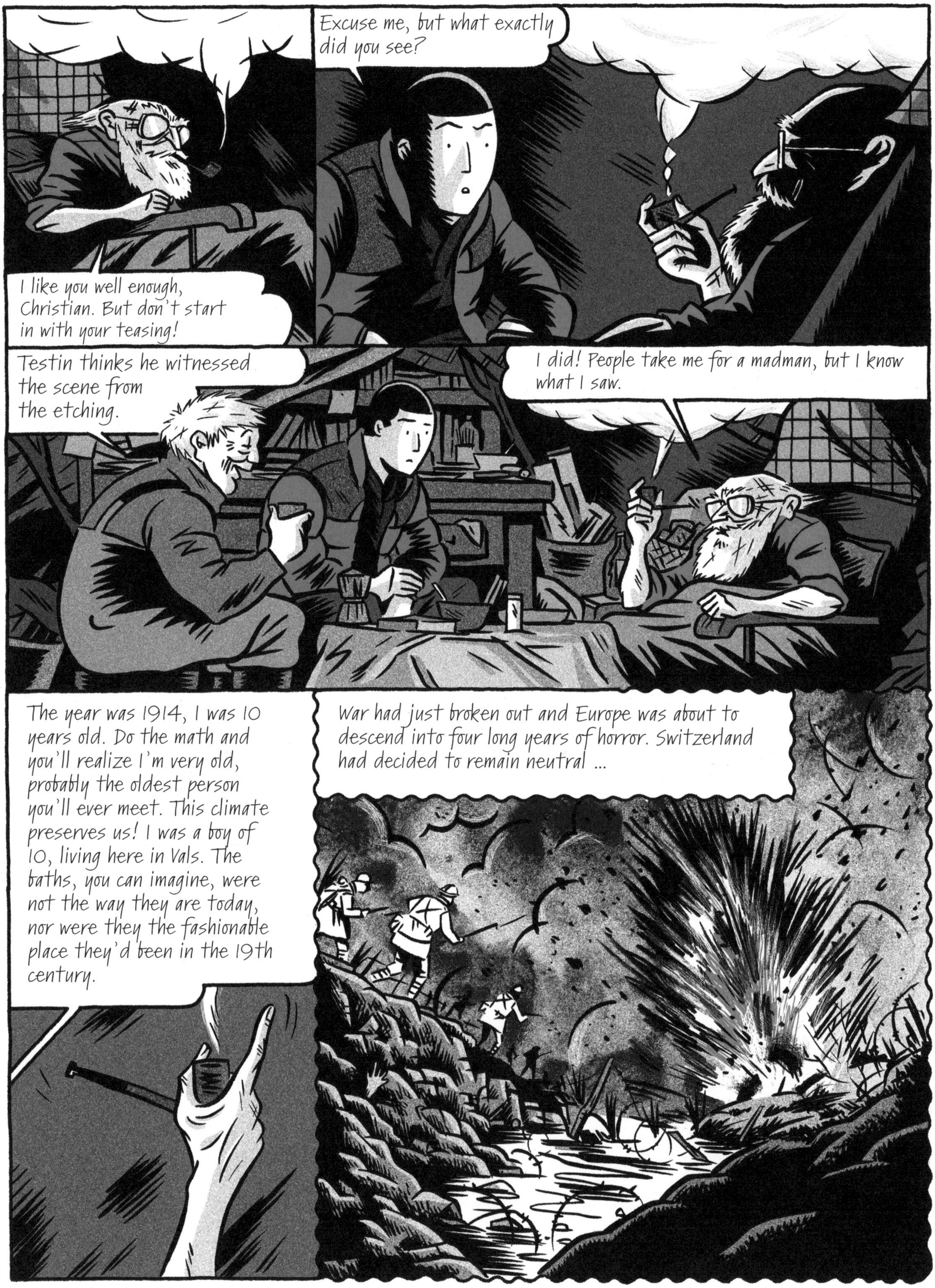

I like you well enough, Christian. But don't start in with your teasing!
Excuse me, but what exactly did you see?
Testin thinks he witnessed the scene from the etching.
I did! People take me for a madman, but I know what I saw.
The year was 1914, I was 10 years old. Do the math and you'll realize I'm very old, probably the oldest person you'll ever meet. This climate preserves us! I was a boy of 10, living here in Vals. The baths, you can imagine, were not the way they are today, nor were they the fashionable place they'd been in the 19th century.
War had just broken out and Europe was about to descend into four long years of horror. Switzerland had decided to remain neutral ...

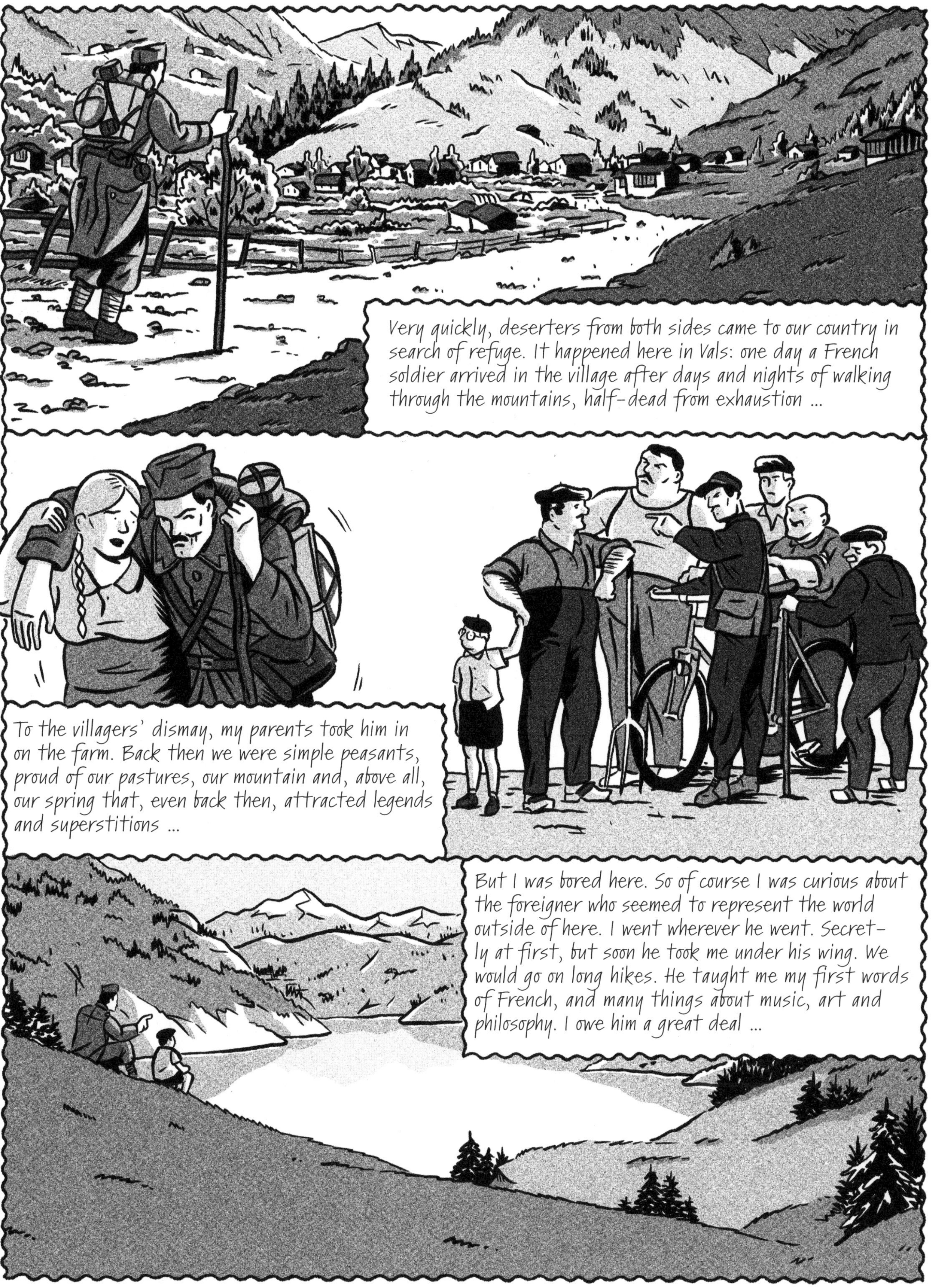
Very quickly, deserters from both sides came to our country in search of refuge. It happened here in Vals: one day a French soldier arrived in the village after days and nights of walking through the mountains, half-dead from exhaustion ...
To the villagers' dismay, my parents took him in on the farm. Back then we were simple peasants, proud of our pastures, our mountain and, above all, our spring that, even back then, attracted legends and superstitions ...
But I was bored here. So of course I was curious about the foreigner who seemed to represent the world outside of here. I went wherever he went. Secretly at first, but soon he took me under his wing. We would go on long hikes. He taught me my first words of French, and many things about music, art and philosophy. I owe him a great deal ...

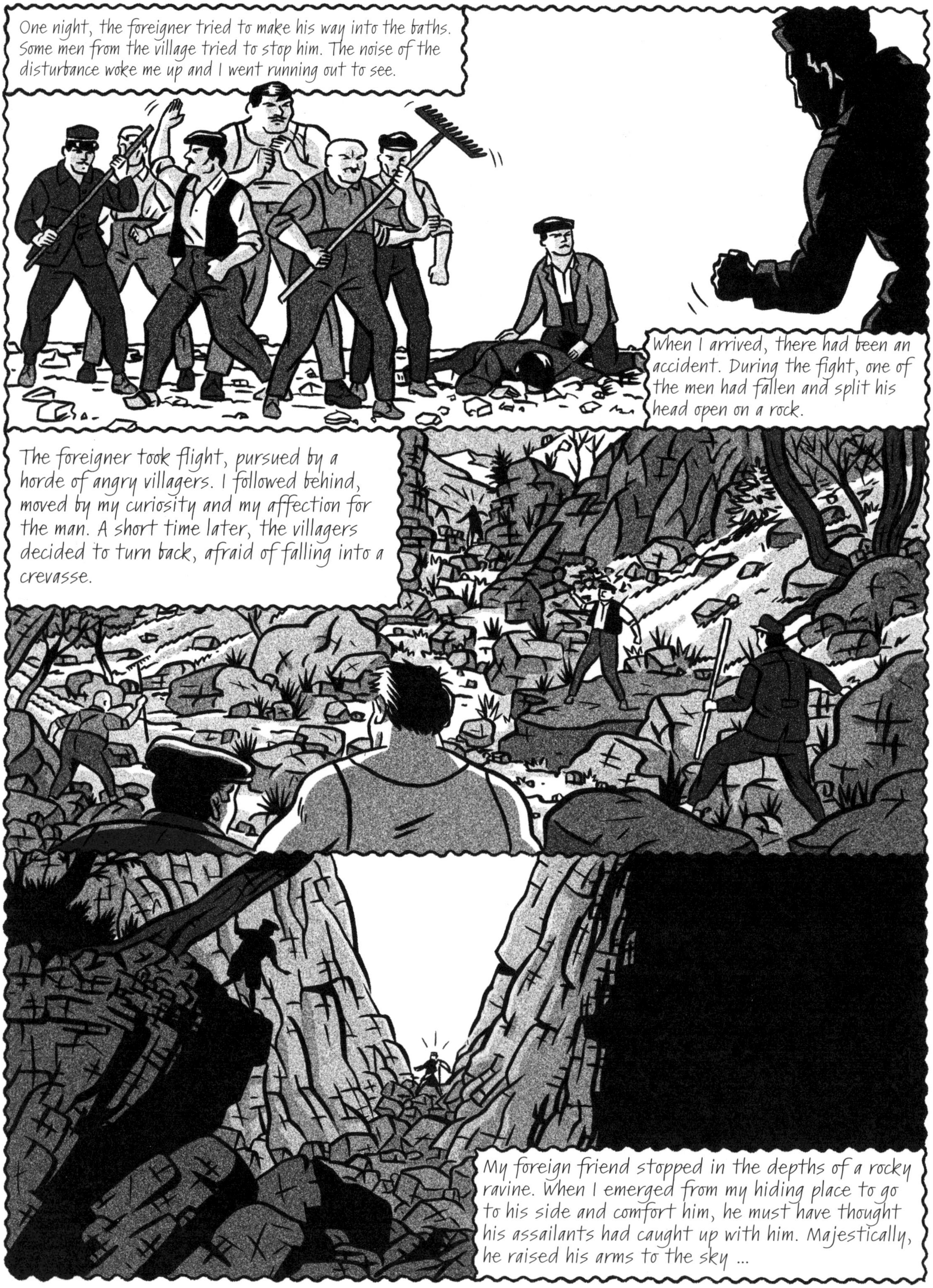
One night, the foreigner tried to make his way into the baths. Some men from the village tried to stop him. The noise of the disturbance woke me up and I went running out to see.
When I arrived, there had been an accident. During the fight, one of the men had fallen and split his head open on a rock.
The foreigner took flight, pursued by a horde of angry villagers. I followed behind, moved by my curiosity and my affection for the man. A short time later, the villagers decided to turn back, afraid of falling into a crevasse.
My foreign friend stopped in the depths of a rocky ravine. When I emerged from my hiding place to go to his side and comfort him, he must have thought his assailants had caught up with him. Majestically, he raised his arms to the sky ...

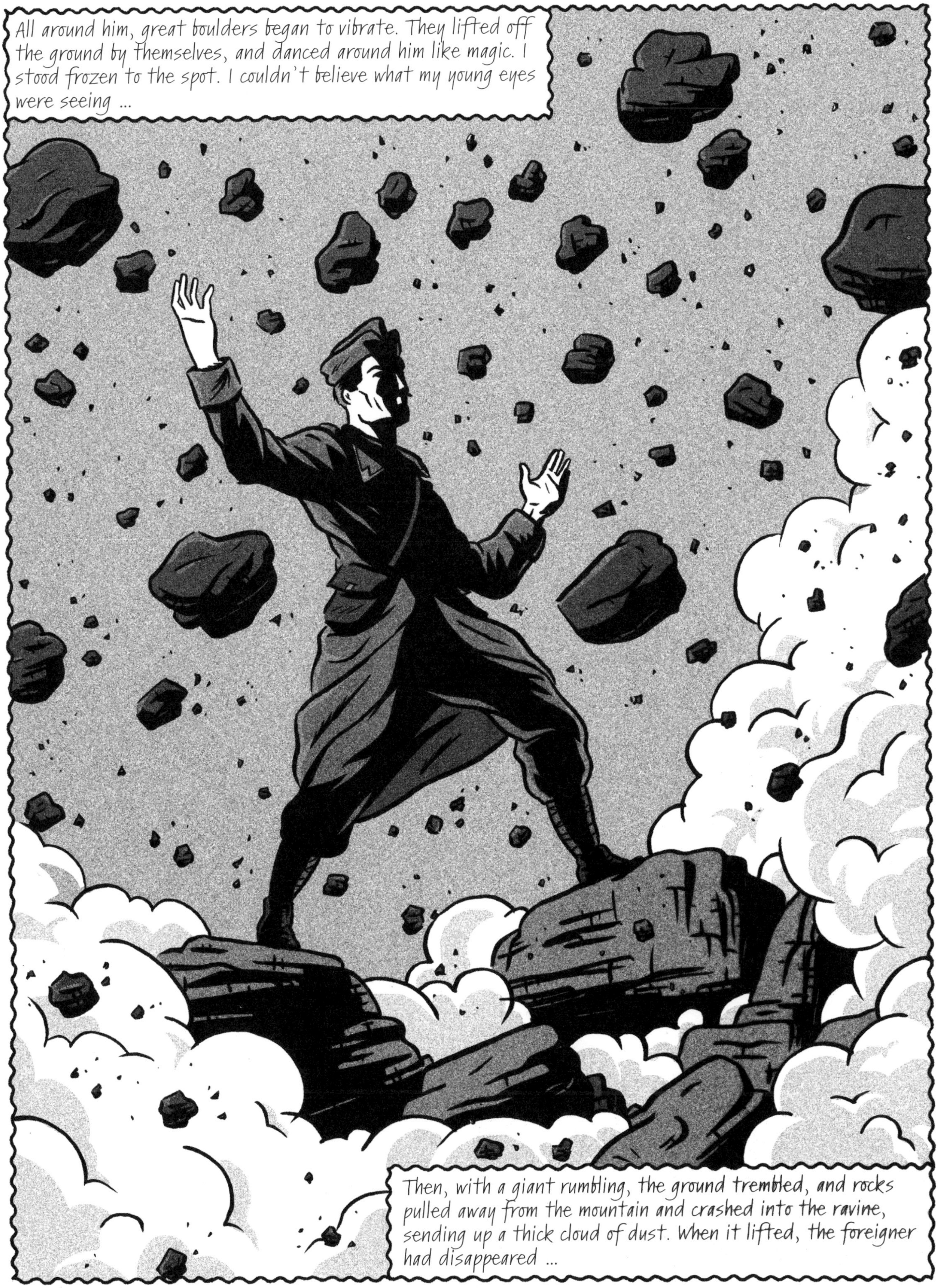
All around him, great boulders began to vibrate. They lifted off the ground by themselves, and danced around him like magic. I stood frozen to the spot. I couldn't believe what my young eyes were seeing ...
Then, with a giant rumbling, the ground trembled, and rocks pulled away from the mountain and crashed into the ravine, sending up a thick cloud of dust. When it lifted, the foreigner had disappeared ...

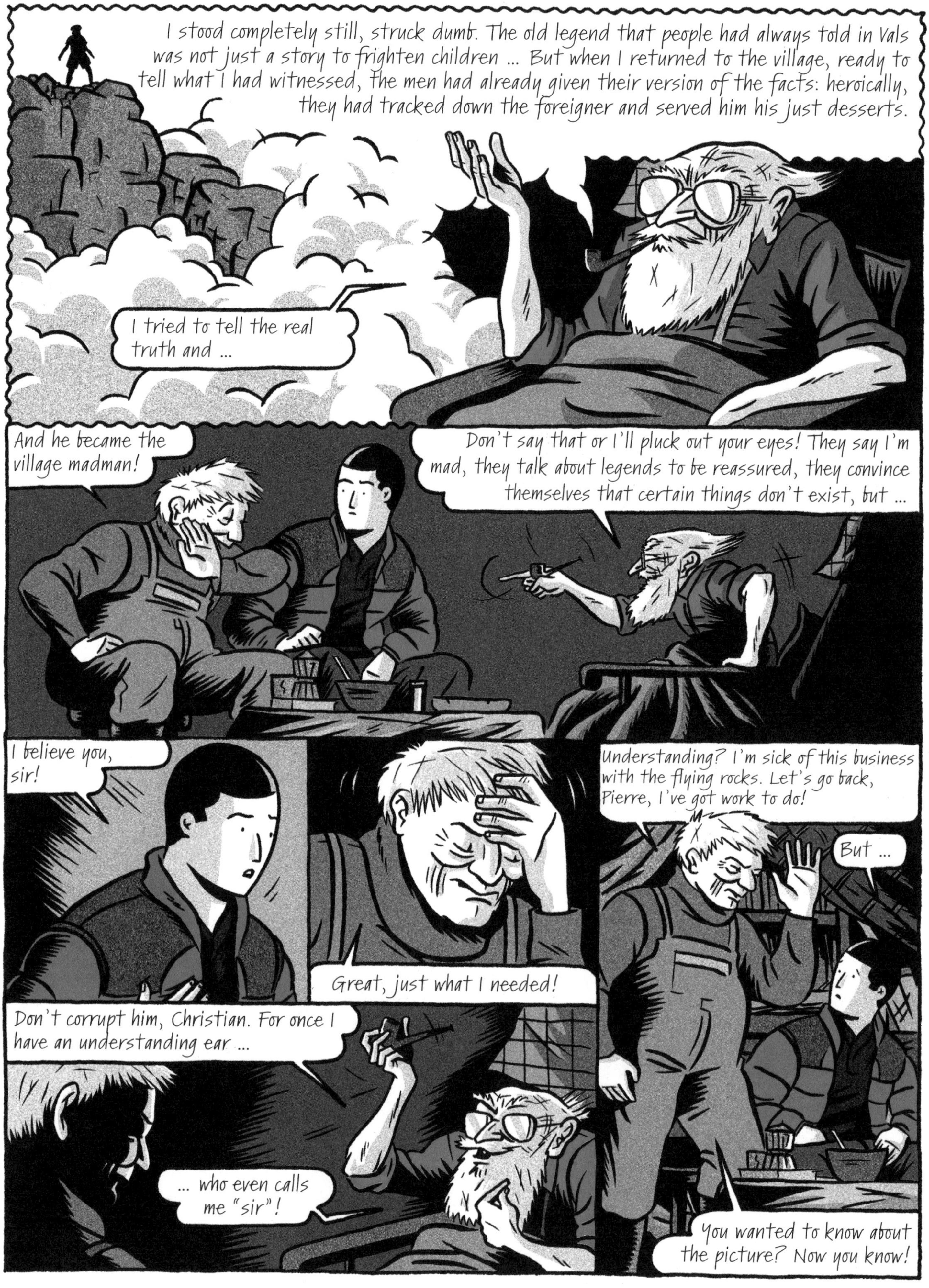
I stood completely still, struck dumb. The old legend that people had always told in Vals was not just a story to frighten children ... But when I returned to the village, ready to tell what I had witnessed, the men had already given their version of the facts: heroically, they had tracked down the foreigner and served him his just desserts.
I tried to tell the real truth and ...
And he became the village madman!
Don't say that or I'll pluck out your eyes! They say I'm mad, they talk about legends to be reassured, they convince themselves that certain things don't exist, but ...
I believe you, sir!
Great, just what I needed!
Understanding? I'm sick of this business with the flying rocks. Let's go back, Pierre, I've got work to do!
But ...
Don't corrupt him, Christian. For once I have an understanding ear ...
... who even calls me "sir"!
You wanted to know about the picture? Now you know!

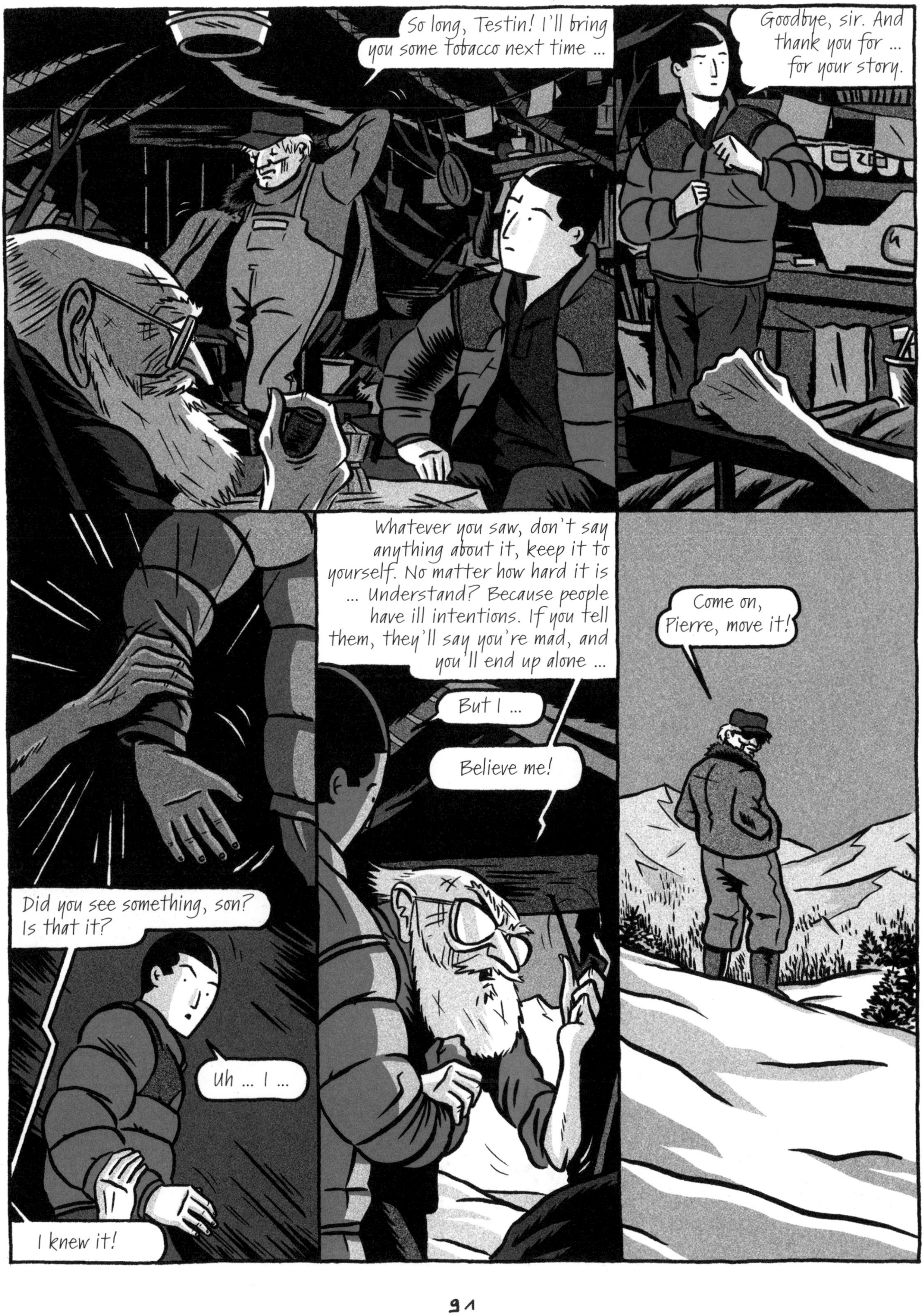
So long, Testin! I'll bring you some tobacco next time ...
Goodbye, sir. And thank you for ... for your story.
Did you see something, son? Is that it?
Uh ... I ...
I knew it!
Whatever you saw, don't say anything about it, keep it to yourself. No matter how hard it is ... Understand? Because people have ill intentions. If you tell them, they'll say you're mad, and you'll end up alone ...
But I ...
Believe me!
Come on, Pierre, move it!

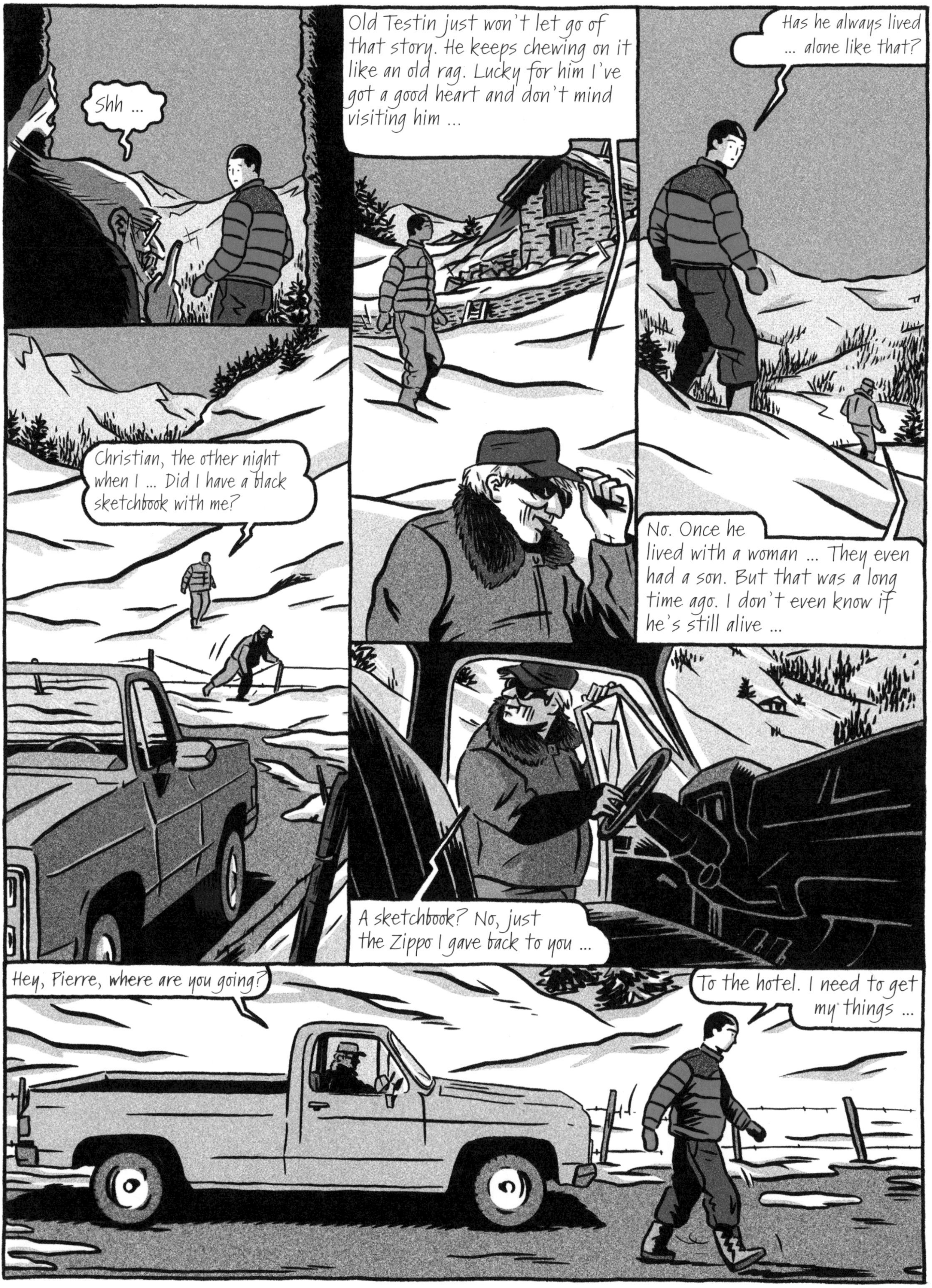
Shh ...
Old Testin just won't let go of that story. He keeps chewing on it like an old rag. Lucky for him I've got a good heart and don't mind visiting him ...
Has he always lived ... alone like that?
Christian, the other night when I ... Did I have a black sketchbook with me?
No. Once he lived with a woman ... They even had a son. But that was a long time ago. I don't even know if he's still alive ...
A sketchbook? No, just the Zippo I gave back to you ...
Hey, Pierre, where are you going?
To the hotel. I need to get my things ...

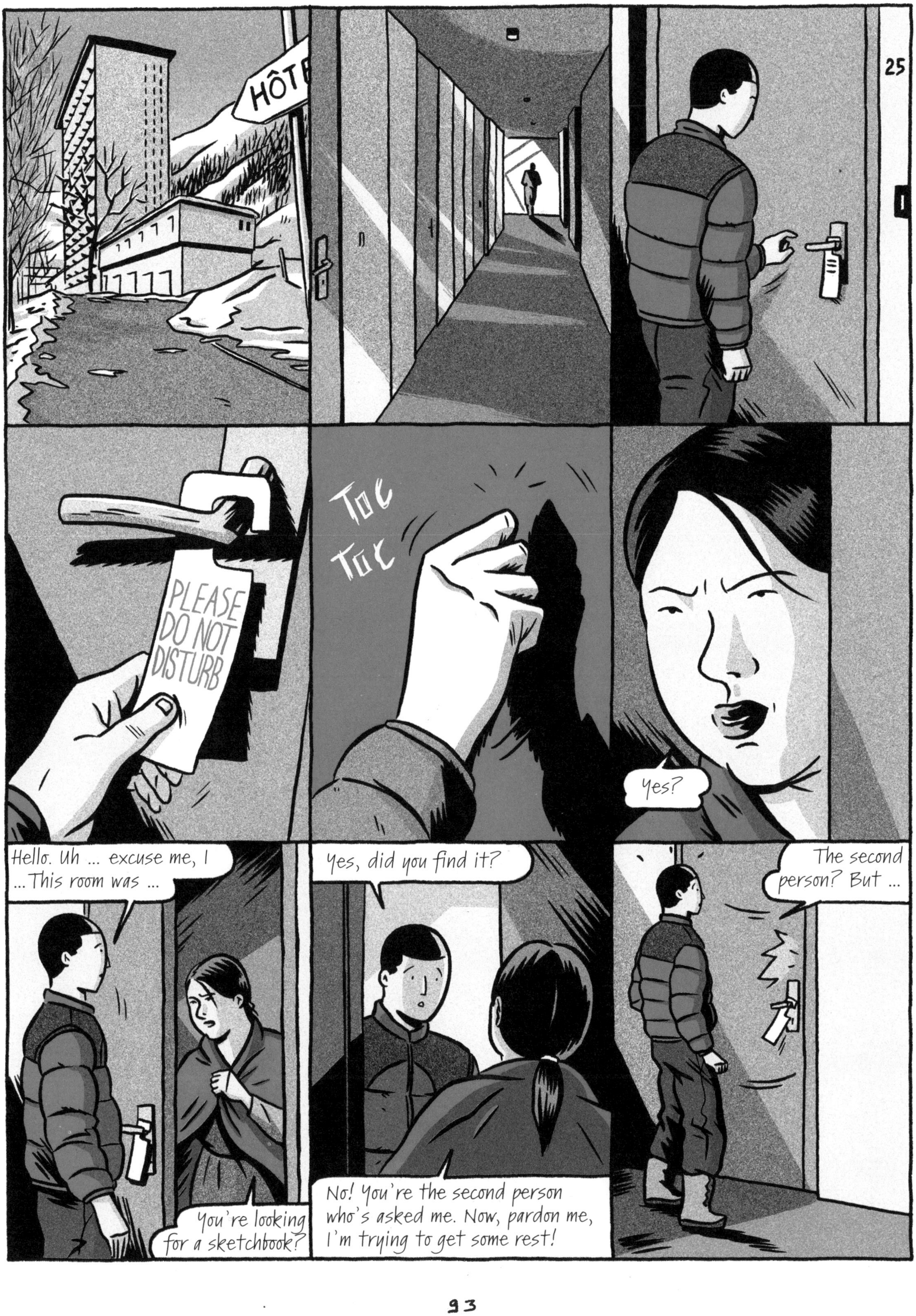
HÔTE
25
PLEASE DO NOT DISTURB
TOC TOC
Yes?
Hello. Uh ... excuse me, I ... This room was ...
You're looking for a sketchbook?
Yes, did you find it?
No! You're the second person who's asked me. Now, pardon me, I'm trying to get some rest!
The second person? But ...

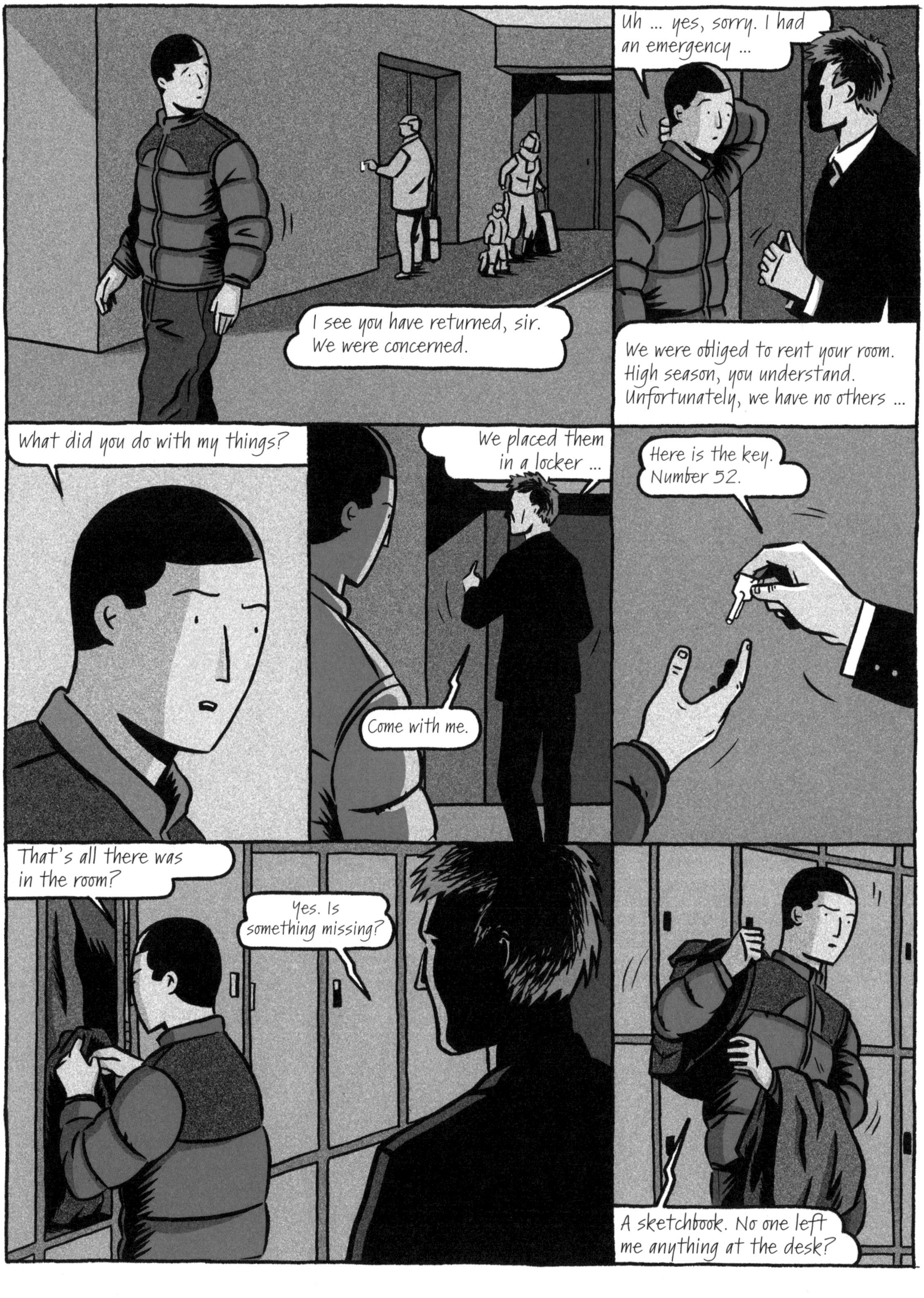
I see you have returned, sir.
We were concerned.
Uh ... yes, sorry. I had an emergency ...
We were obliged to rent your room. High season, you understand. Unfortunately, we have no others ...
What did you do with my things?
We placed them in a locker ...
Come with me.
Here is the key. Number 52.
That's all there was in the room?
Yes. Is something missing?
A sketchbook. No one left me anything at the desk?

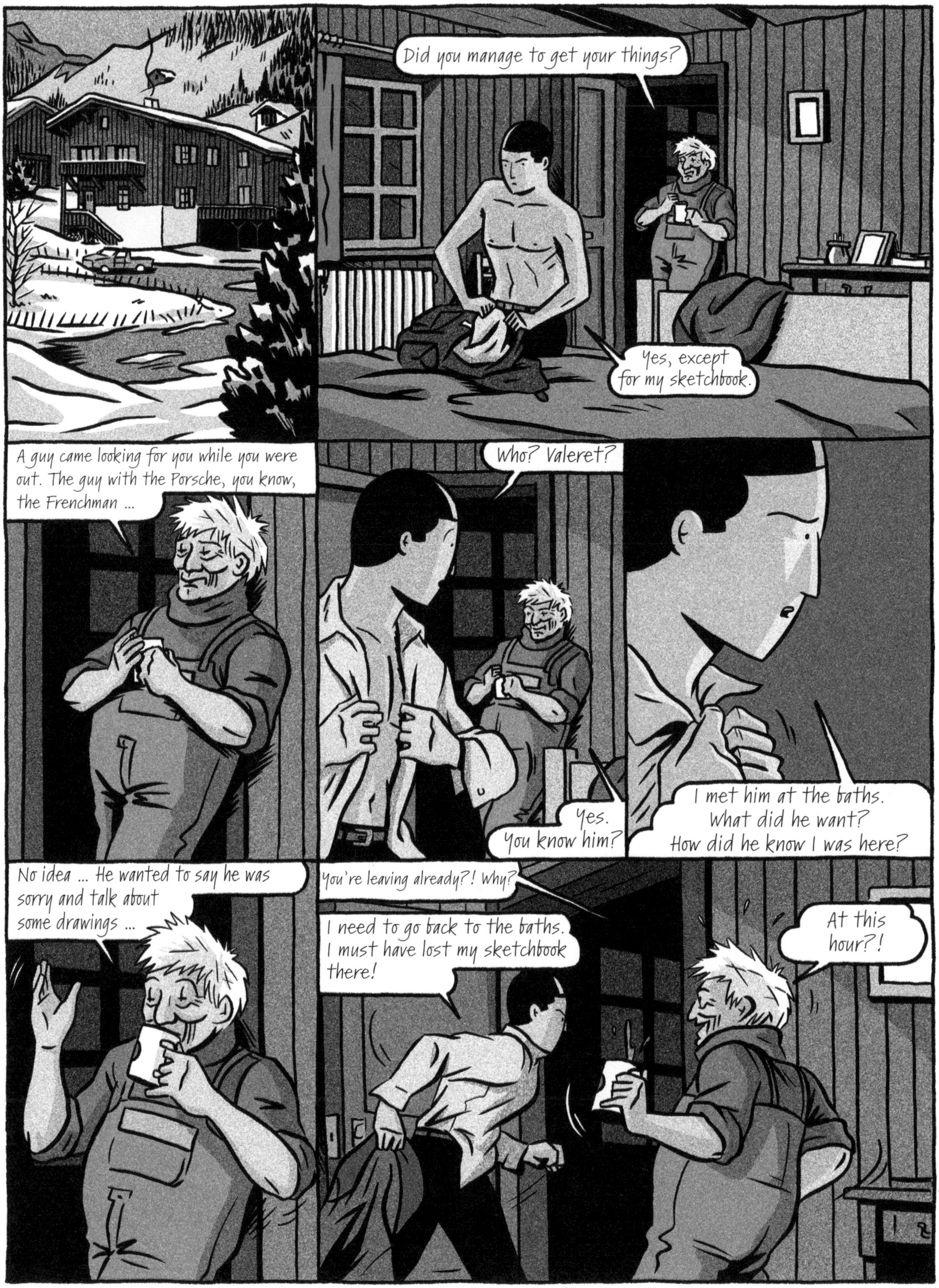
Did you manage to get your things?
Yes, except for my sketchbook.
A guy came looking for you while you were out. The guy with the Porsche, you know, the Frenchman ...
Who? Valeret?
Yes. You know him?
I met him at the baths. What did he want? How did he know I was here?
No idea ... He wanted to say he was sorry and talk about some drawings ...
You're leaving already?! Why?
I need to go back to the baths. I must have lost my sketchbook there!
At this hour?!

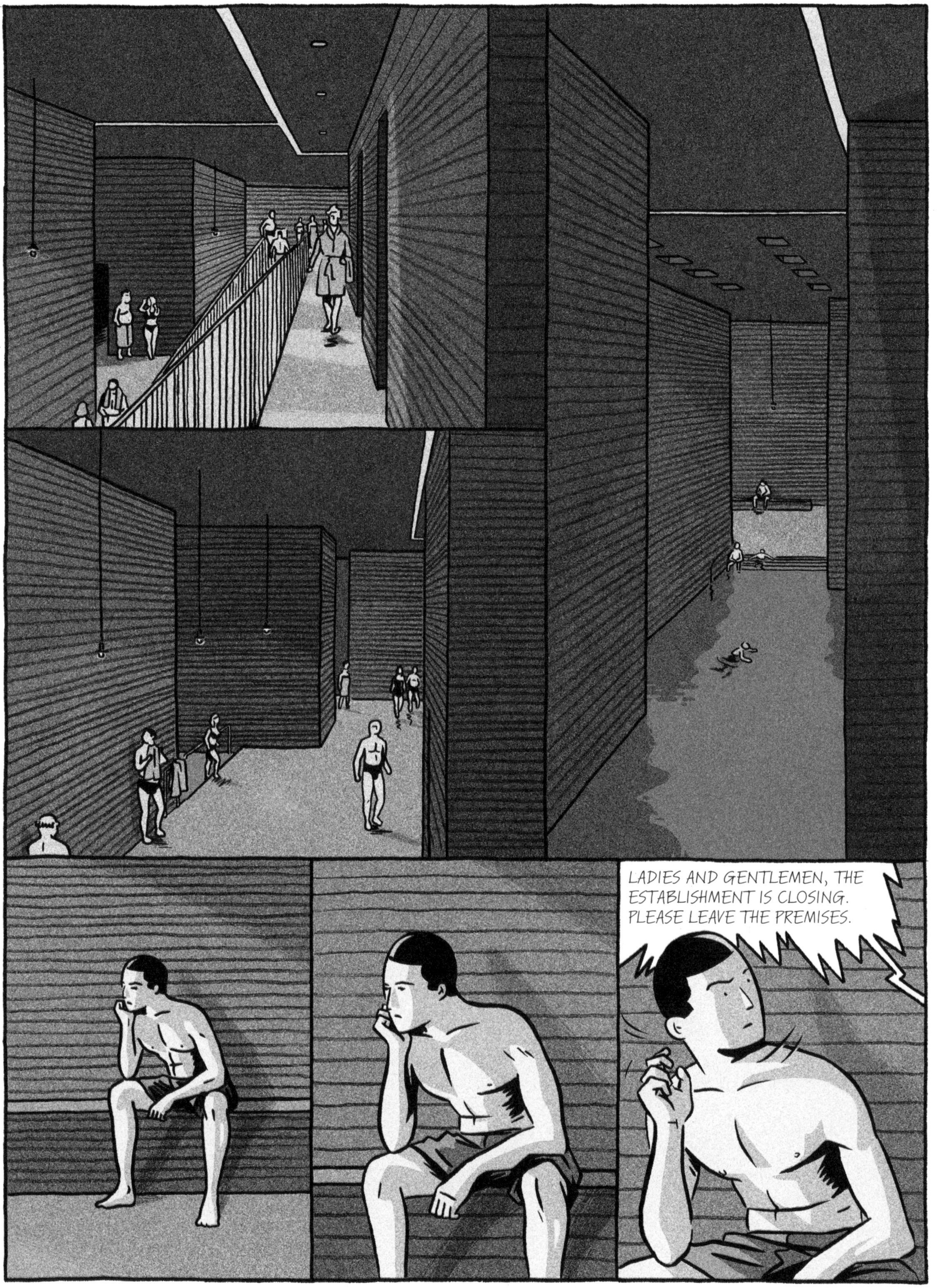
LADIES AND GENTLEMEN, THE ESTABLISHMENT IS CLOSING. PLEASE LEAVE THE PREMISES.

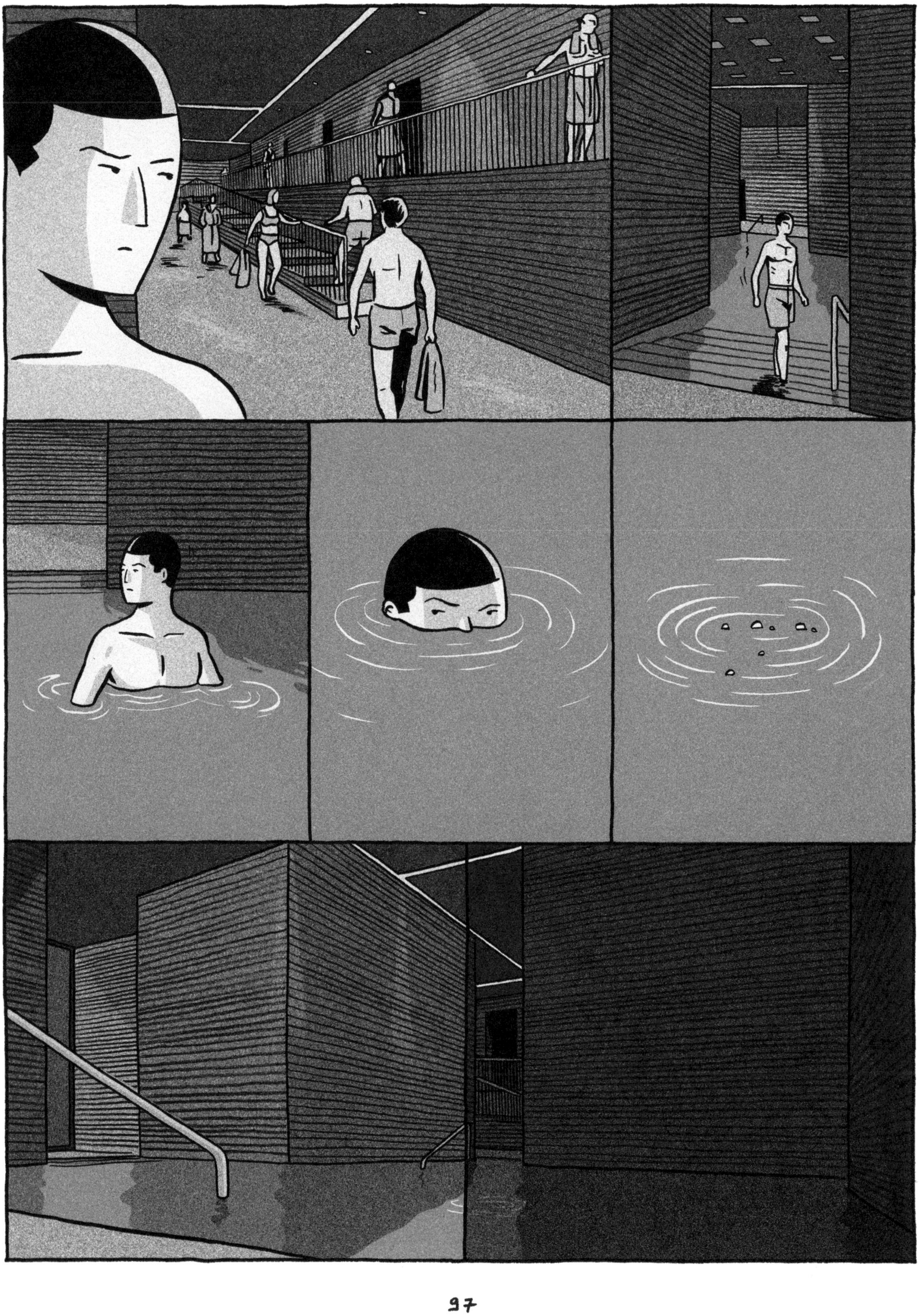

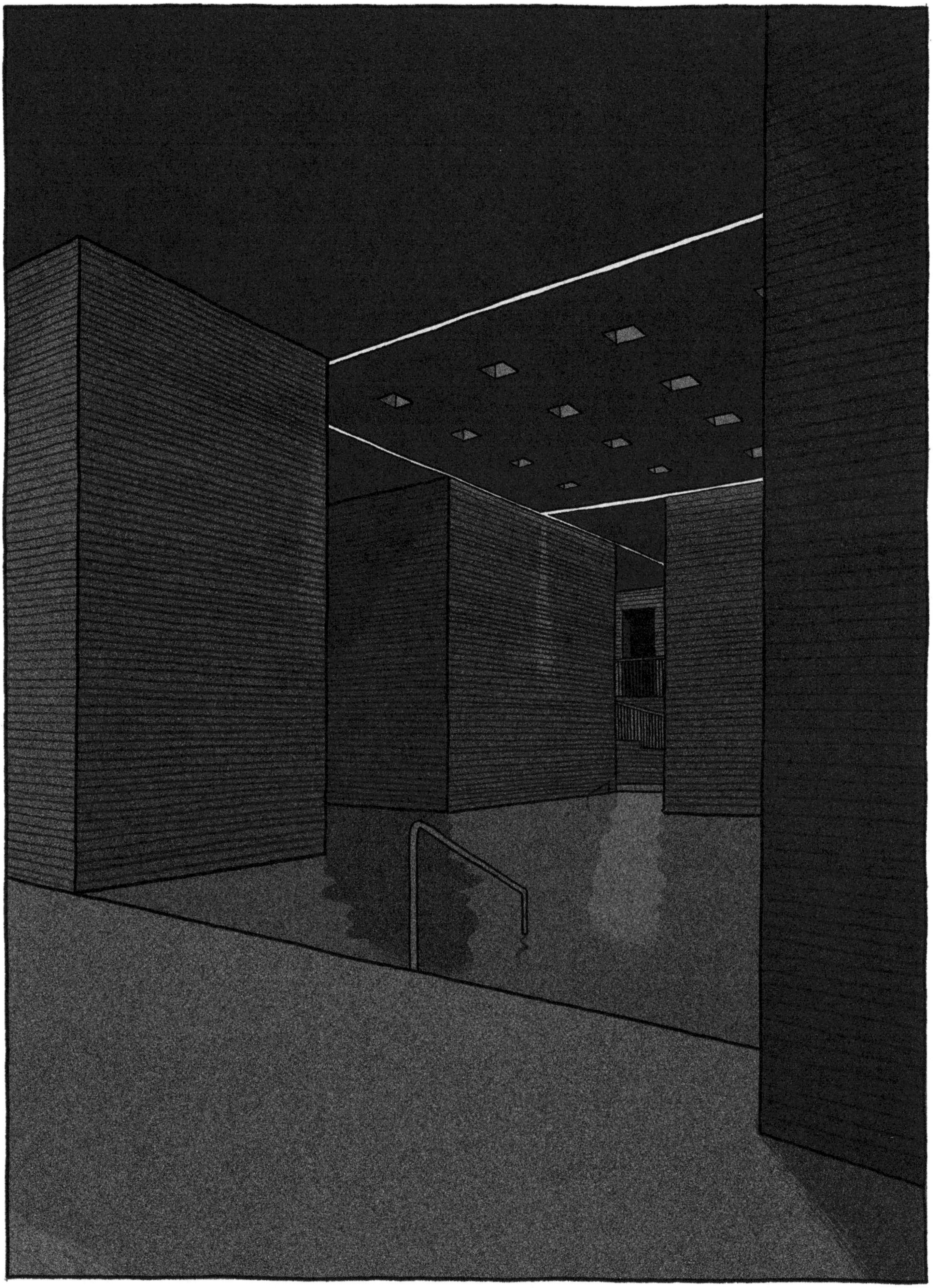

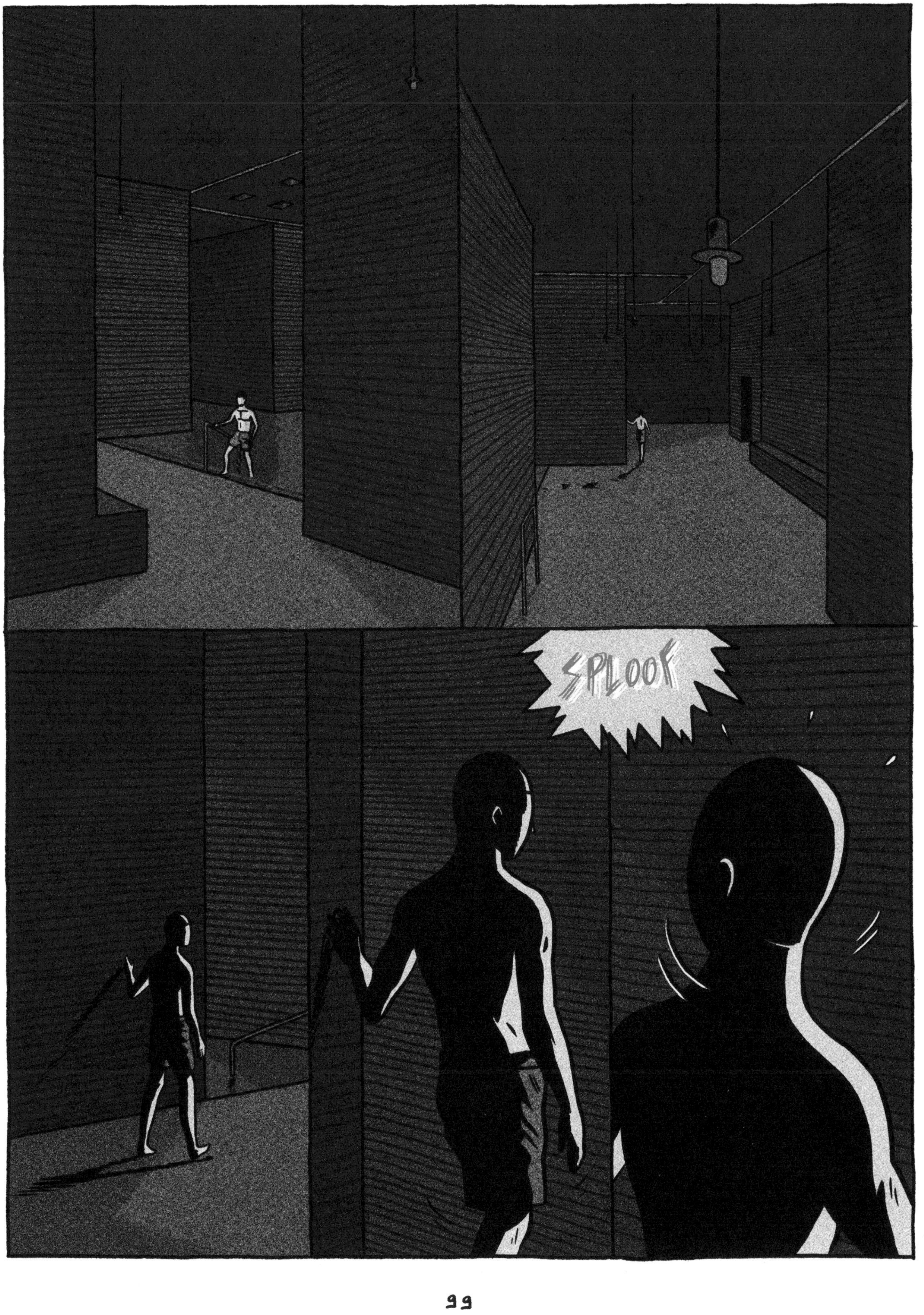
SPLOOF

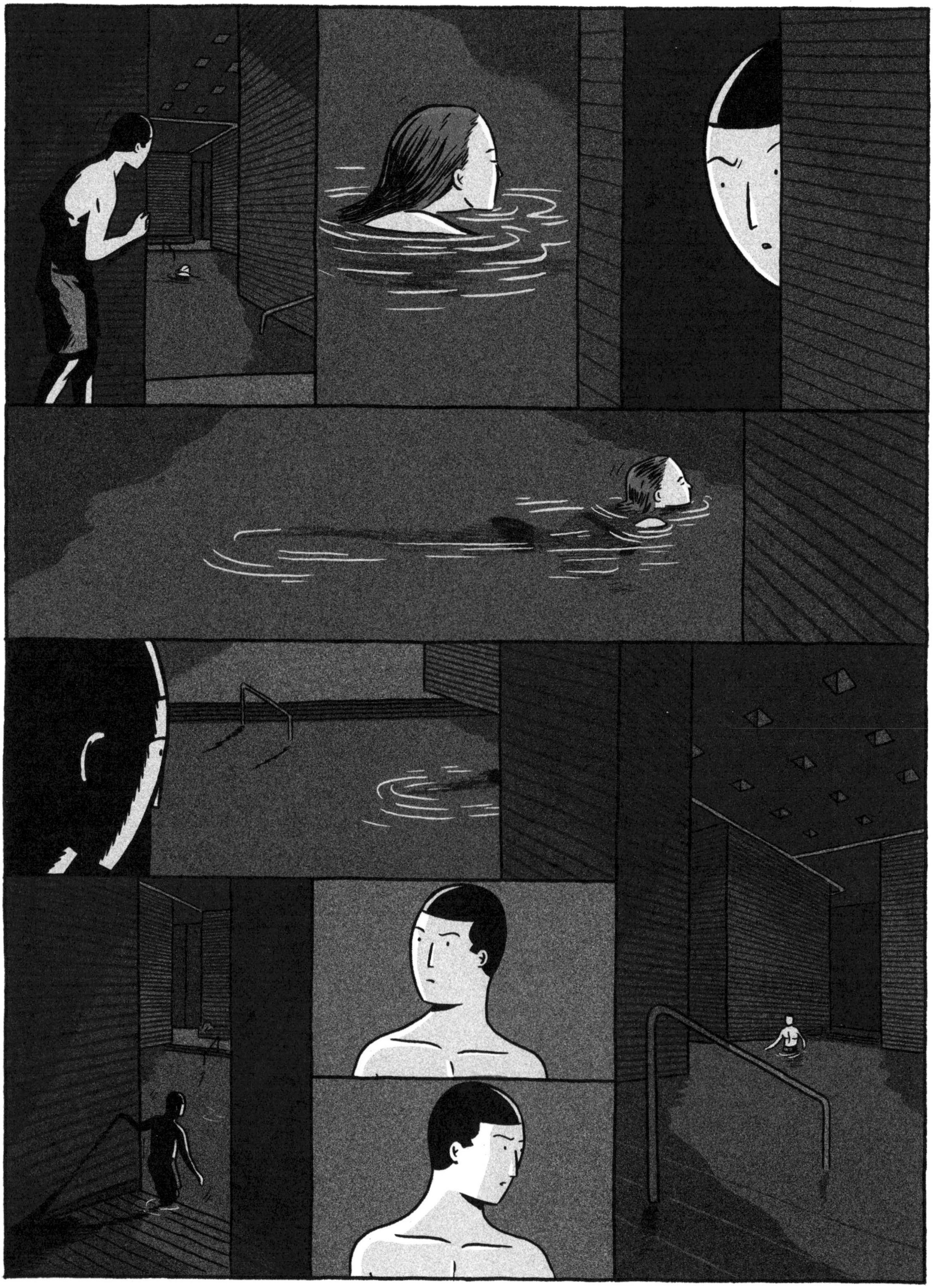

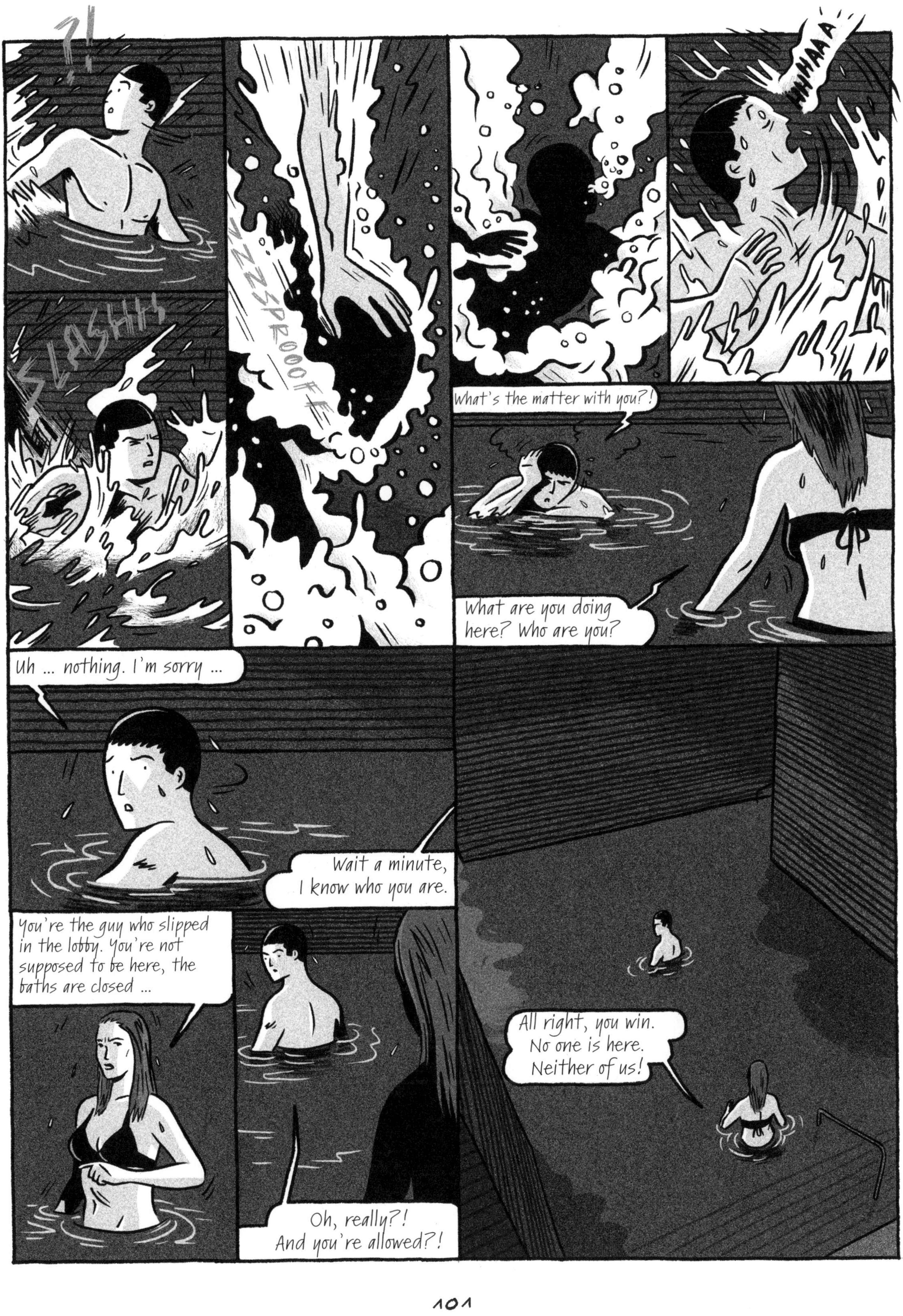
?!
SLASHHH
ZZZSPROOOFF
AHHAAA
What's the matter with you?!
What are you doing here? Who are you?
Uh ... nothing. I'm sorry ...
Wait a minute, I know who you are.
You're the guy who slipped in the lobby. You're not supposed to be here, the baths are closed ...
Oh, really?! And you're allowed?!
All right, you win. No one is here. Neither of us!

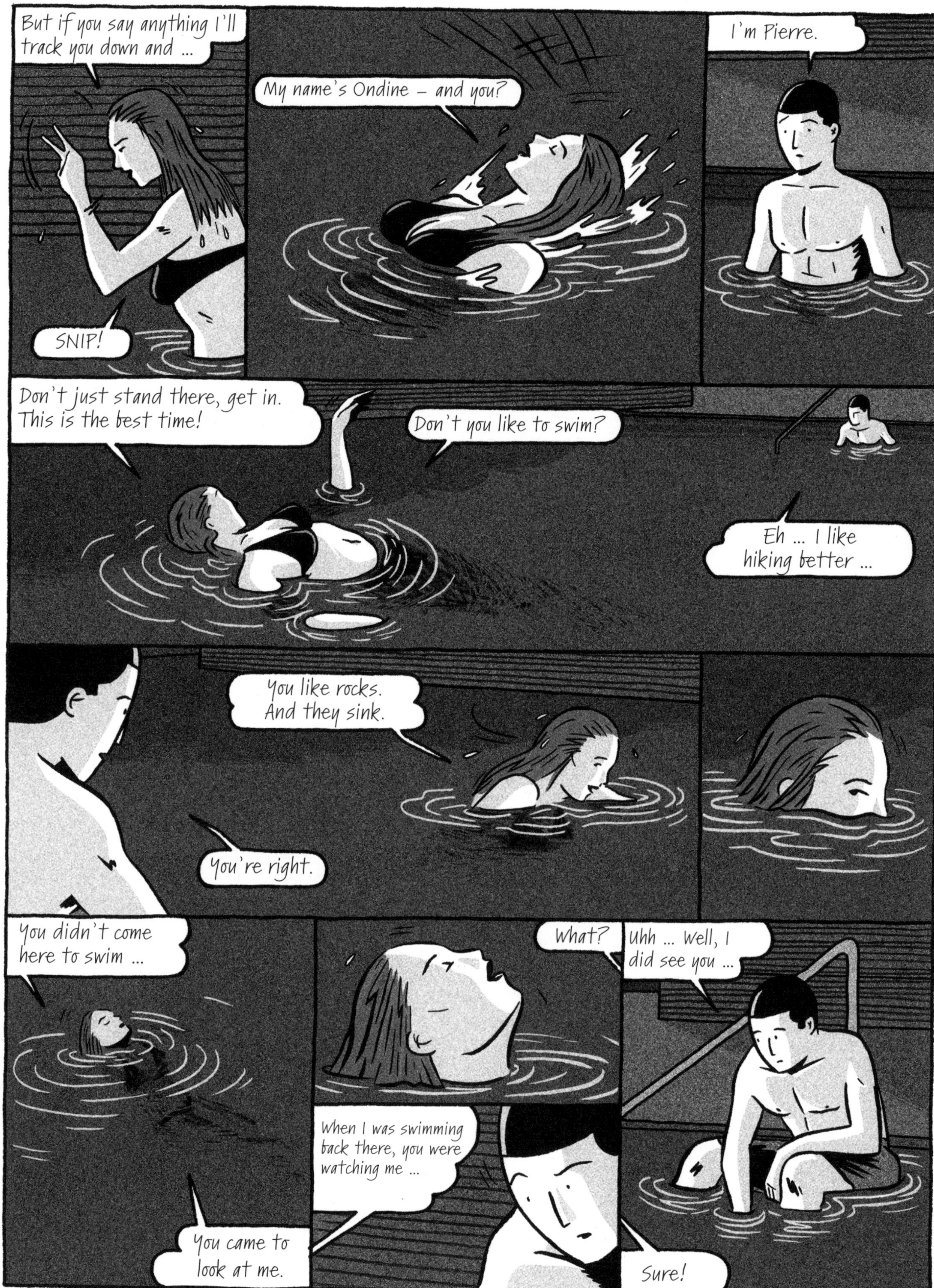
But if you say anything I'll track you down and ...
SNIP!
My name's Ondine – and you?
I'm Pierre.
Don't just stand there, get in. This is the best time!
Don't you like to swim?
Eh ... I like hiking better ...
You like rocks. And they sink.
You're right.
You didn't come here to swim ...
You came to look at me.
What?
When I was swimming back there, you were watching me ...
Uhh ... Well, I did see you ...
Sure!

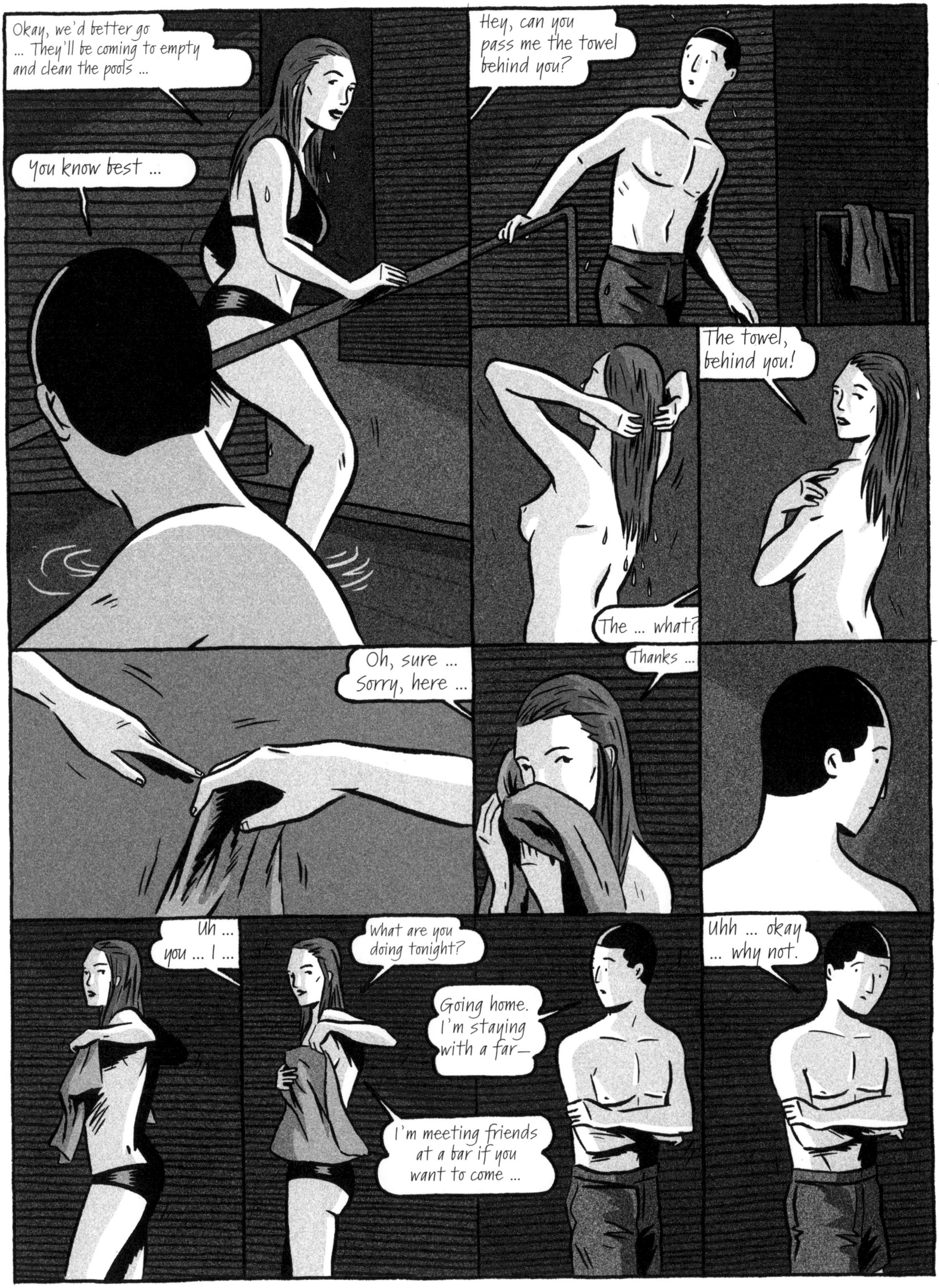
Okay, we'd better go ... They'll be coming to empty and clean the pools ...
You know best ...
Hey, can you pass me the towel behind you?
The ... what?
The towel, behind you!
Oh, sure ... Sorry, here ...
Thanks ...
Uh ... you ... I ...
What are you doing tonight?
Going home. I'm staying with a far—
I'm meeting friends at a bar if you want to come ...
Uhh ... okay ... why not.

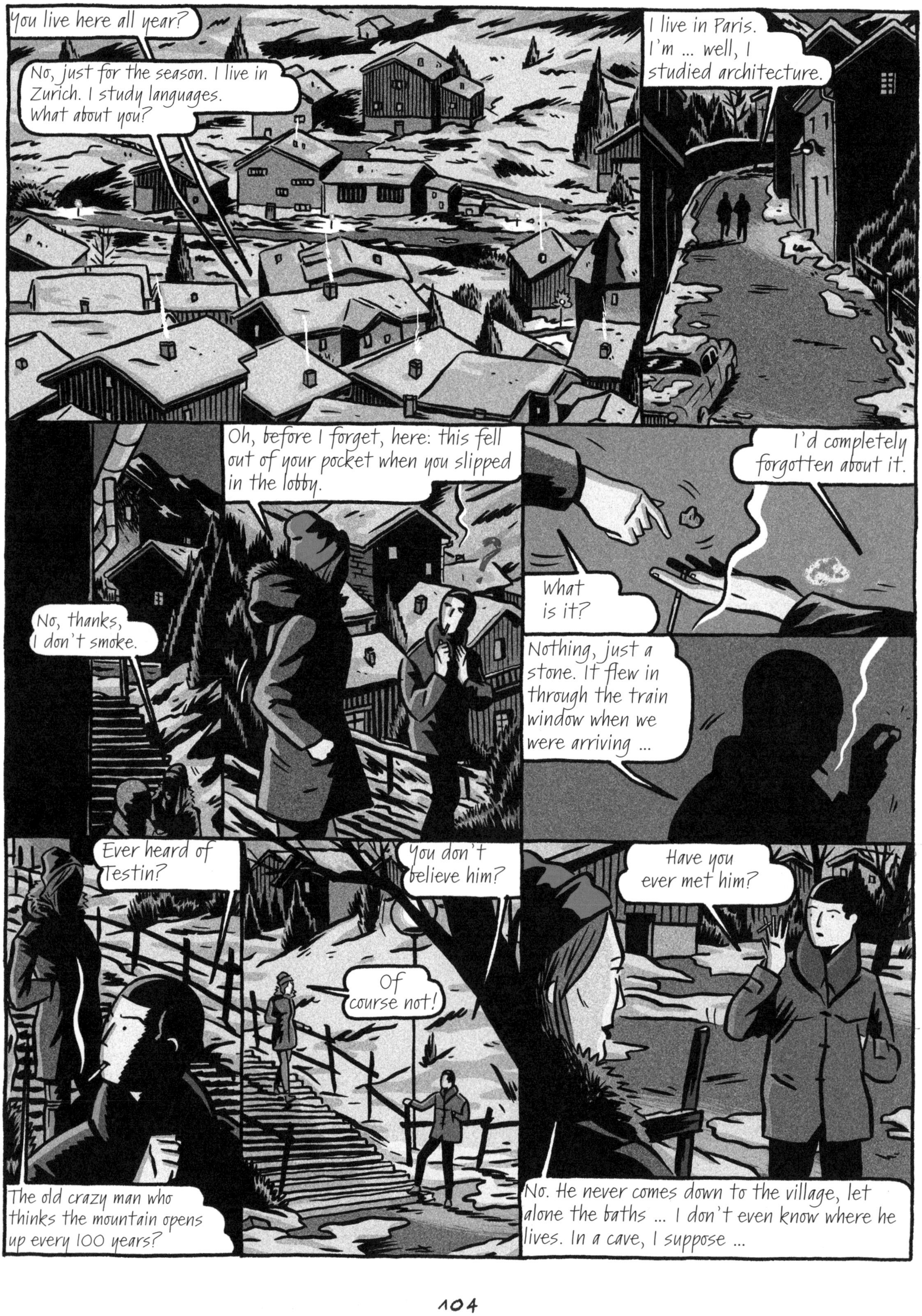
You live here all year?
No, just for the season. I live in Zurich. I study languages. What about you?
I live in Paris. I'm ... well, I studied architecture.
Oh, before I forget, here: this fell out of your pocket when you slipped in the lobby.
No, thanks, I don't smoke.
I'd completely forgotten about it.
What is it?
Nothing, just a stone. It flew in through the train window when we were arriving ...
Ever heard of Testin?
The old crazy man who thinks the mountain opens up every 100 years?
You don't believe him?
Of course not!
Have you ever met him?
No. He never comes down to the village, let alone the baths ... I don't even know where he lives. In a cave, I suppose ...

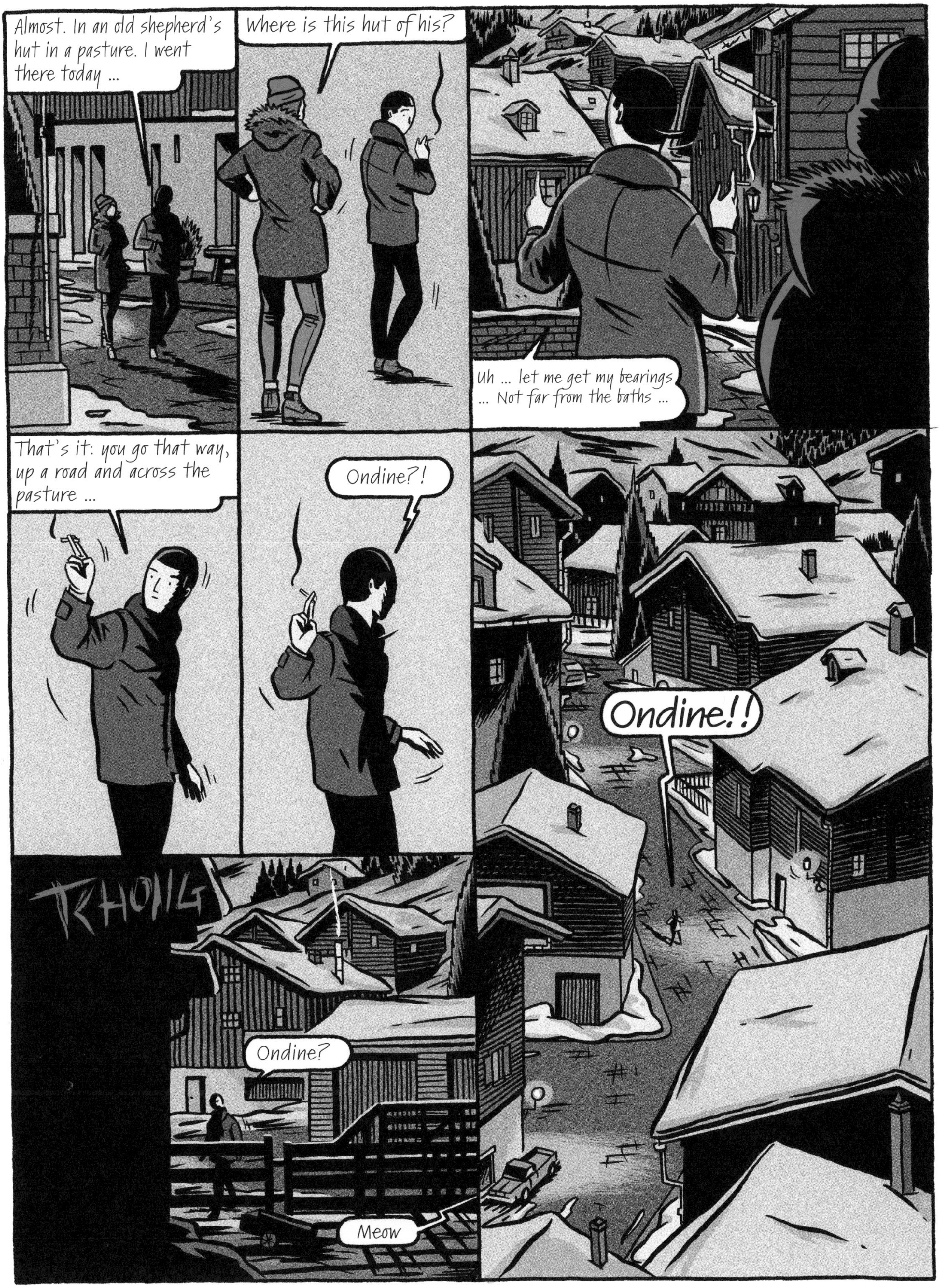
Almost. In an old shepherd's hut in a pasture. I went there today ...
Where is this hut of his?
Uh ... let me get my bearings ... Not far from the baths ...
That's it: you go that way, up a road and across the pasture ...
Ondine?!
Ondine!!
TCHONG
Ondine?
Meow

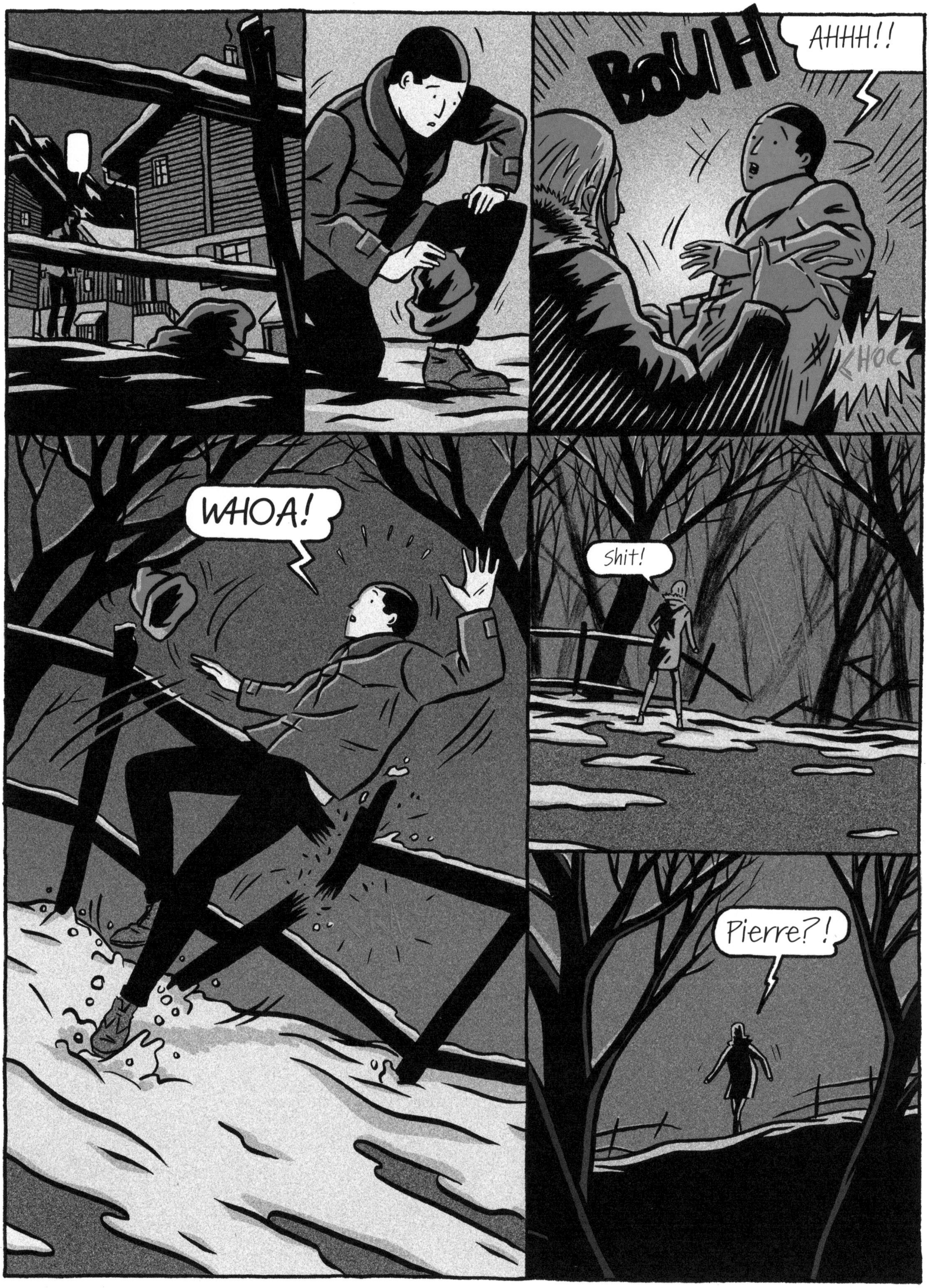
BOUH
AHHH!!
CHOC
WHOA!
Shit!
Pierre?!

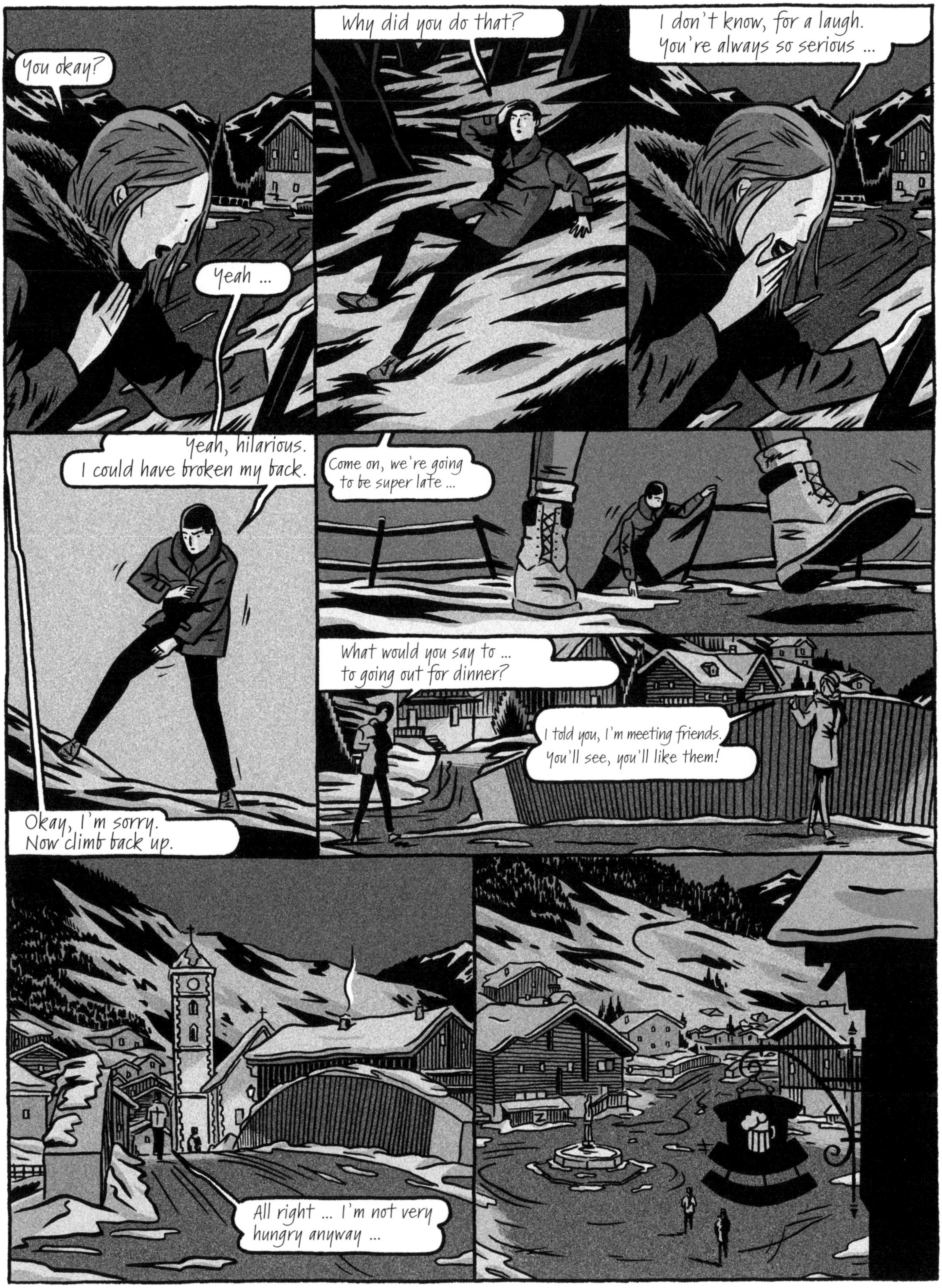
You okay?
Yeah ...
Why did you do that?
I don't know, for a laugh. You're always so serious ...
Yeah, hilarious. I could have broken my back.
Okay, I'm sorry. Now climb back up.
Come on, we're going to be super late ...
What would you say to ... to going out for dinner?
I told you, I'm meeting friends. You'll see, you'll like them!
All right ... I'm not very hungry anyway ...

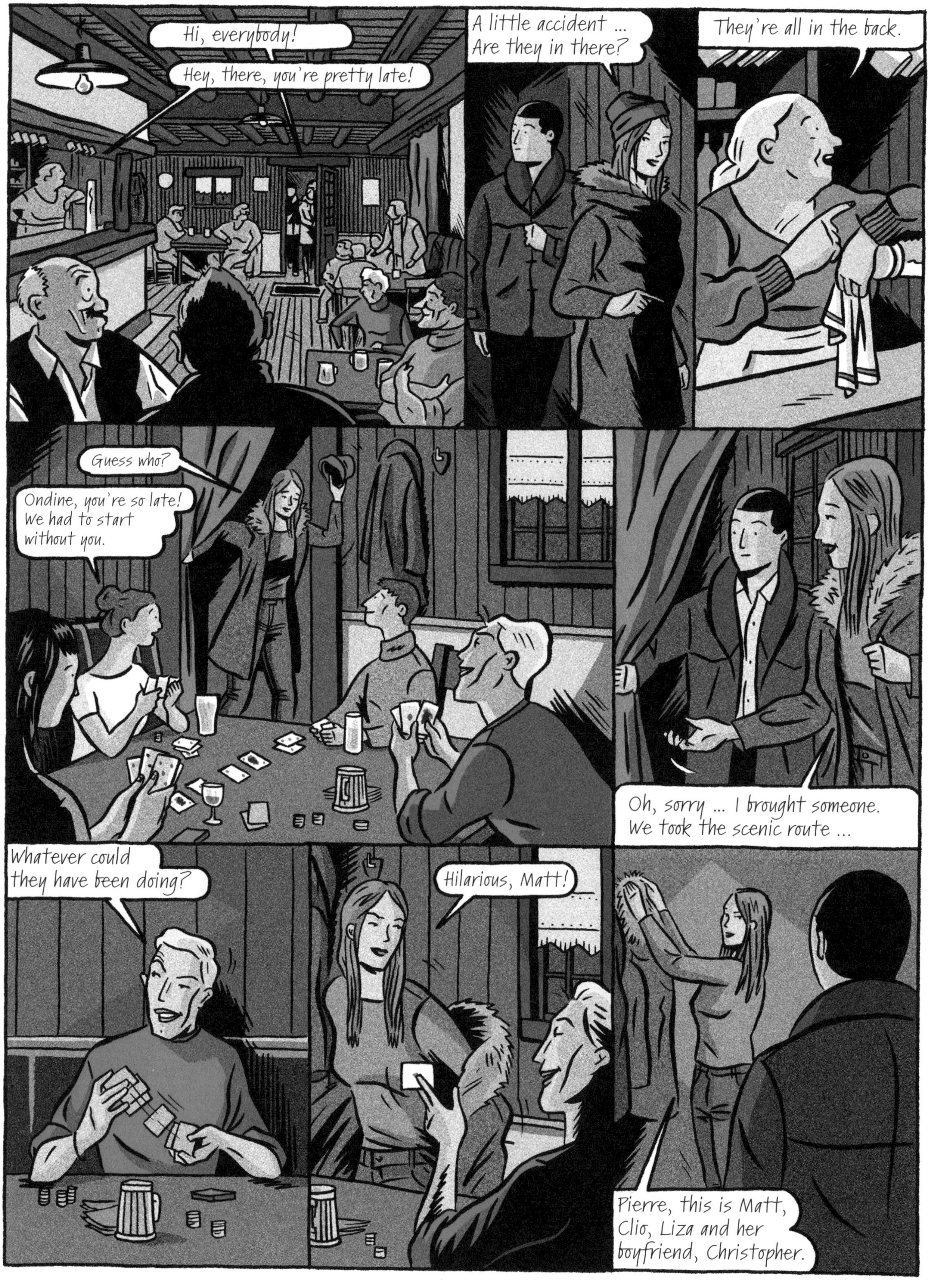
Hi, everybody!
Hey, there, you're pretty late!
A little accident ...
Are they in there?
They're all in the back.
Guess who?
Ondine, you're so late! We had to start without you.
Oh, sorry ... I brought someone. We took the scenic route ...
Whatever could they have been doing?
Hilarious, Matt!
Pierre, this is Matt, Clio, Liza and her boyfriend, Christopher.

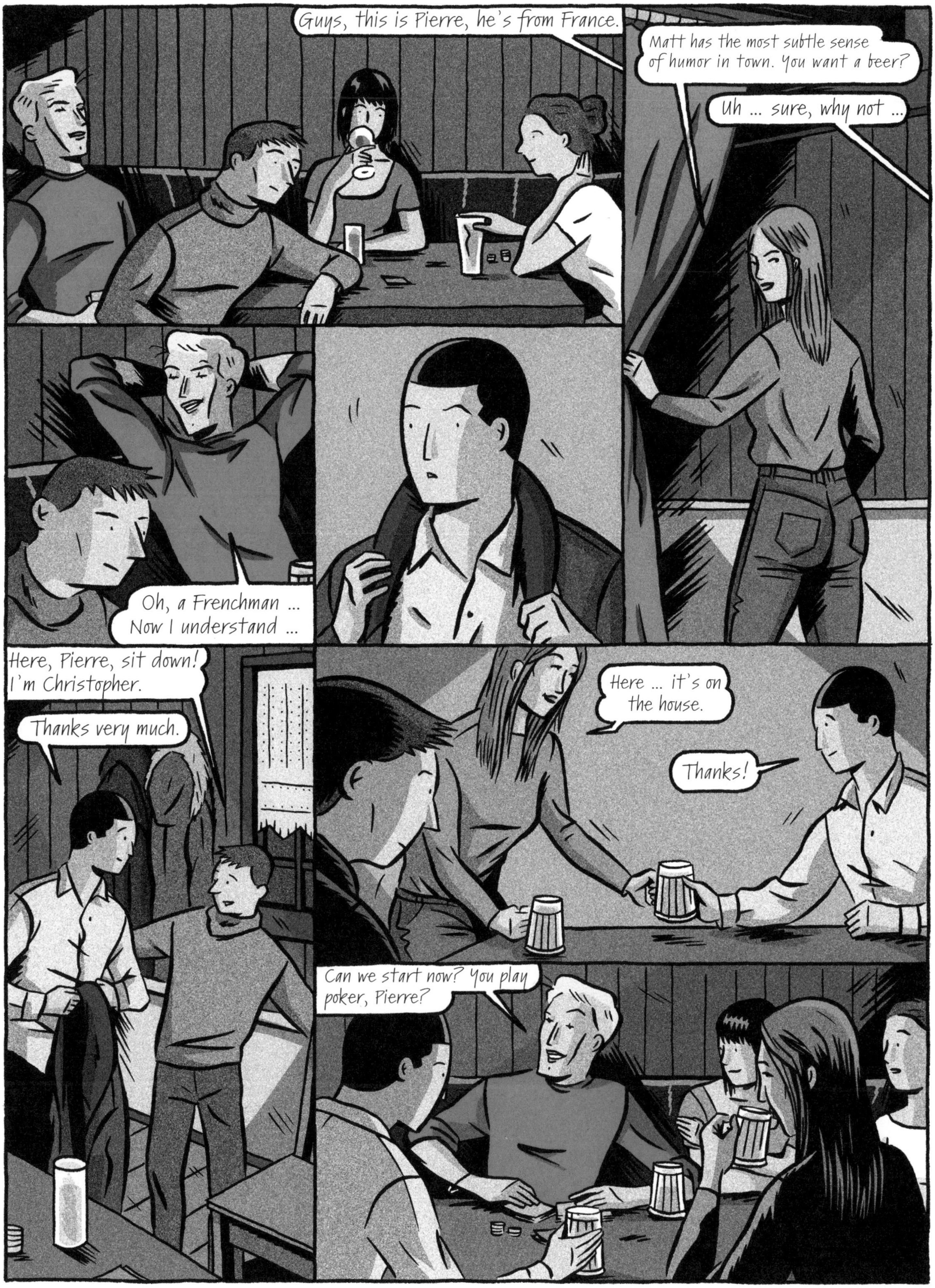
Guys, this is Pierre, he's from France.
Matt has the most subtle sense of humor in town. You want a beer?
Uh ... sure, why not ...
Oh, a Frenchman ... Now I understand ...
Here, Pierre, sit down! I'm Christopher.
Thanks very much.
Here ... it's on the house.
Thanks!
Can we start now? You play poker, Pierre?

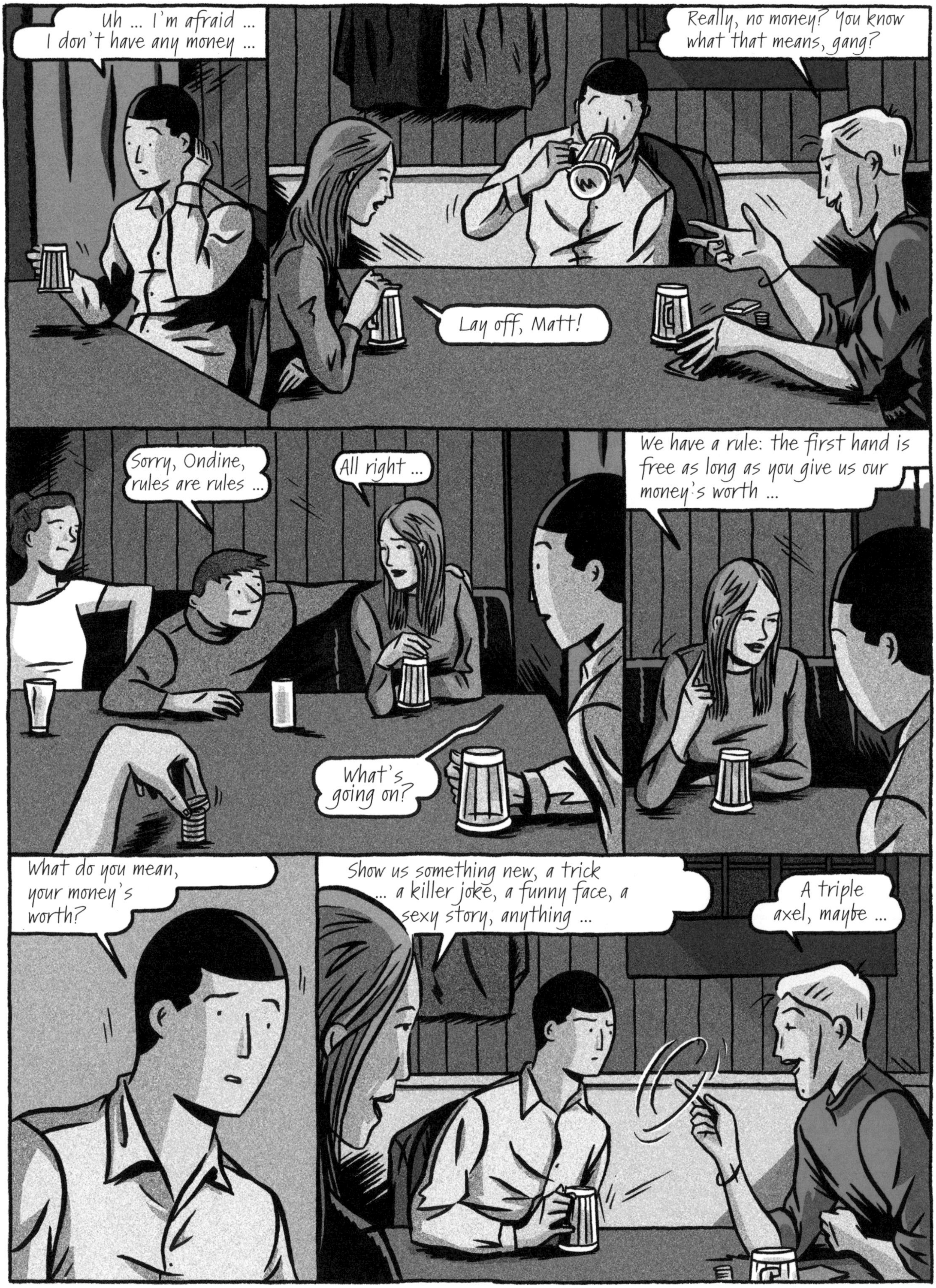
Uh ... I'm afraid ... I don't have any money ...
Really, no money? You know what that means, gang?
Lay off, Matt!
Sorry, Ondine, rules are rules ...
All right ...
What's going on?
We have a rule: the first hand is free as long as you give us our money's worth ...
What do you mean, your money's worth?
Show us something new, a trick ... a killer joke, a funny face, a sexy story, anything ...
A triple axel, maybe ...

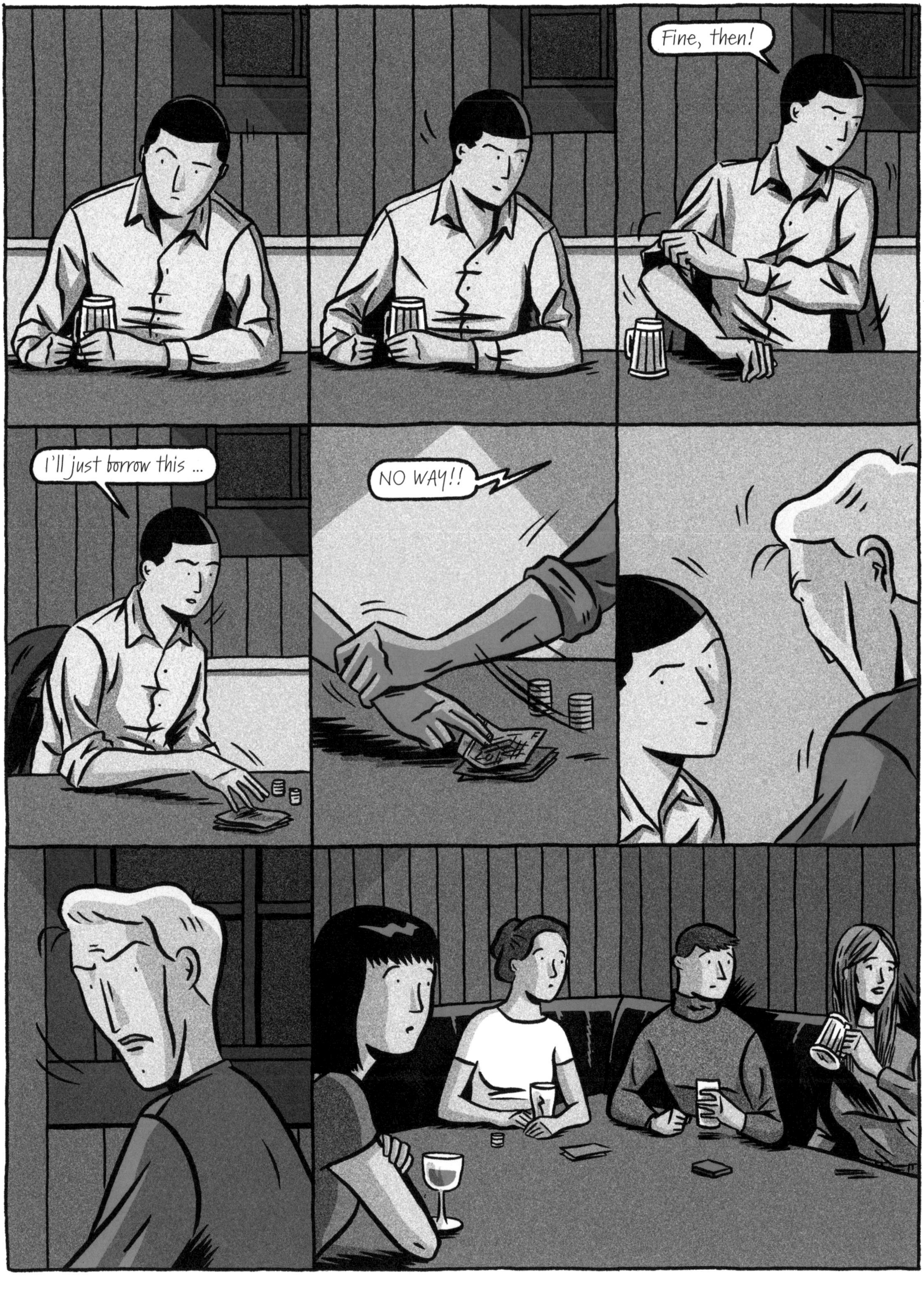
Fine, then!
I'll just borrow this ...
NO WAY!!

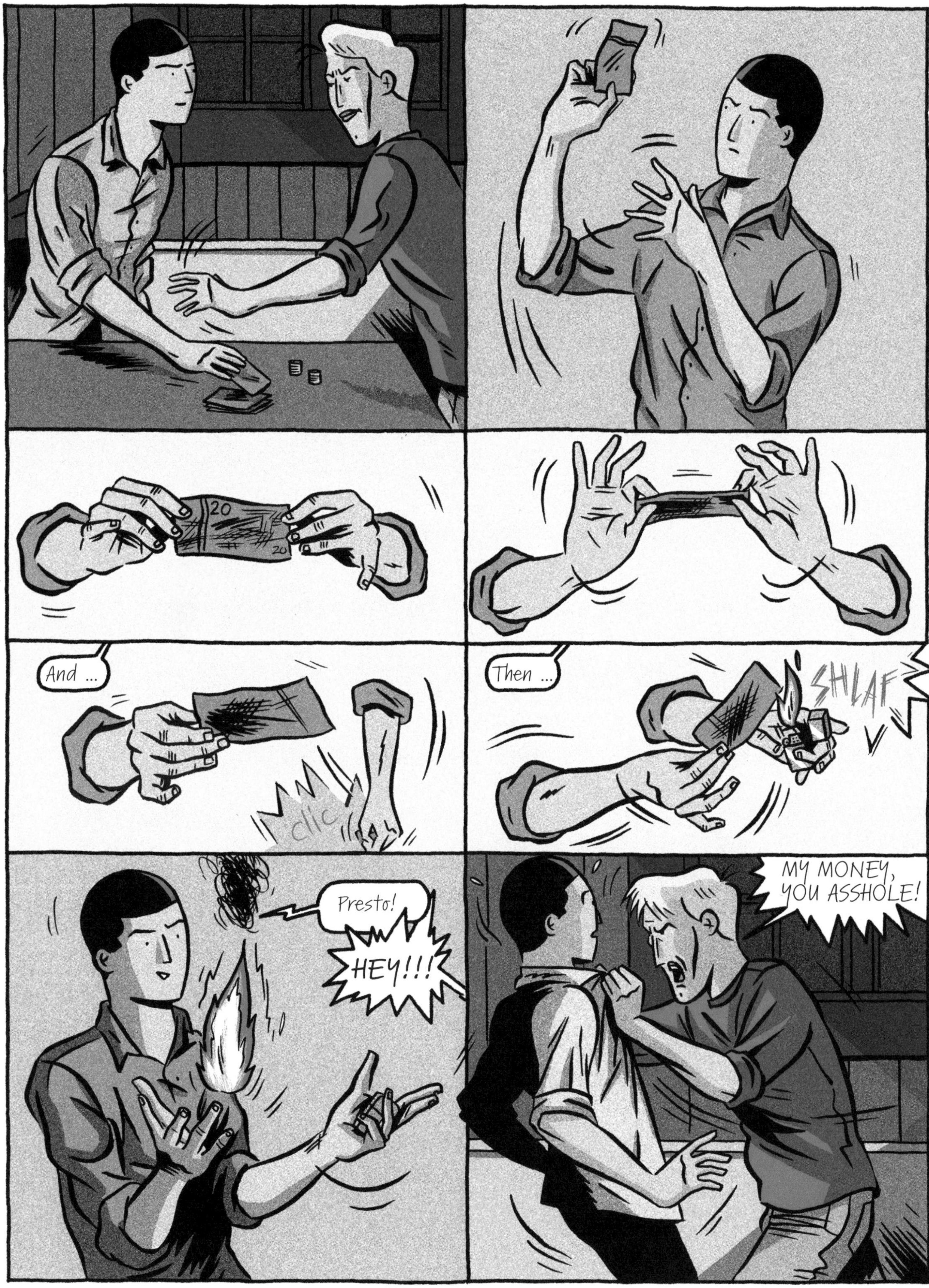
And ...
clic
Then ...
SHLAF
Presto!
HEY!!!
MY MONEY, YOU ASSHOLE!

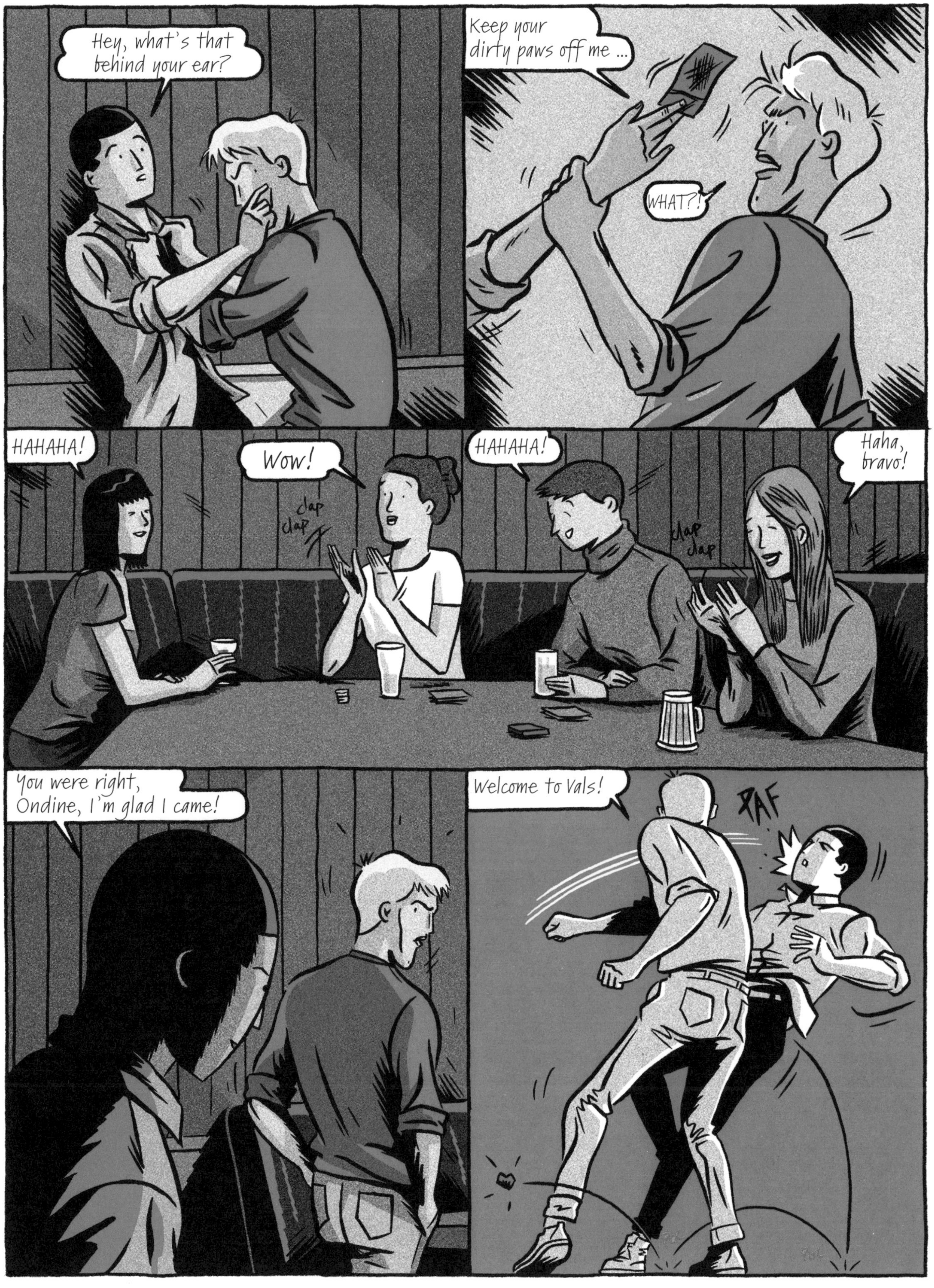
Hey, what's that behind your ear?
Keep your dirty paws off me ...
WHAT?!
HAHAHA!
Wow!
clap clap
HAHAHA!
clap clap
Haha, bravo!
You were right, Ondine, I'm glad I came!
Welcome to Vals!
PAF

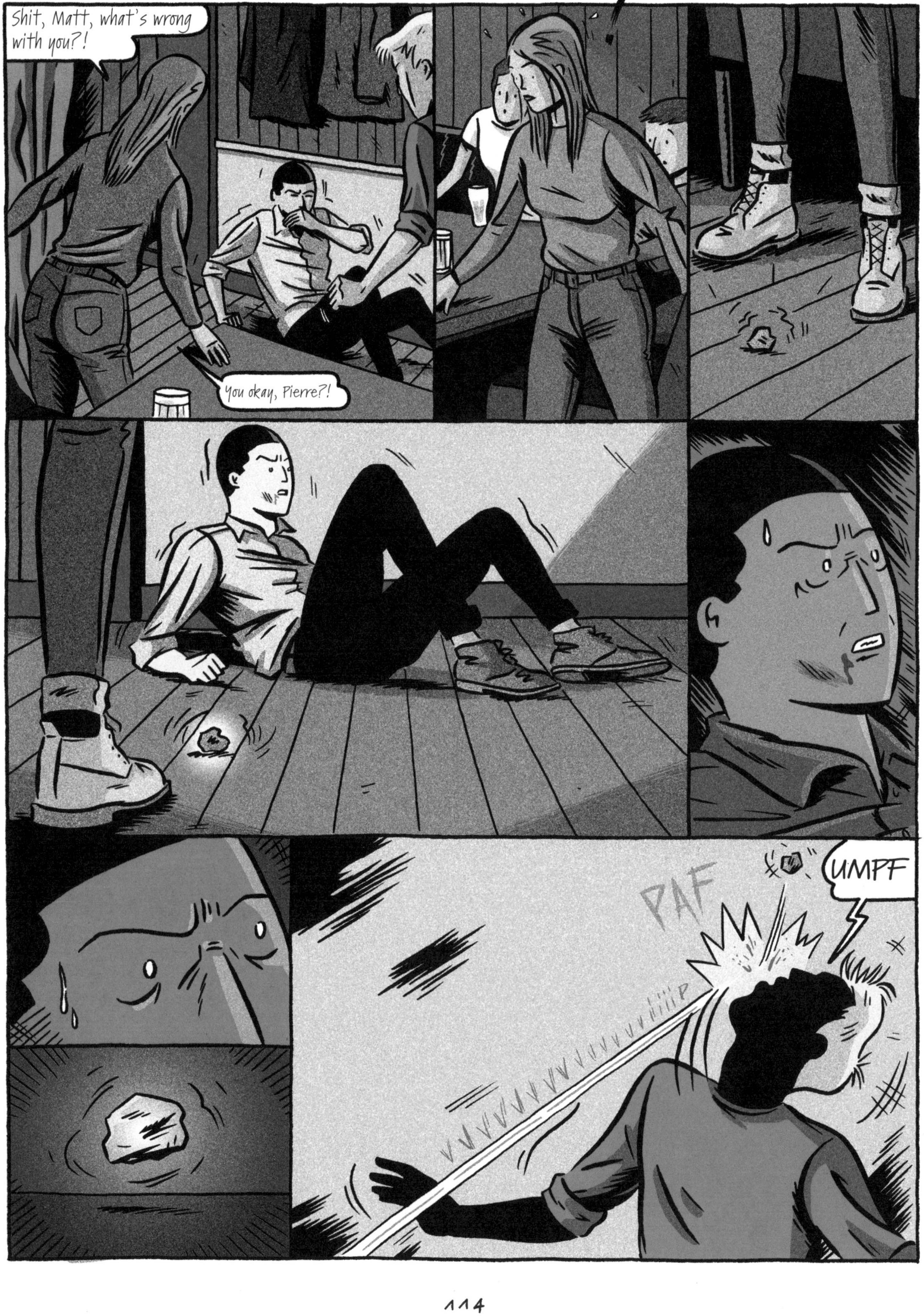
Shit, Matt, what's wrong with you?!
You okay, Pierre?!
PAF
UMPF

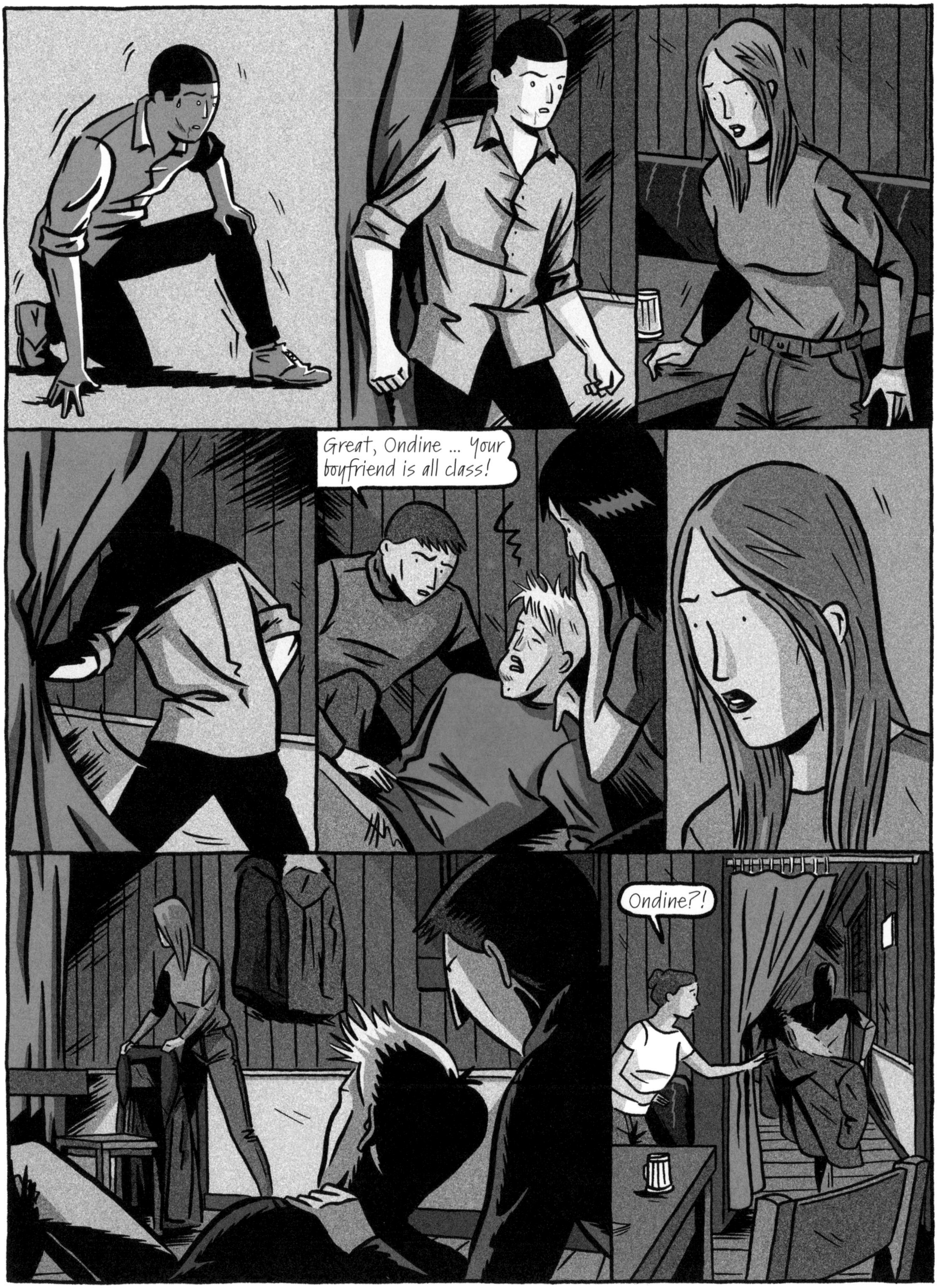
Great, Ondine ... Your boyfriend is all class!
Ondine?!

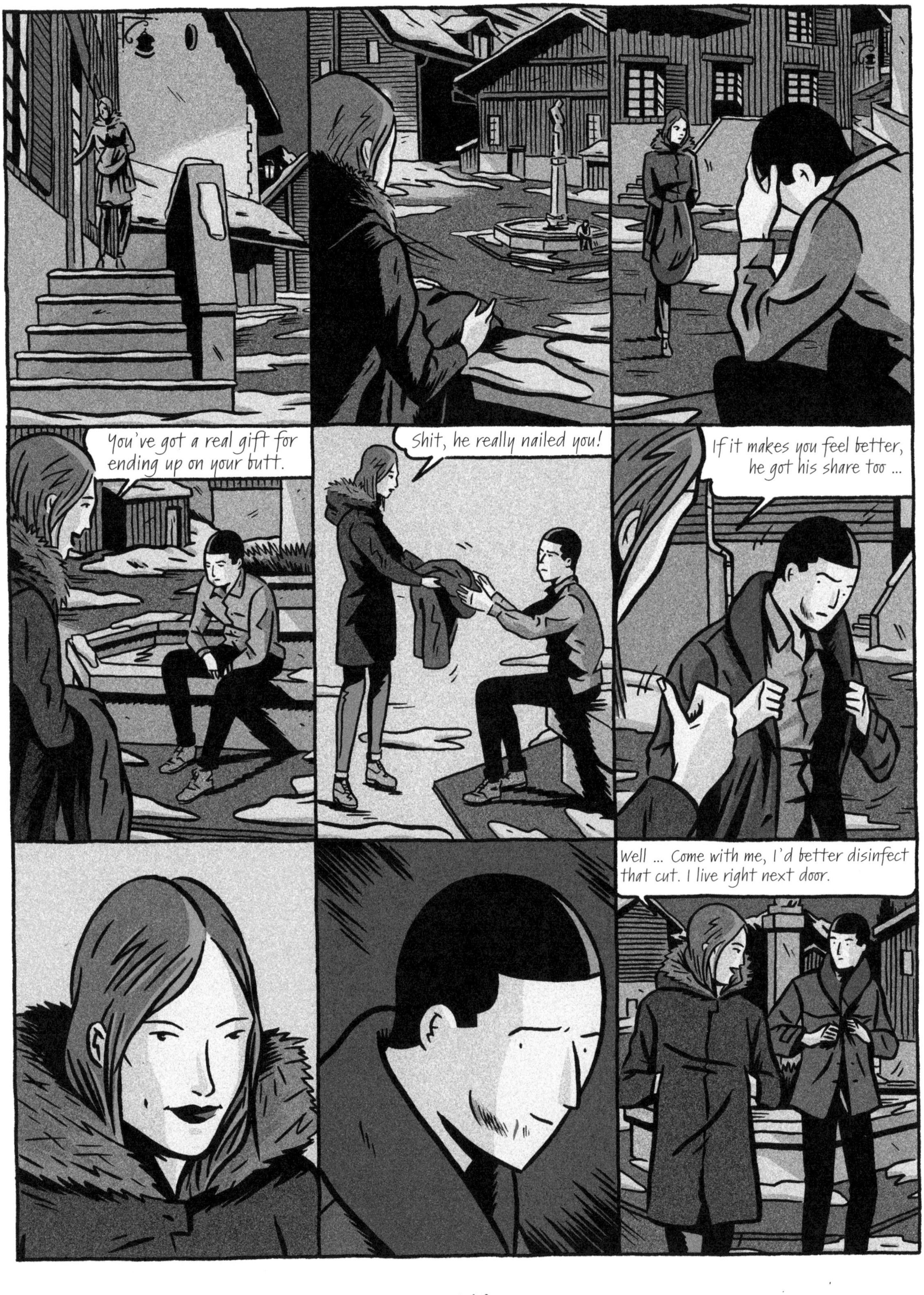
You've got a real gift for ending up on your butt.
Shit, he really nailed you!
If it makes you feel better, he got his share too ...
Well ... Come with me, I'd better disinfect that cut. I live right next door.

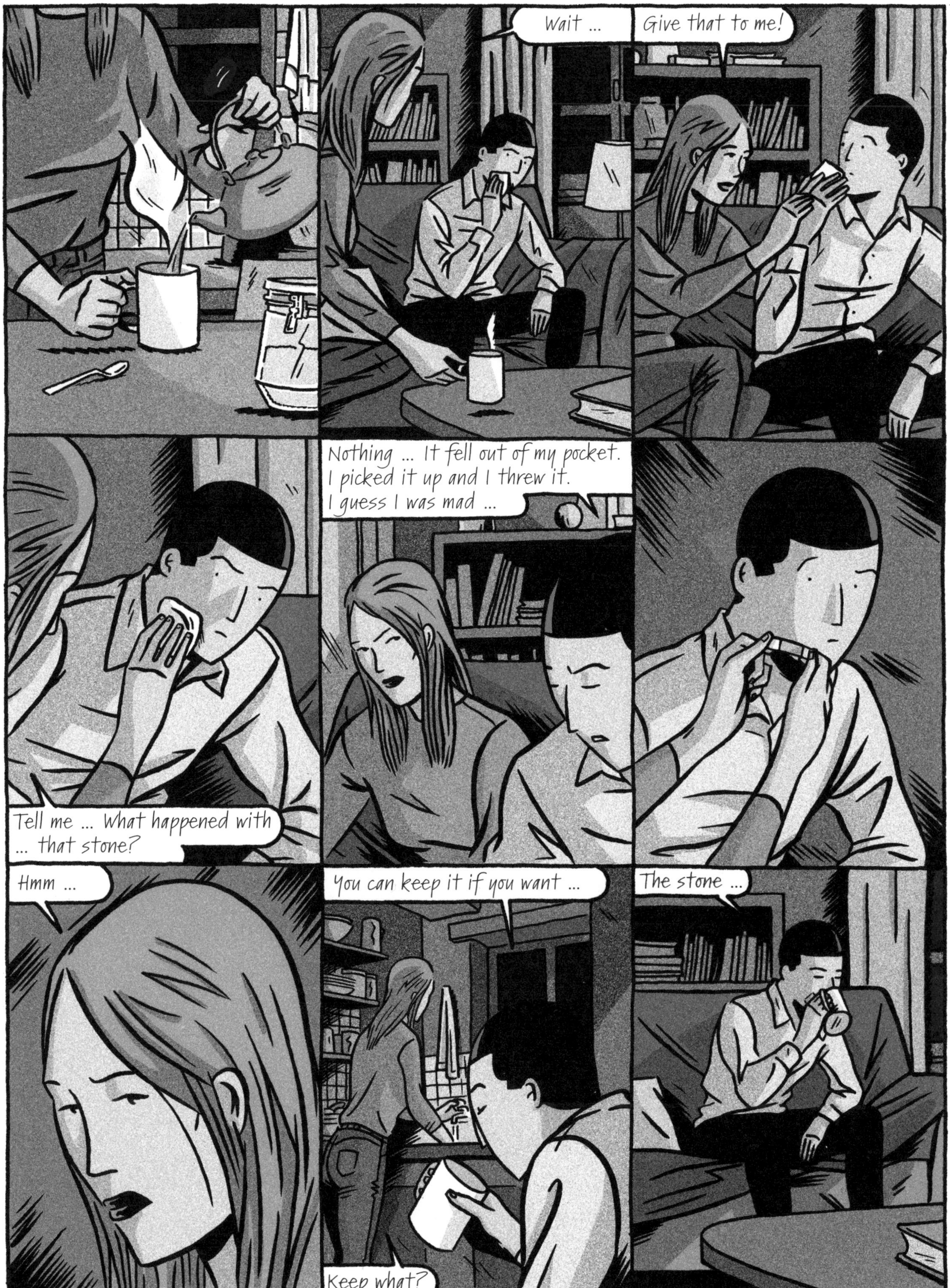
Wait ...
Give that to me!
Tell me ... What happened with ... that stone?
Nothing ... It fell out of my pocket. I picked it up and I threw it. I guess I was mad ...
Hmm ...
You can keep it if you want ...
Keep what?
The stone ...

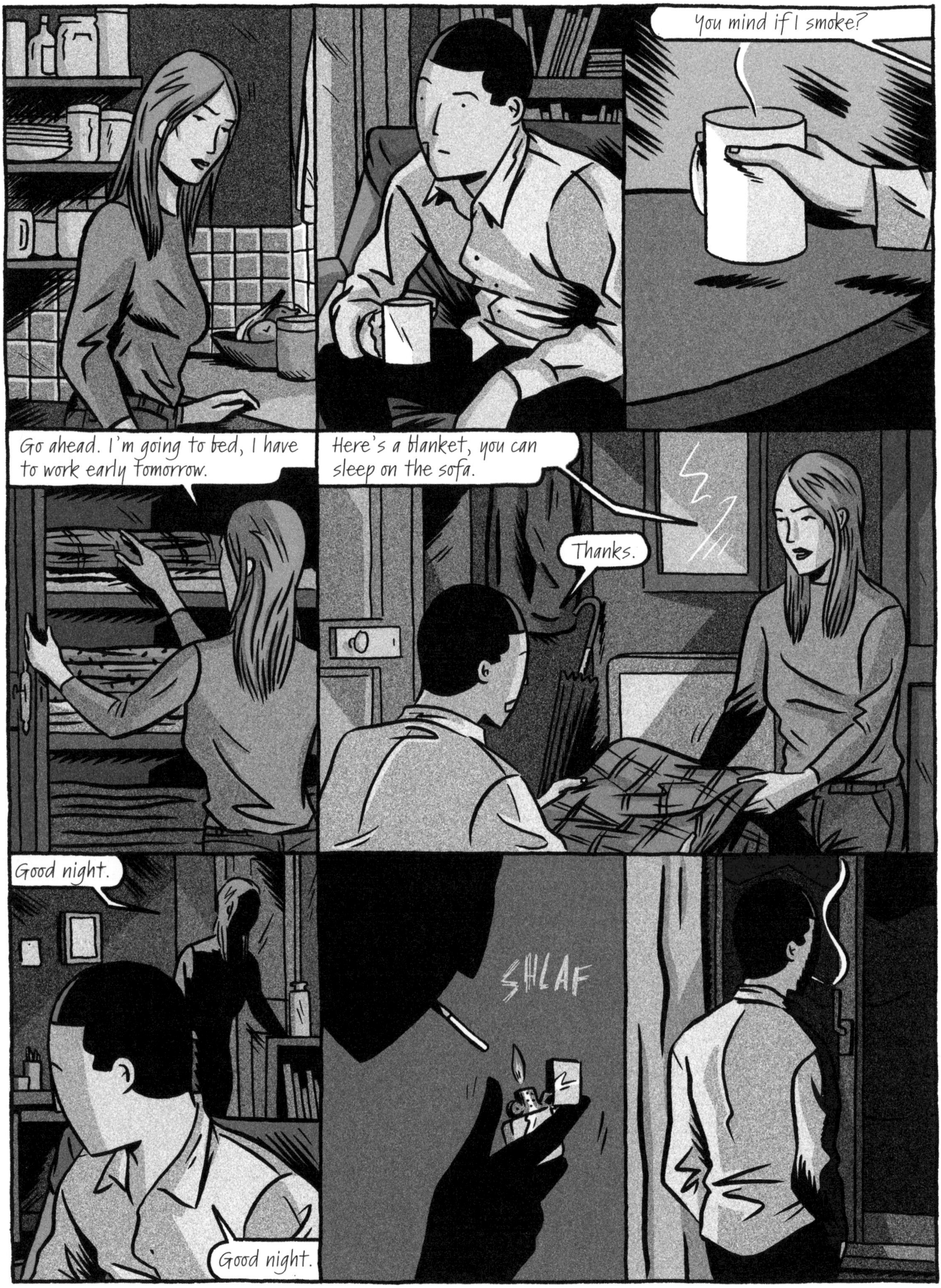
You mind if I smoke?
Go ahead. I'm going to bed, I have to work early tomorrow.
Here's a blanket, you can sleep on the sofa.
Thanks.
Good night.
Good night.
SHLAF

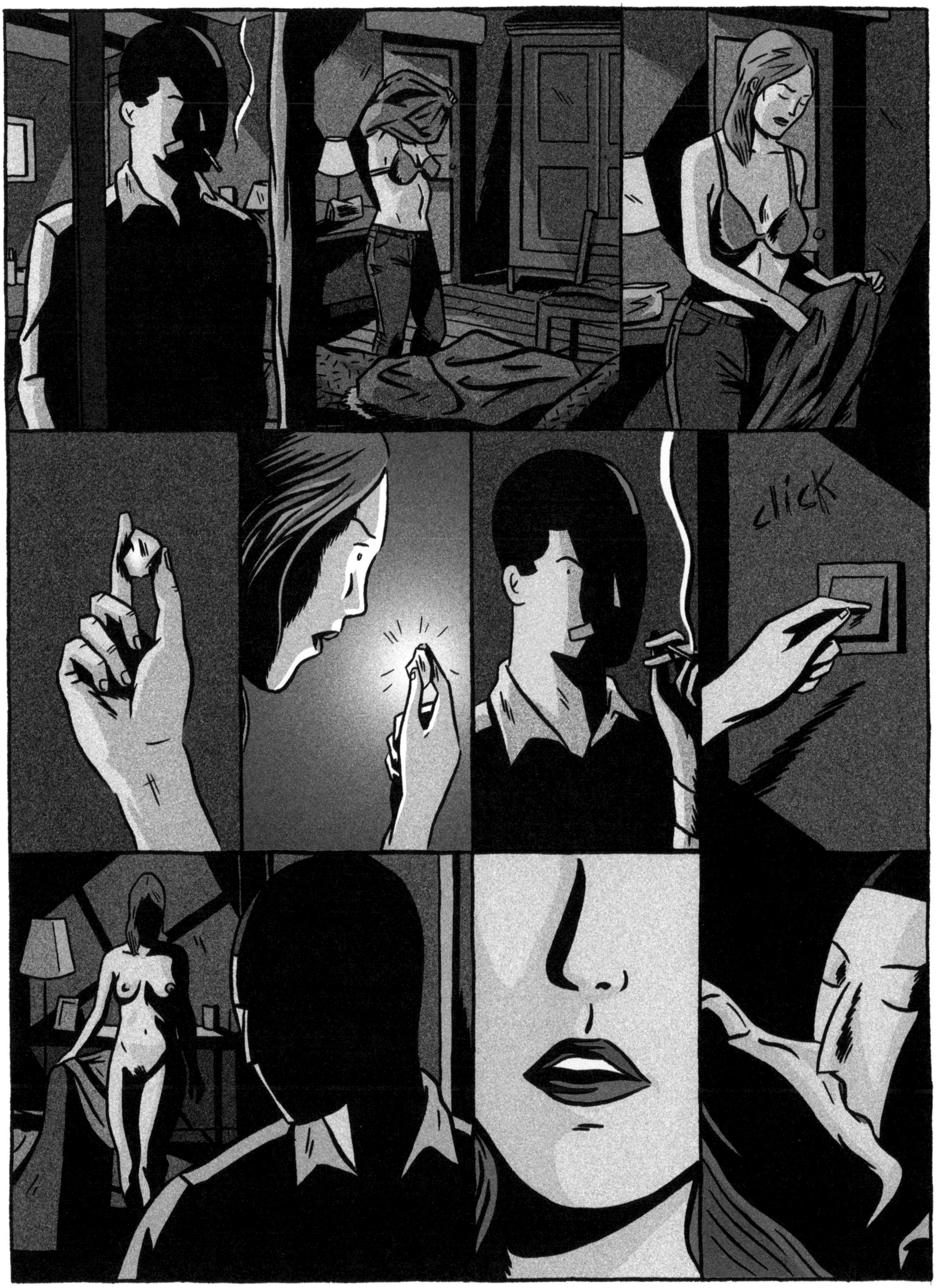
click

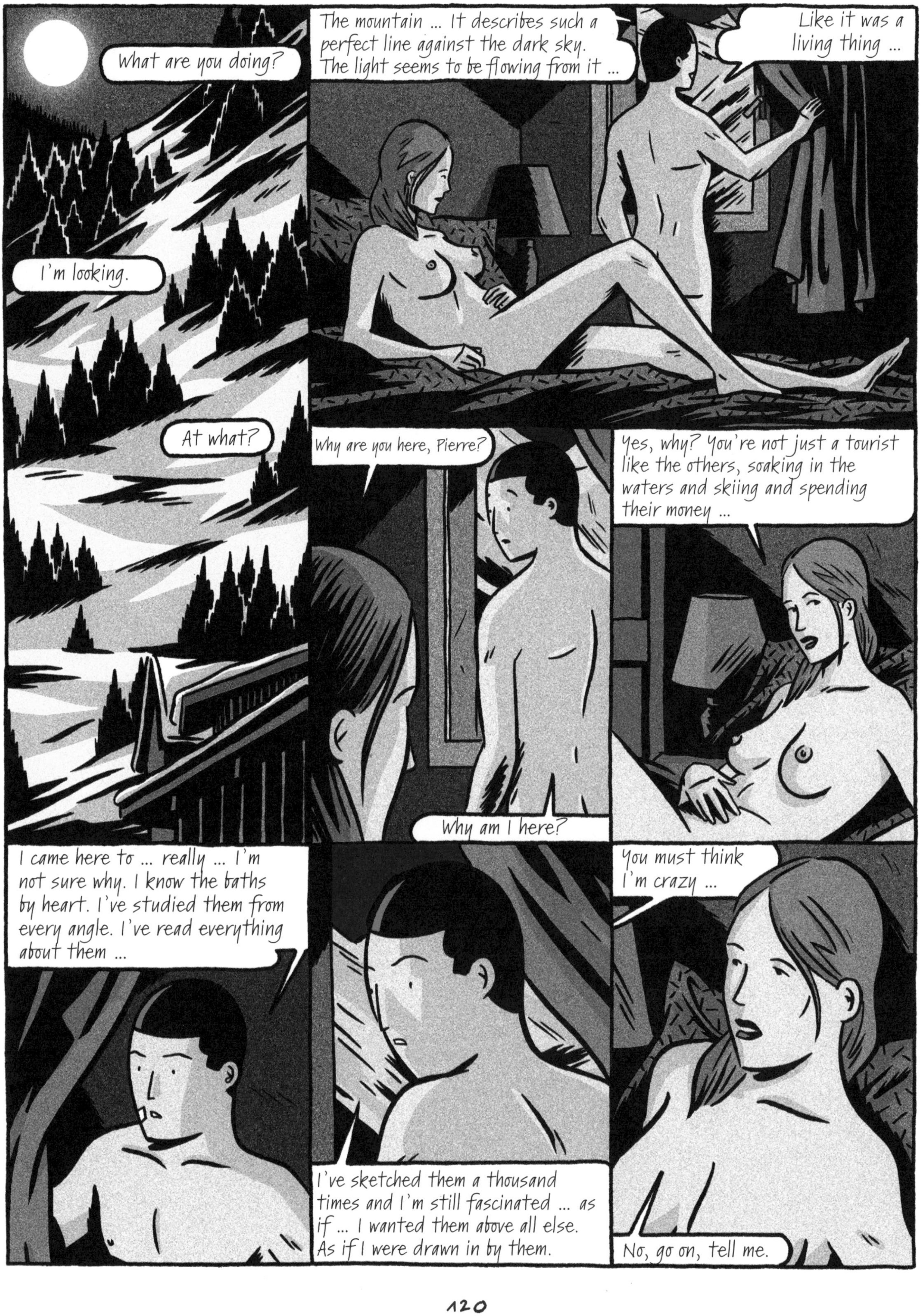
What are you doing?
I'm looking.
At what?
The mountain ... It describes such a perfect line against the dark sky. The light seems to be flowing from it ...
Like it was a living thing ...
Why are you here, Pierre?
Why am I here?
Yes, why? You're not just a tourist like the others, soaking in the waters and skiing and spending their money ...
I came here to ... really ... I'm not sure why. I know the baths by heart. I've studied them from every angle. I've read everything about them ...
I've sketched them a thousand times and I'm still fascinated ... as if ... I wanted them above all else. As if I were drawn in by them.
You must think I'm crazy ...
No, go on, tell me.

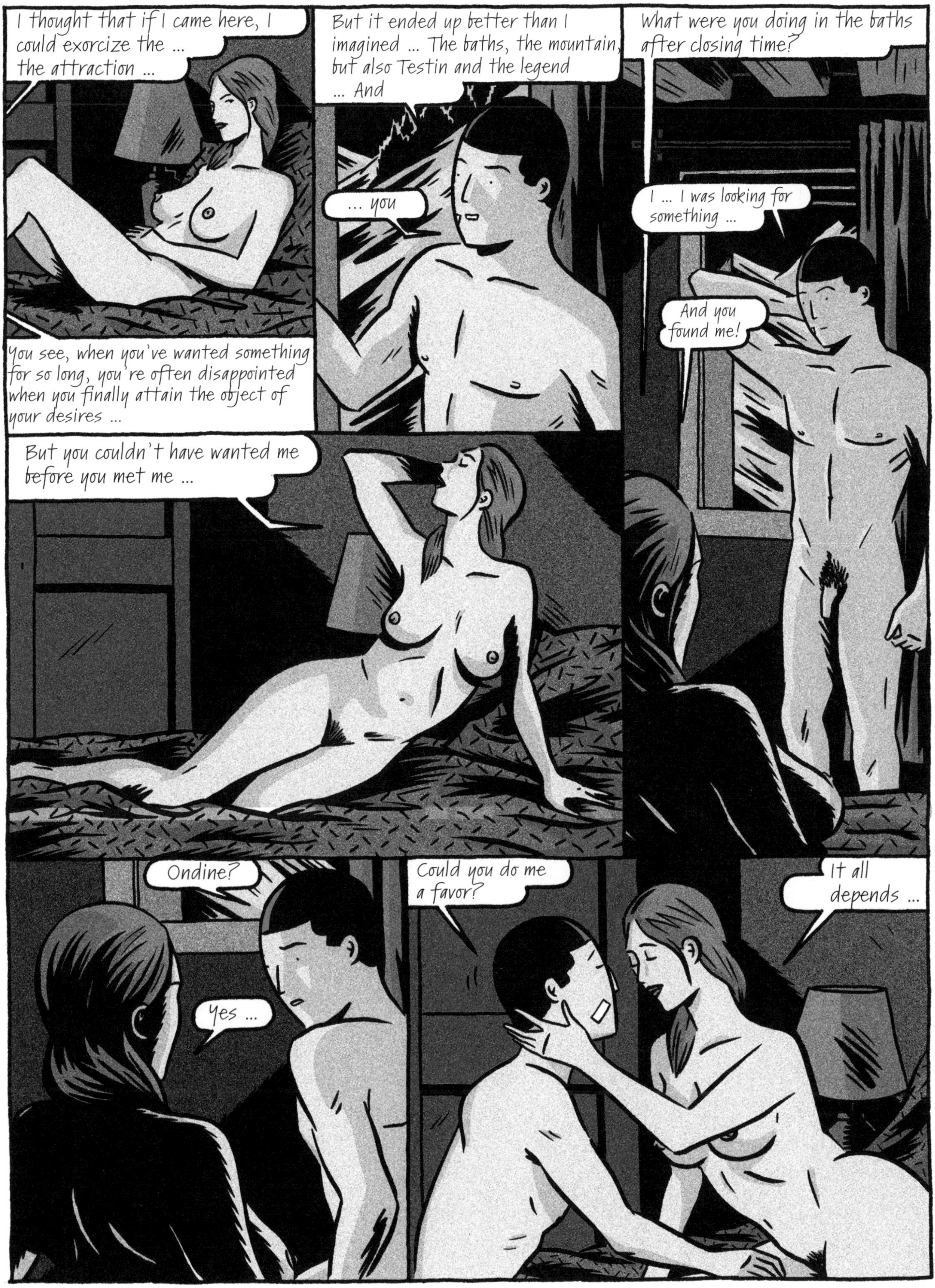
I thought that if I came here, I could exorcize the ... the attraction ...
You see, when you've wanted something for so long, you're often disappointed when you finally attain the object of your desires ...
But it ended up better than I imagined ... The baths, the mountain, but also Testin and the legend ... And
... you
What were you doing in the baths after closing time?
I ... I was looking for something ...
And you found me!
But you couldn't have wanted me before you met me ...
Ondine?
Yes ...
Could you do me a favor?
It all depends ...

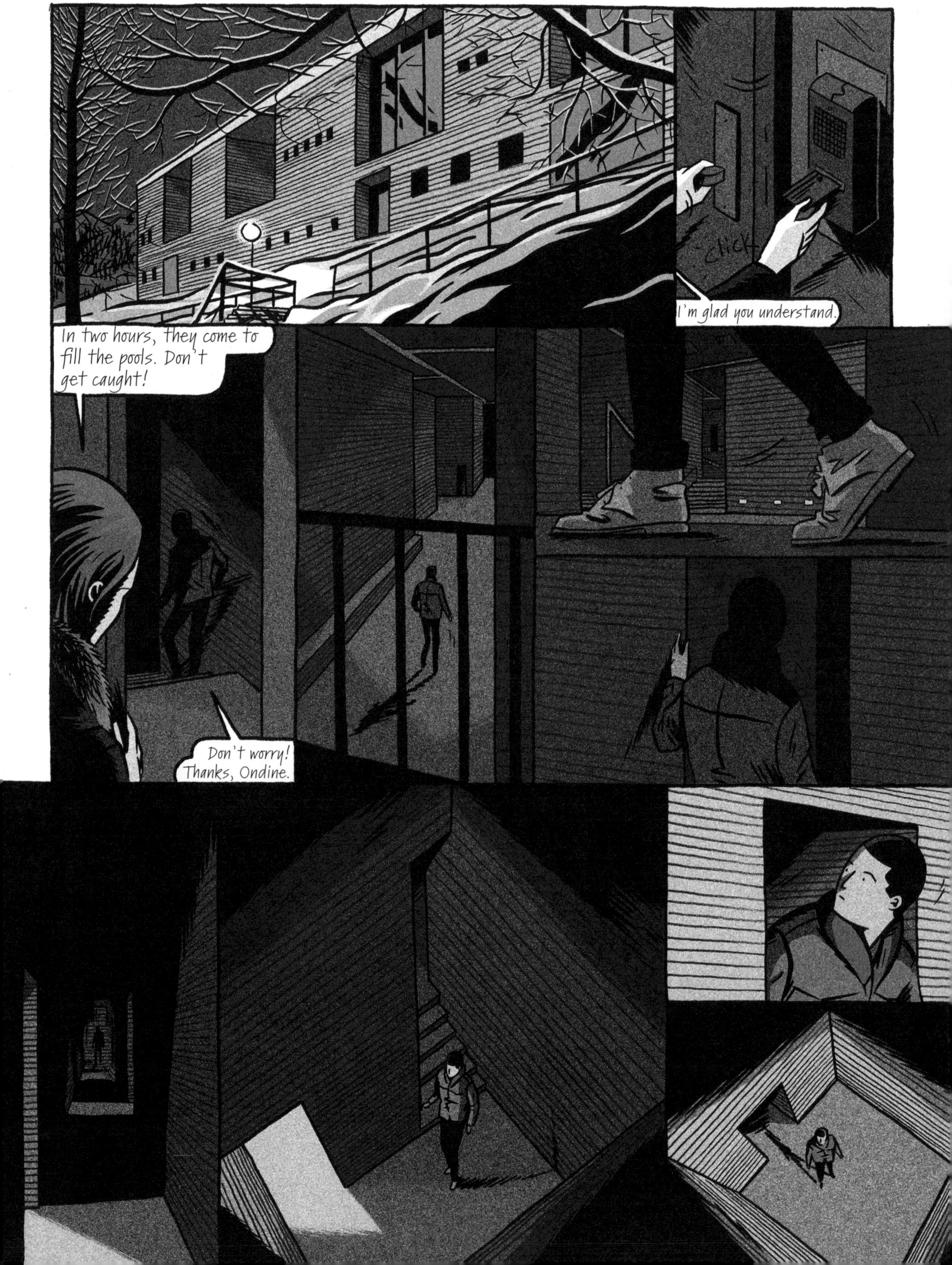
click
I'm glad you understand.
In two hours, they come to fill the pools. Don't get caught!
Don't worry! Thanks, Ondine.

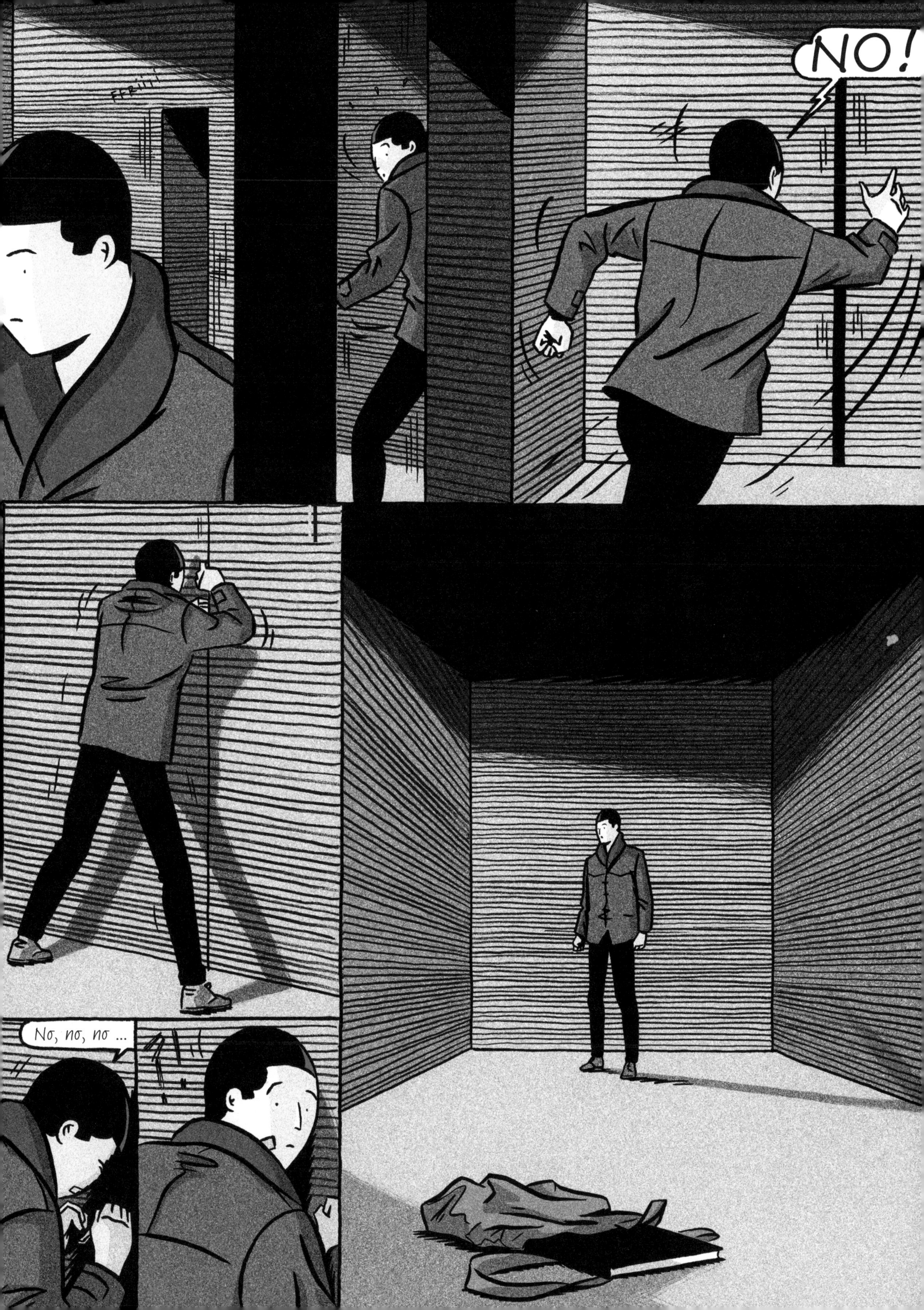
FFRiiii
NO!
No, no, no ...

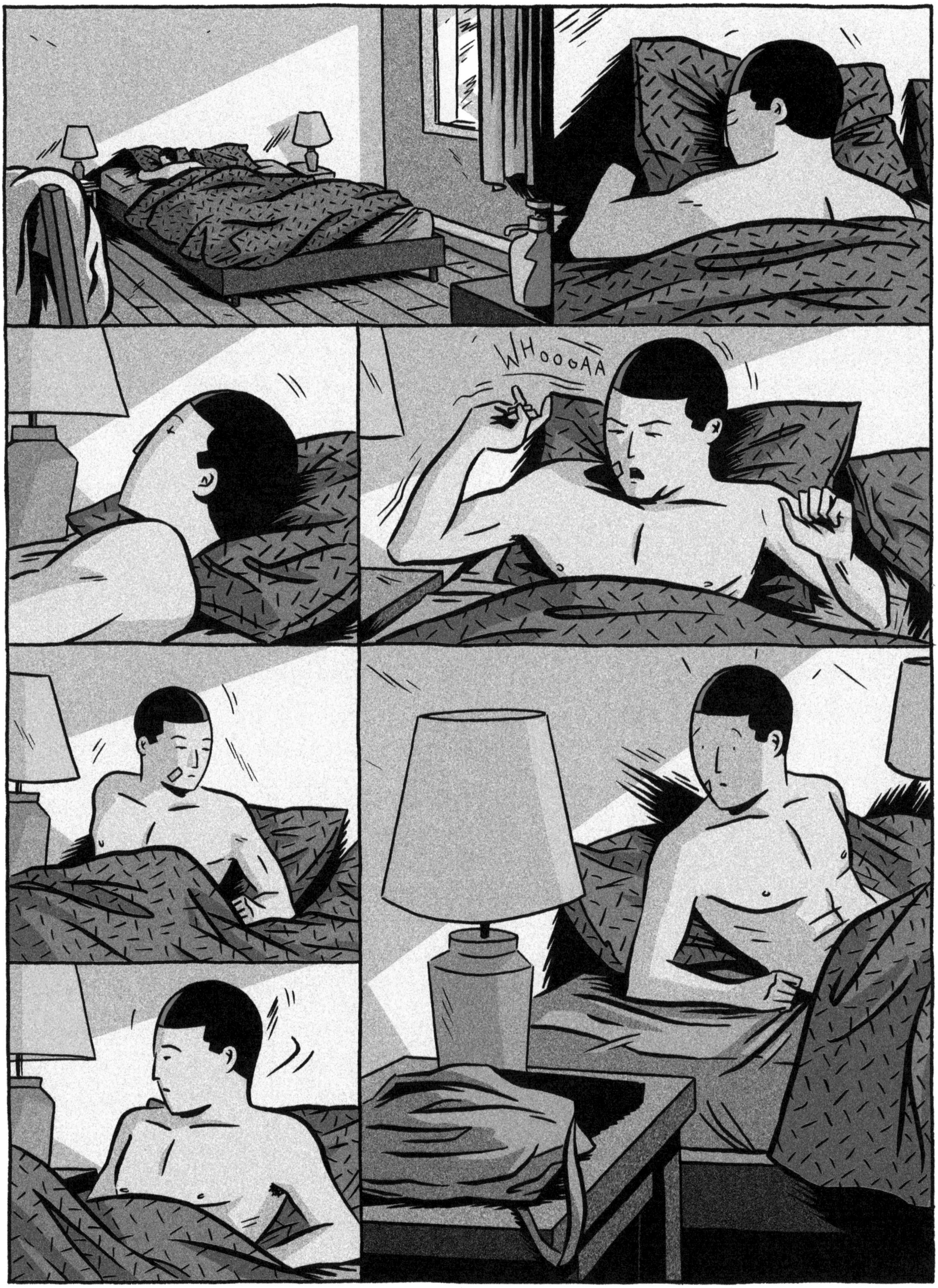
WHOOOAA

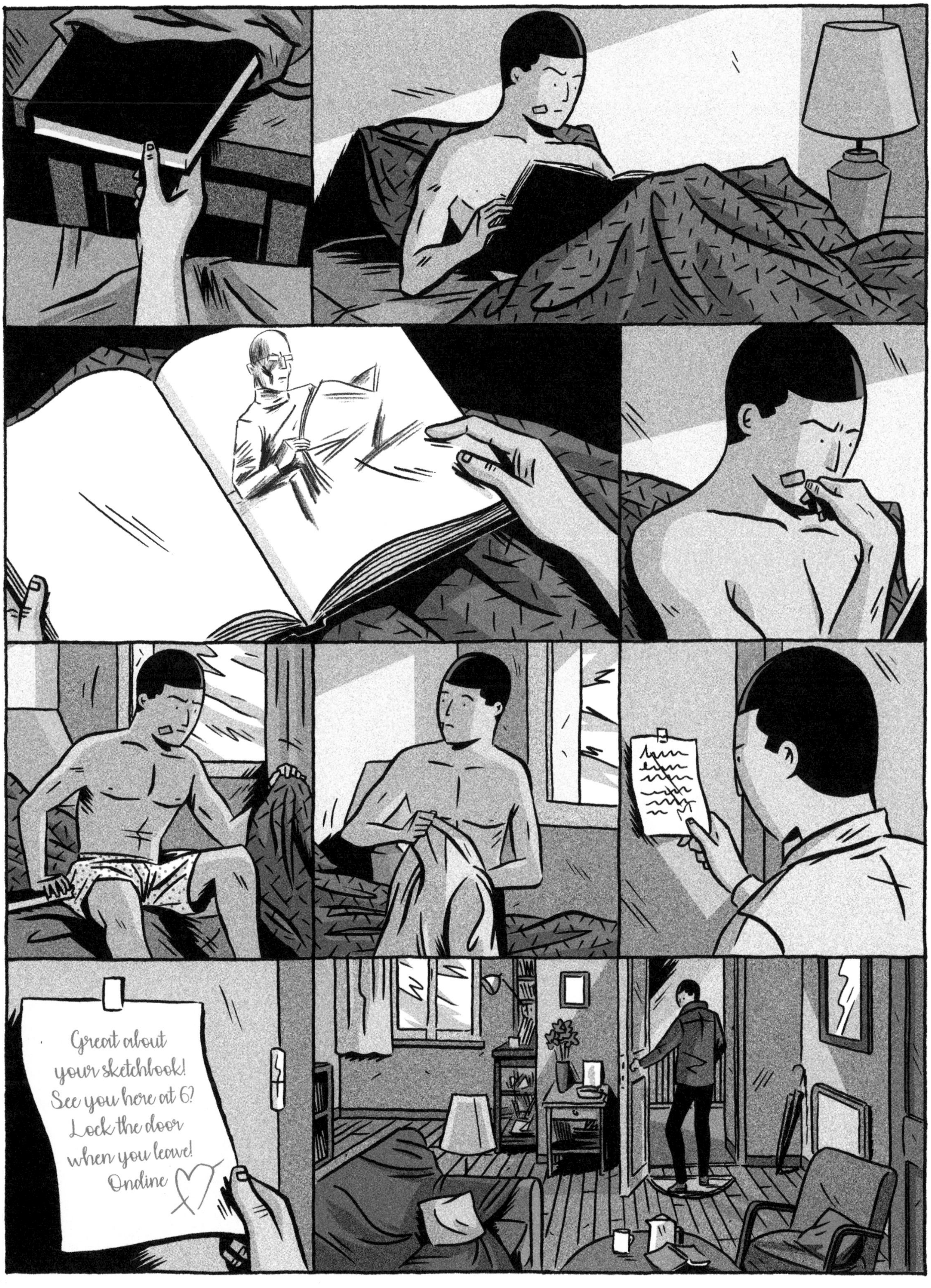
Great about
your sketchbook!
See you here at 6?
Lock the door
when you leave!
Ondine

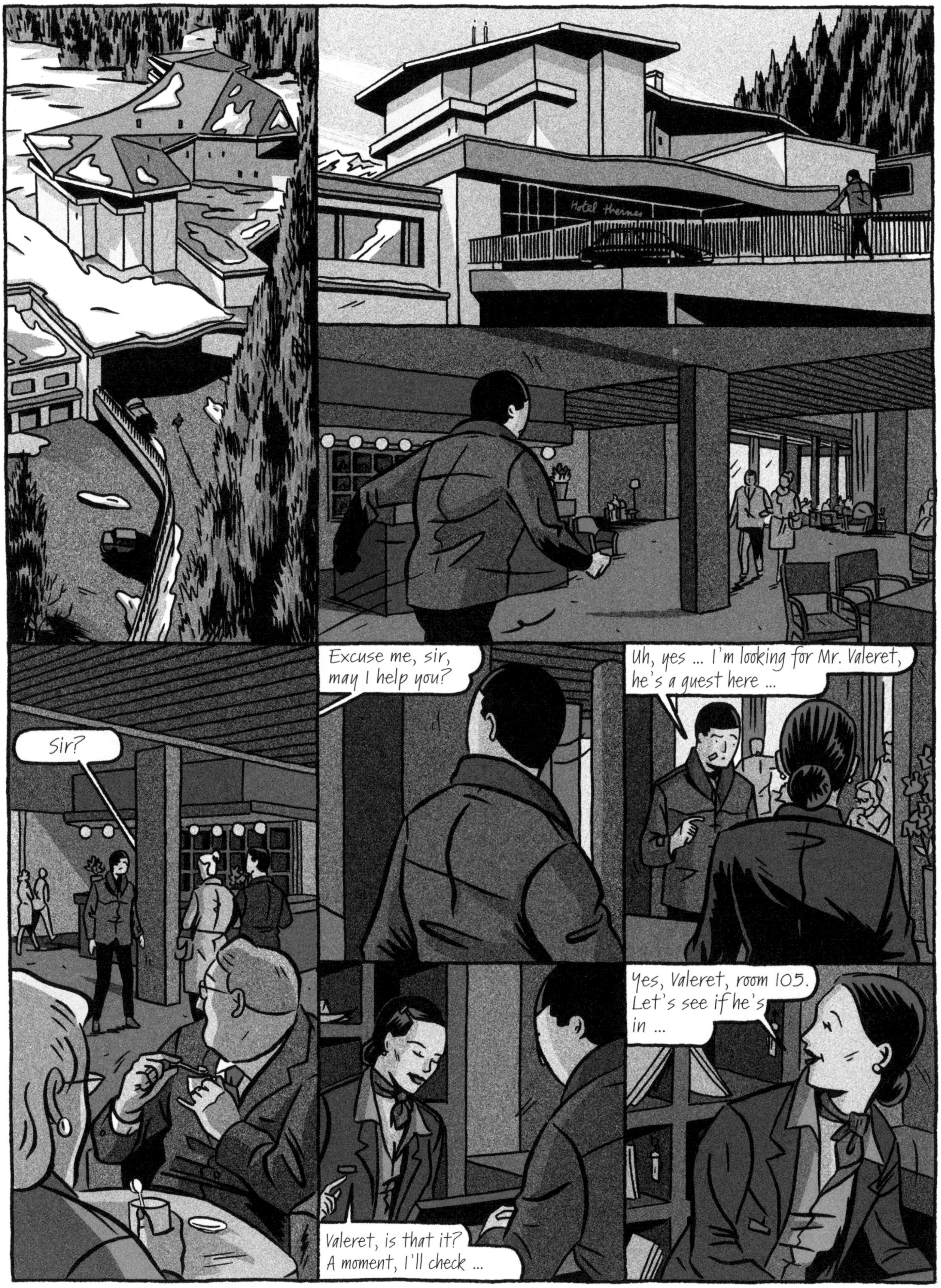
Hotel thermes
Excuse me, sir, may I help you?
Uh, yes ... I'm looking for Mr. Valeret, he's a guest here ...
Sir?
Valeret, is that it? A moment, I'll check ...
Yes, Valeret, room 105. Let's see if he's in ...

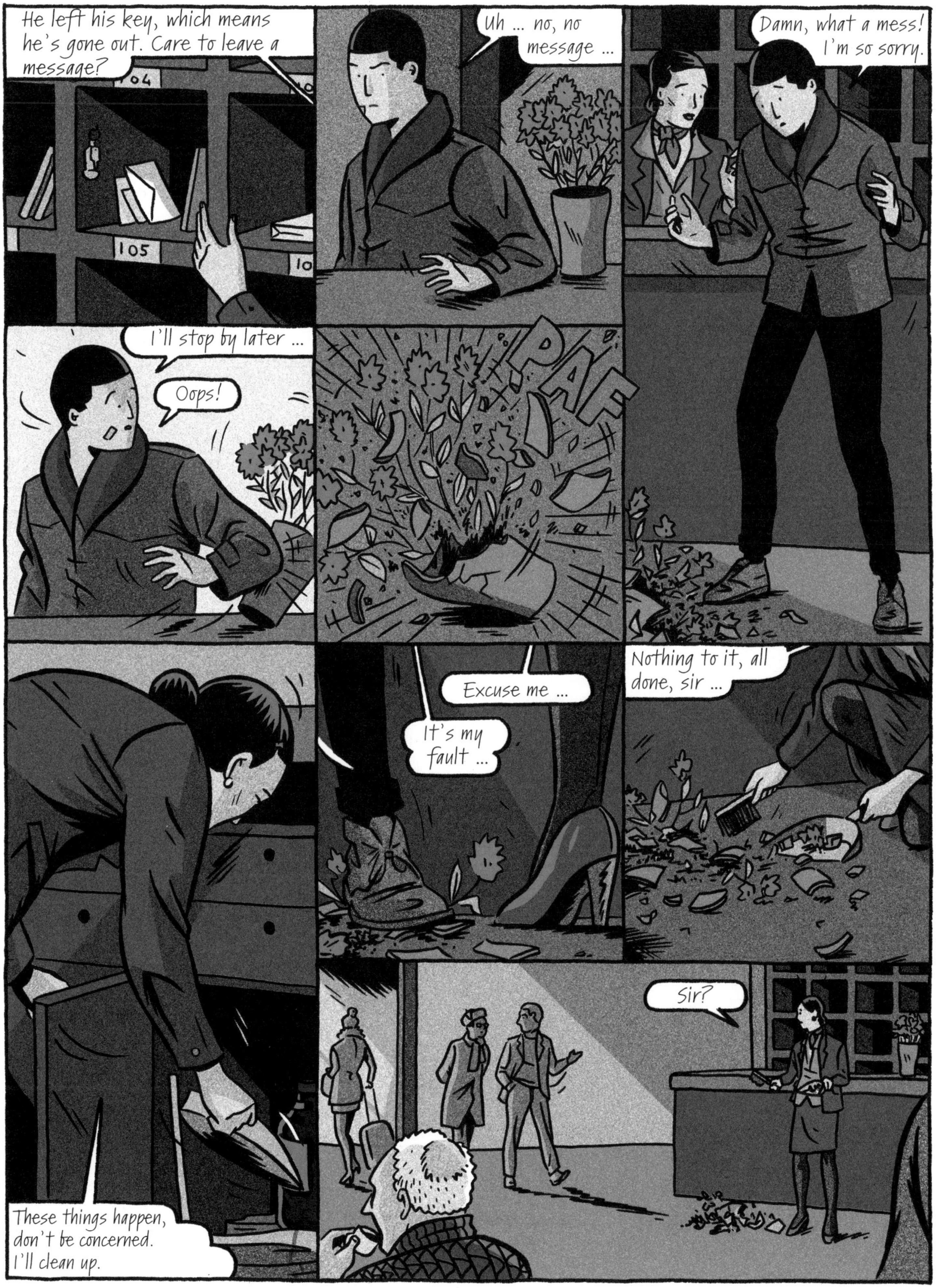
He left his key, which means he's gone out. Care to leave a message?
104
105
Uh ... no, no message ...
Damn, what a mess! I'm so sorry.
I'll stop by later ...
Oops!
PAF
Excuse me ...
It's my fault ...
Nothing to it, all done, sir ...
These things happen, don't be concerned. I'll clean up.
Sir?

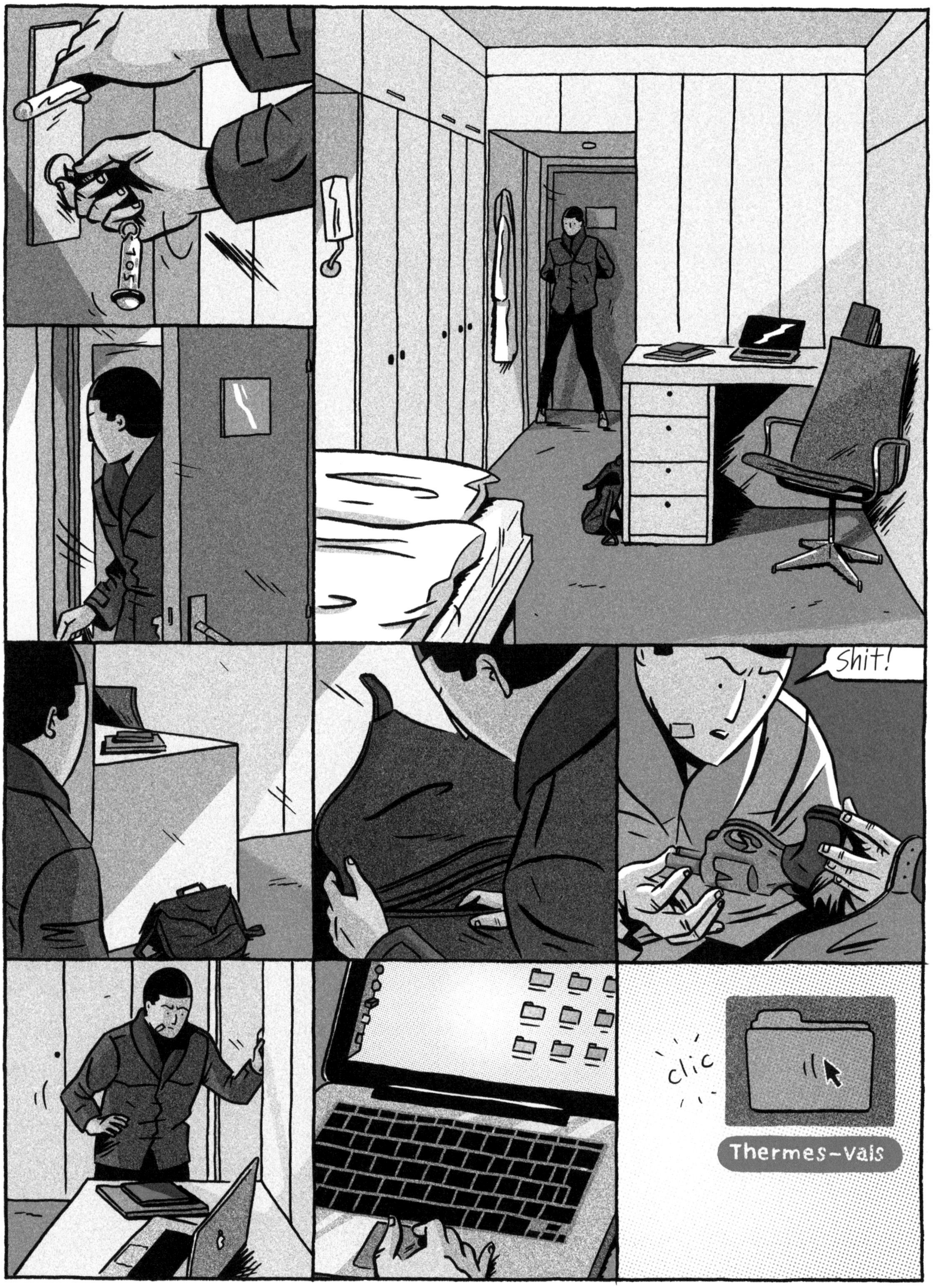
105
Shit!
clic
Thermes-Vals

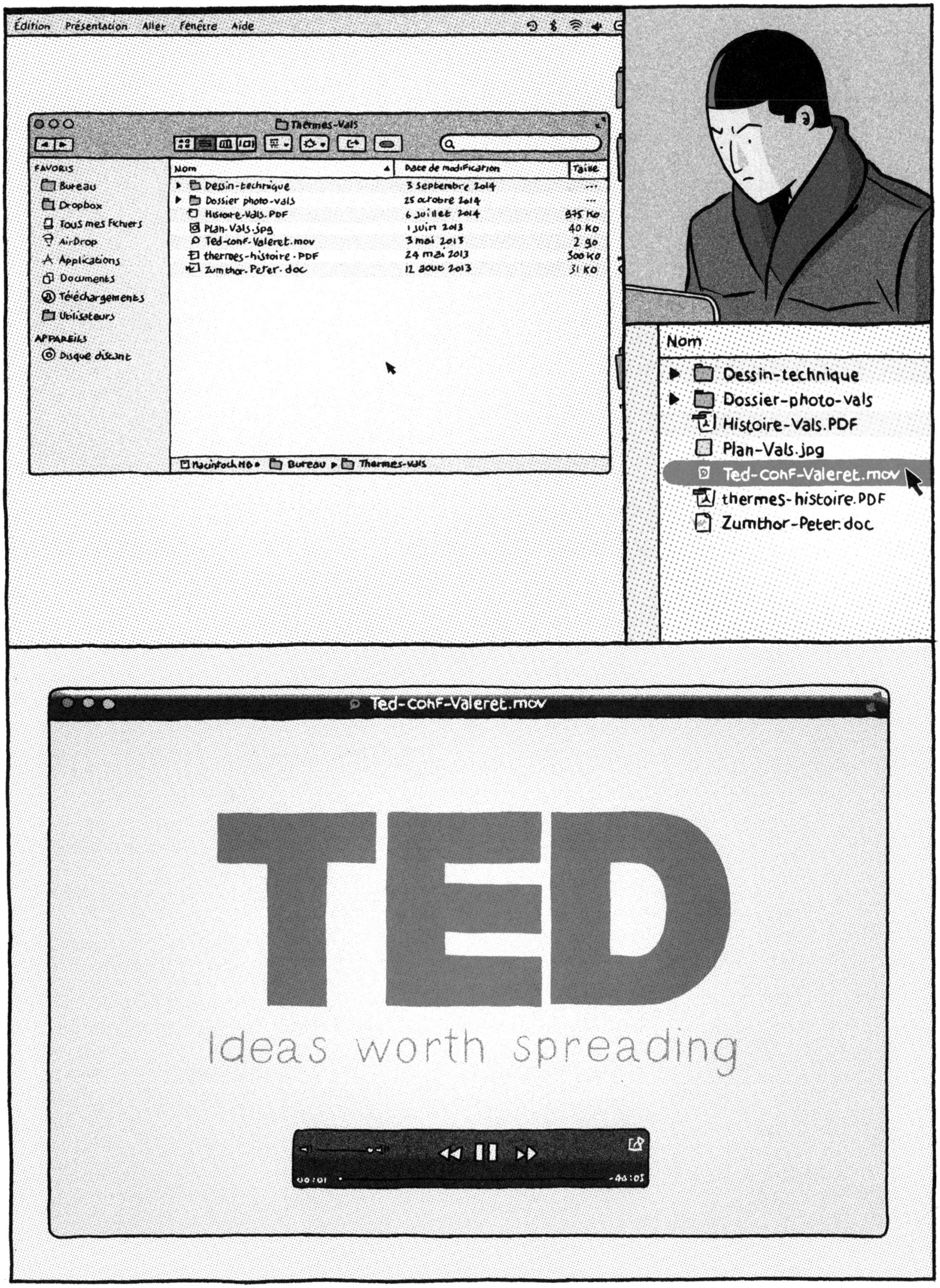
Édition Présentation Aller Fenêtre Aide
Thermes-Vals
FAVORIS
Bureau
Dropbox
Tous mes Fichiers
AirDrop
Applications
Documents
Téléchargements
Utilisateurs
APPAREILS
Disque distant
Nom
Date de modification
Taille
Dessin-technique 3 septembre 2014
Dossier photo-vals 25 octobre 2014
Histoire-Vals.PDF 6 juillet 2014 975 Ko
Plan-Vals.jpg 1 juin 2013 40 Ko
Ted-conf-Valeret.mov 3 mai 2013 2 go
thermes-histoire.PDF 24 mai 2013 300 Ko
Zumthor-Peter.doc 12 août 2013 31 Ko
Bureau
Thermes-Vals
Nom
Dessin-technique
Dossier-photo-vals
Histoire-Vals.PDF
Plan-Vals.jpg
Ted-conf-Valeret.mov
thermes-histoire.PDF
Zumthor-Peter.doc
Ted-conf-Valeret.mov
TED
ideas worth spreading

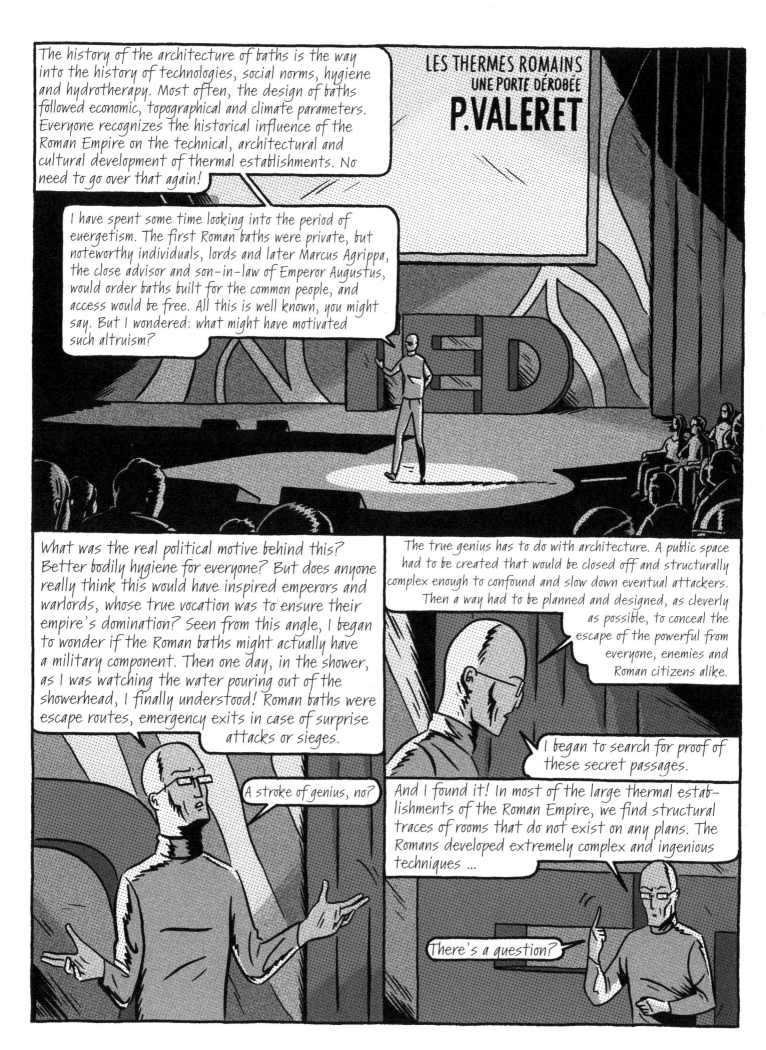

The history of the architecture of baths is the way into the history of technologies, social norms, hygiene and hydrotherapy. Most often, the design of baths followed economic, topographical and climate parameters. Everyone recognizes the historical influence of the Roman Empire on the technical, architectural and cultural development of thermal establishments. No need to go over that again!

I have spent some time looking into the period of euergetism. The first Roman baths were private, but noteworthy individuals, lords and later Marcus Agrippa, the close advisor and son-in-law of Emperor Augustus, would order baths built for the common people, and access would be free. All this is well known, you might say. But I wondered: what might have motivated such altruism?

LES THERMES ROMAINS
UNE PORTE DÉROBÉE
P.VALERET

What was the real political motive behind this? Better bodily hygiene for everyone? But does anyone really think this would have inspired emperors and warlords, whose true vocation was to ensure their empire's domination? Seen from this angle, I began to wonder if the Roman baths might actually have a military component. Then one day, in the shower, as I was watching the water pouring out of the showerhead, I finally understood! Roman baths were escape routes, emergency exits in case of surprise attacks or sieges.

A stroke of genius, no?

The true genius has to do with architecture. A public space had to be created that would be closed off and structurally complex enough to confound and slow down eventual attackers. Then a way had to be planned and designed, as cleverly as possible, to conceal the escape of the powerful from everyone, enemies and Roman citizens alike.

I began to search for proof of these secret passages.

And I found it! In most of the large thermal establishments of the Roman Empire, we find structural traces of rooms that do not exist on any plans. The Romans developed extremely complex and ingenious techniques ...

There's a question?

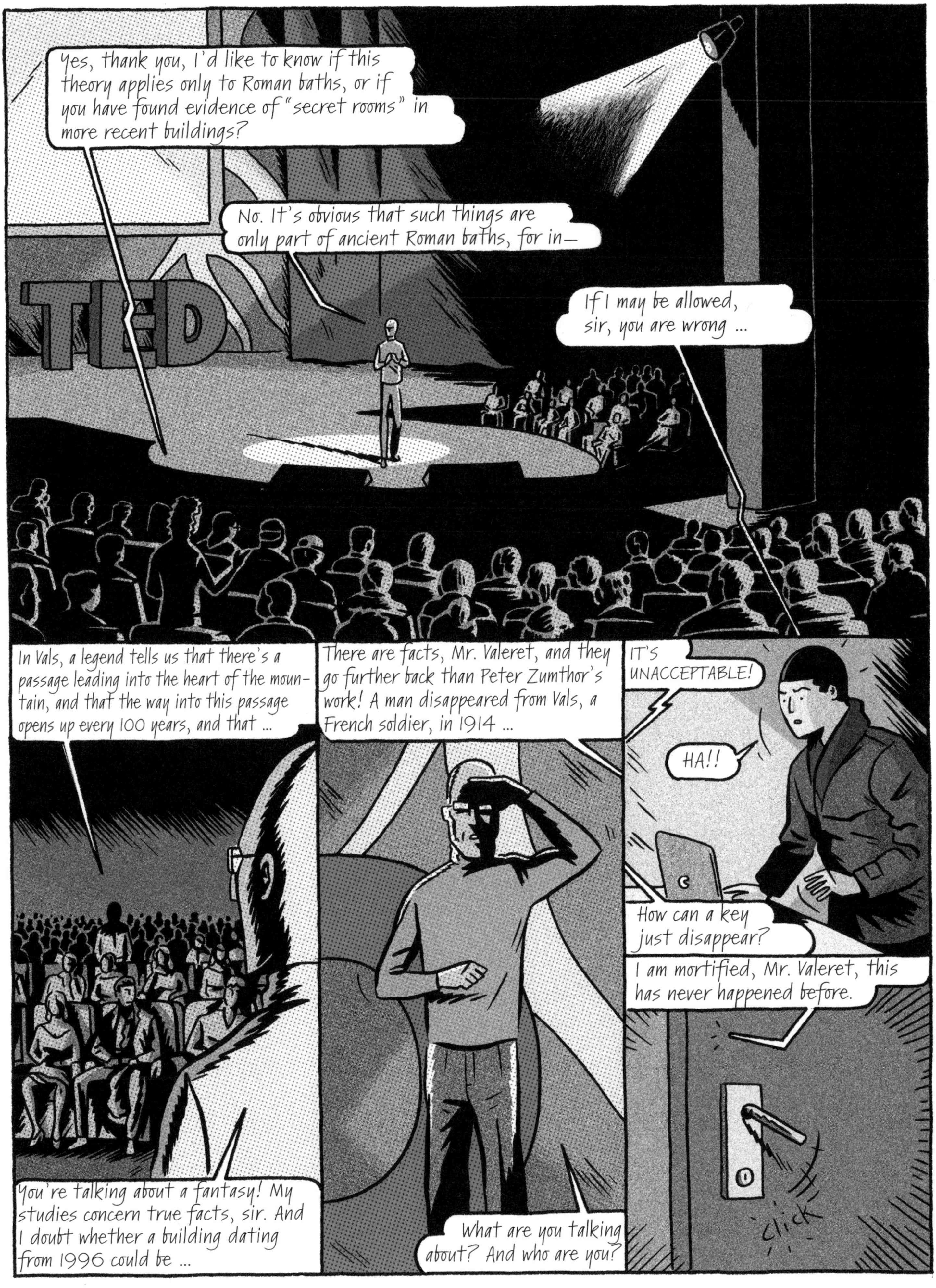
Yes, thank you, I'd like to know if this theory applies only to Roman baths, or if you have found evidence of "secret rooms" in more recent buildings?
No. It's obvious that such things are only part of ancient Roman baths, for in—
TED
If I may be allowed, sir, you are wrong ...
In Vals, a legend tells us that there's a passage leading into the heart of the mountain, and that the way into this passage opens up every 100 years, and that ...
You're talking about a fantasy! My studies concern true facts, sir. And I doubt whether a building dating from 1996 could be ...
There are facts, Mr. Valeret, and they go further back than Peter Zumthor's work! A man disappeared from Vals, a French soldier, in 1914 ...
What are you talking about? And who are you?
IT'S UNACCEPTABLE!
HA!!
How can a key just disappear?
I am mortified, Mr. Valeret, this has never happened before.
click

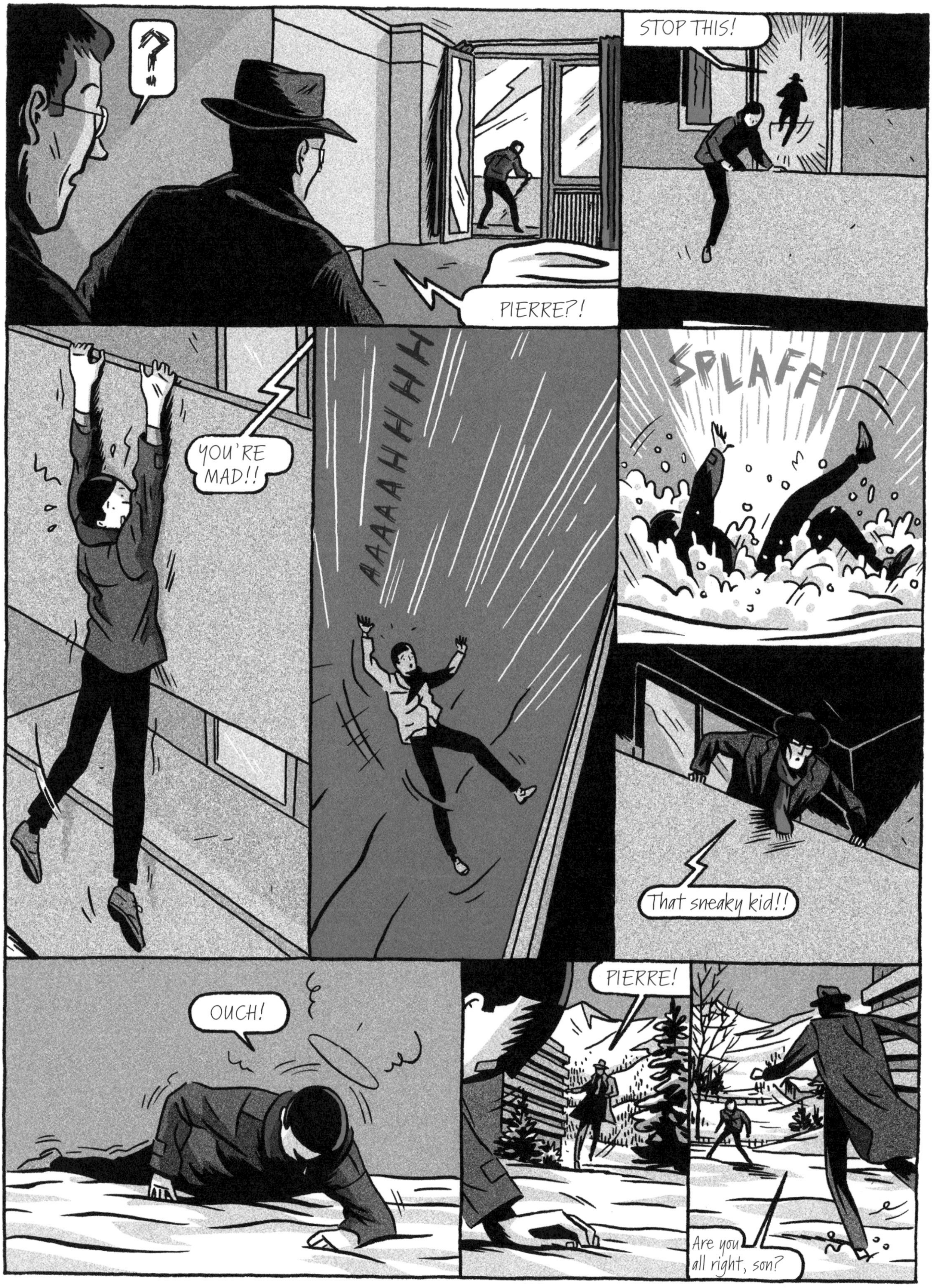
?!
PIERRE?!
STOP THIS!
YOU'RE MAD!!
AAAAAHHHHHH
SPLAFF
That sneaky kid!!
OUCH!
PIERRE!
Are you all right, son?

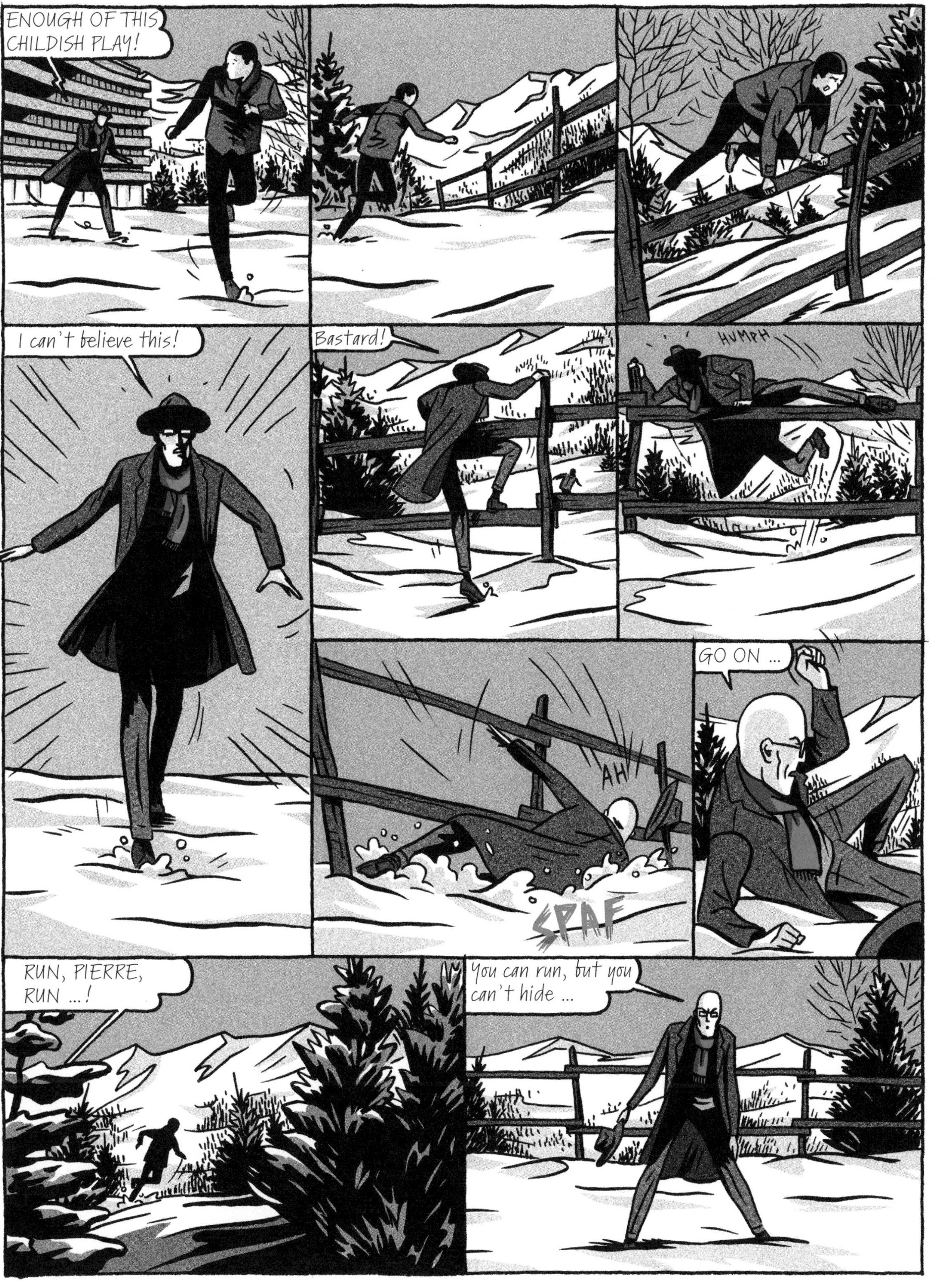
ENOUGH OF THIS CHILDISH PLAY!
I can't believe this!
Bastard!
HUMPH
AH
SPAF
GO ON ...
RUN, PIERRE, RUN ...!
You can run, but you can't hide ...

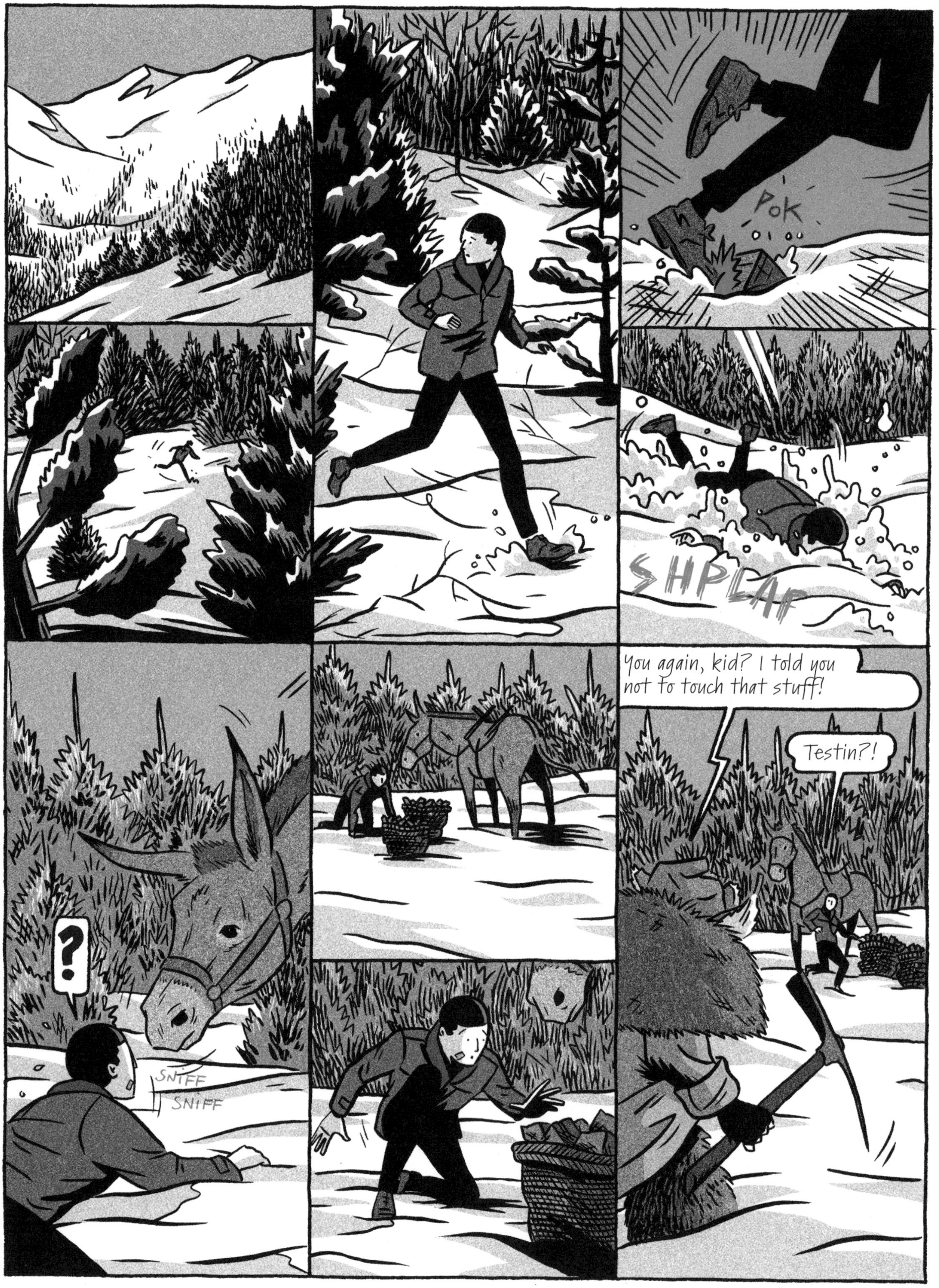
POK
SHPLAF
?
SNIFF
SNIFF
You again, kid? I told you not to touch that stuff!
Testin?!

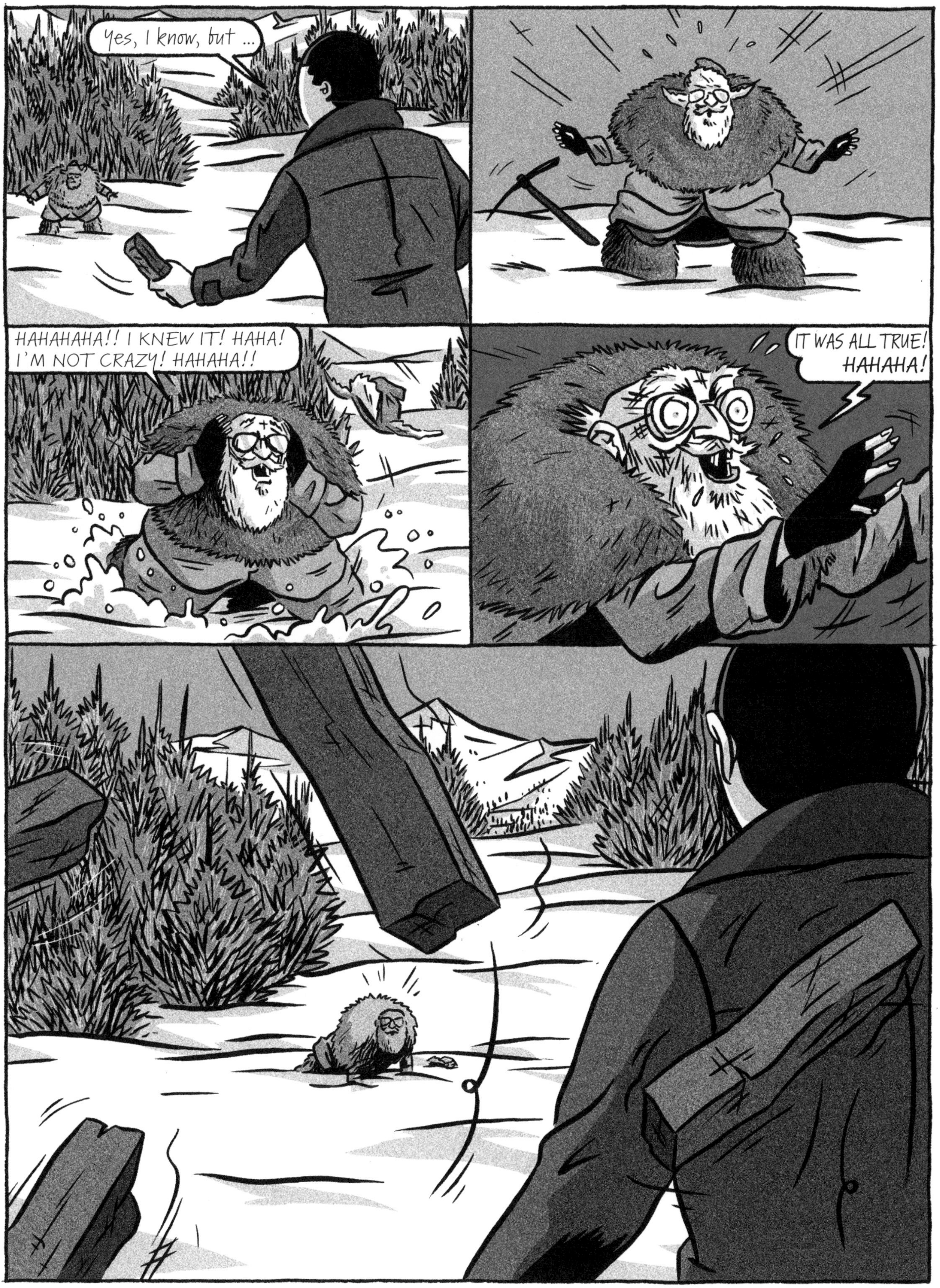
Yes, I know, but ...
HAHAHAHA!! I KNEW IT! HAHA! I'M NOT CRAZY! HAHAHA!!
IT WAS ALL TRUE! HAHAHA!

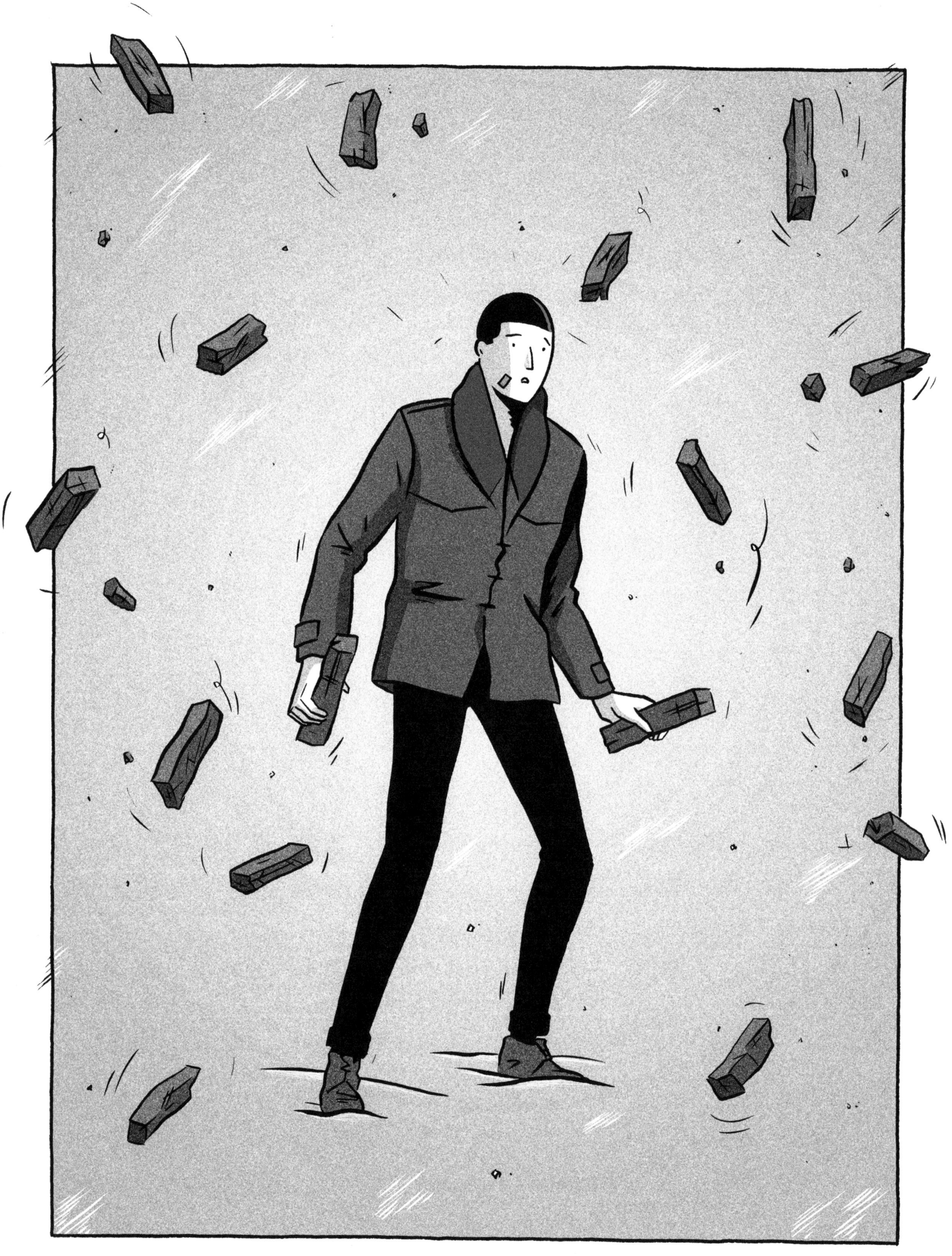

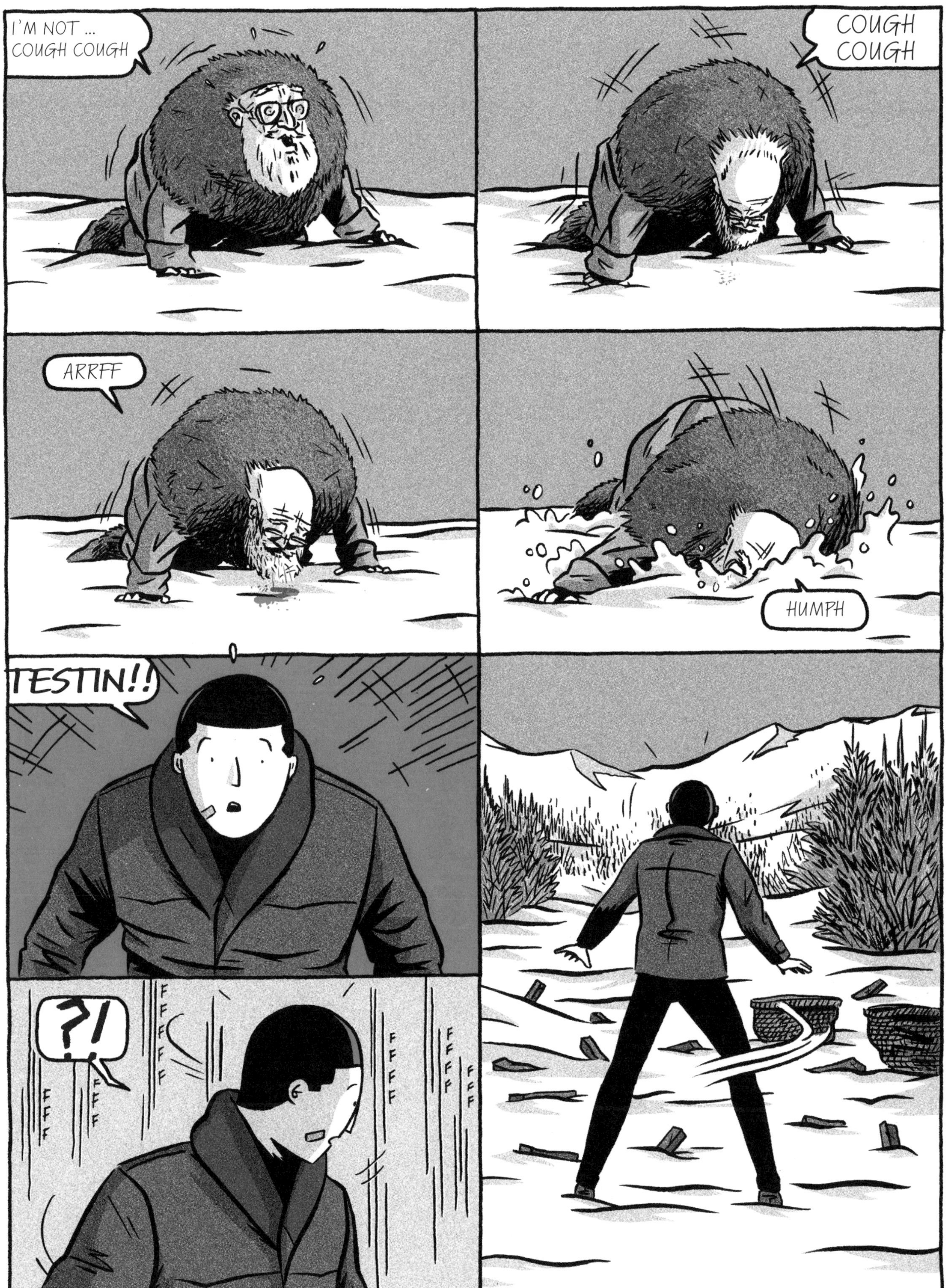
I'M NOT ... COUGH COUGH
COUGH COUGH
ARRFF
HUMPH
TESTIN!!
?!

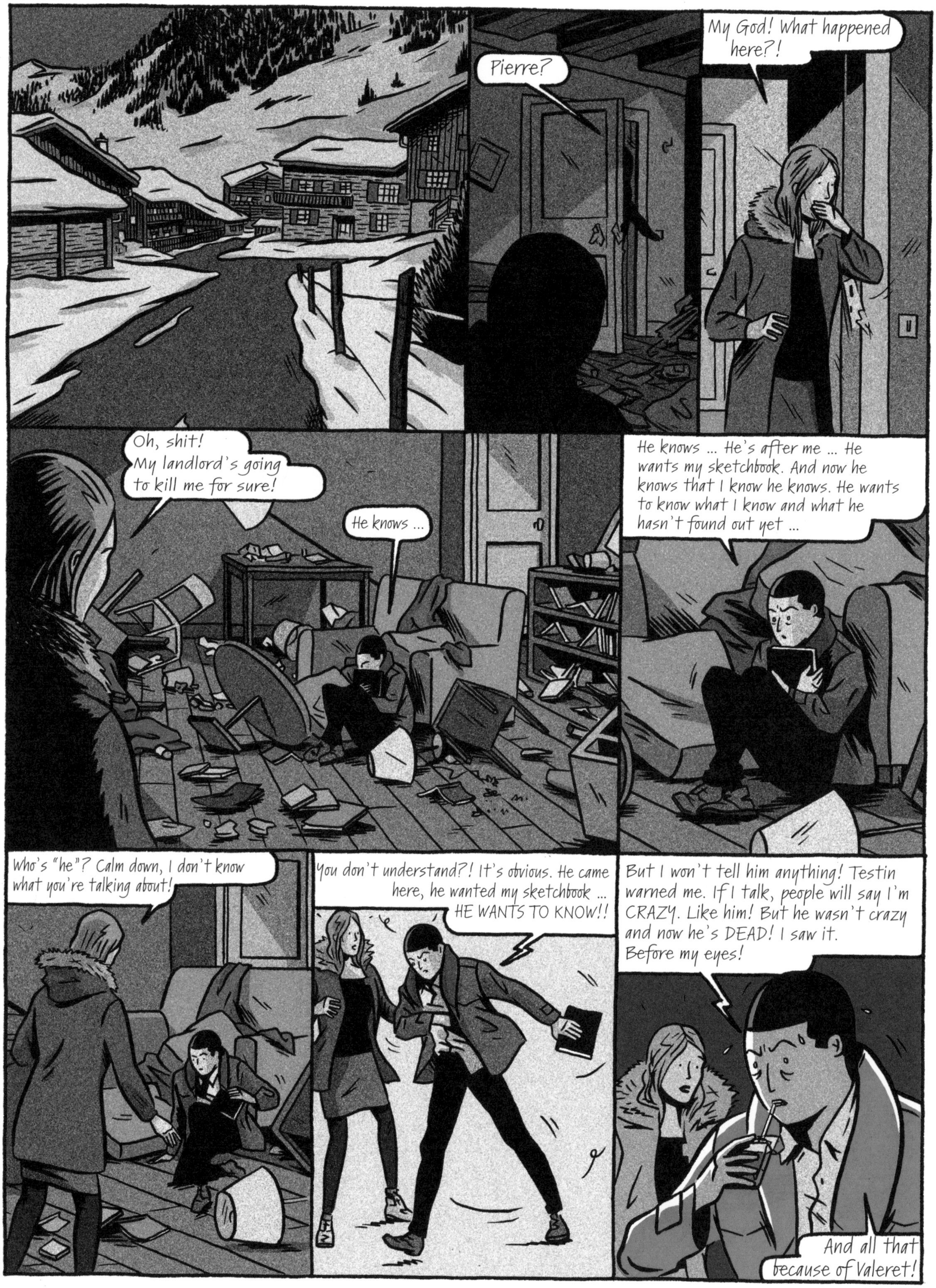
Pierre?
My God! What happened here?!
Oh, shit! My landlord's going to kill me for sure!
He knows ...
He knows ... He's after me ... He wants my sketchbook. And now he knows that I know he knows. He wants to know what I know and what he hasn't found out yet ...
Who's "he"? Calm down, I don't know what you're talking about!
You don't understand?! It's obvious. He came here, he wanted my sketchbook ... HE WANTS TO KNOW!!
But I won't tell him anything! Testin warned me. If I talk, people will say I'm CRAZY. Like him! But he wasn't crazy and now he's DEAD! I saw it. Before my eyes!
And all that because of Valeret!

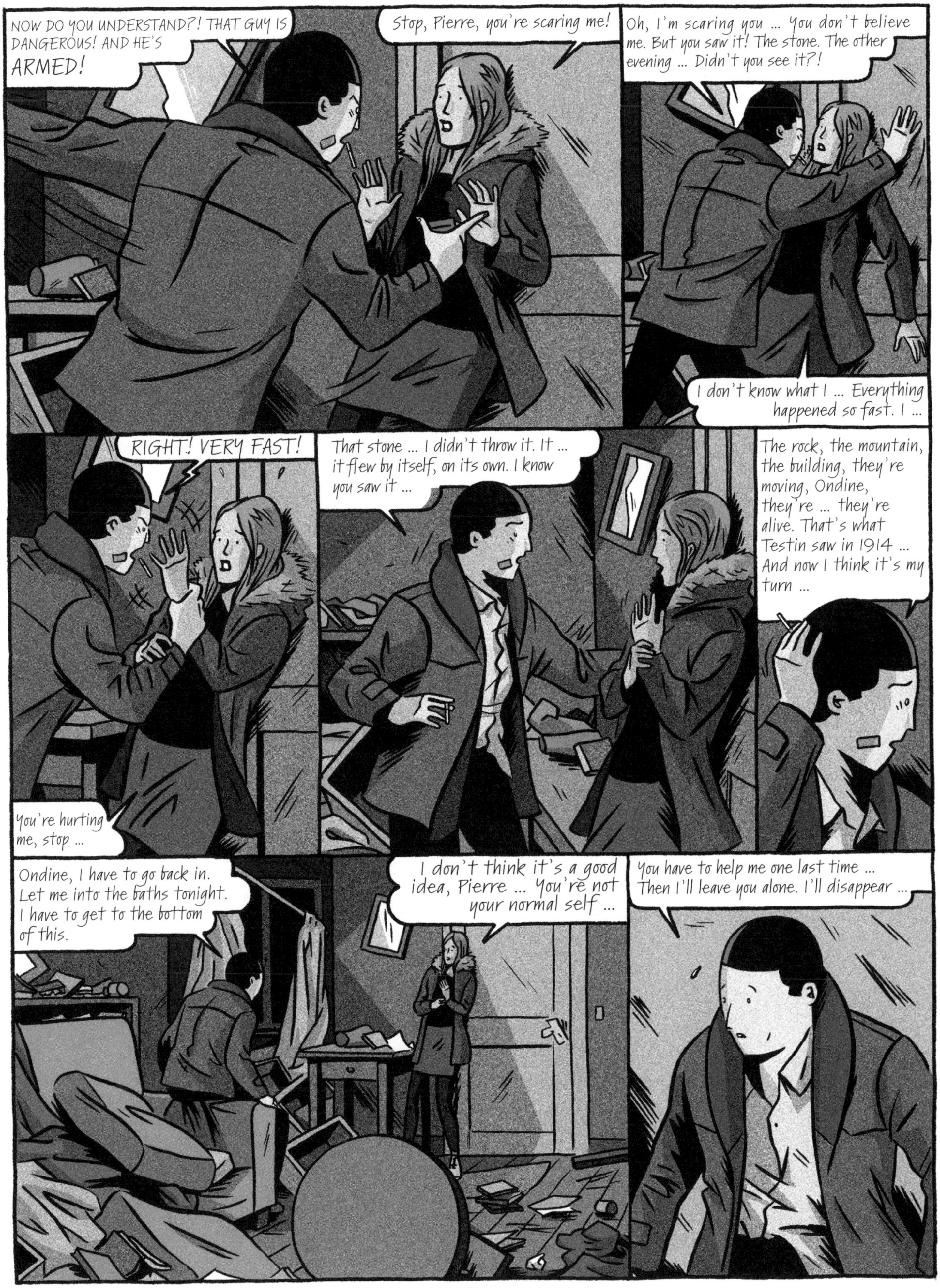
NOW DO YOU UNDERSTAND?! THAT GUY IS DANGEROUS! AND HE'S ARMED!
Stop, Pierre, you're scaring me!
Oh, I'm scaring you ... You don't believe me. But you saw it! The stone. The other evening ... Didn't you see it?!
I don't know what I ... Everything happened so fast. I ...
RIGHT! VERY FAST!
You're hurting me, stop ...
That stone ... I didn't throw it. It ... it flew by itself, on its own. I know you saw it ...
The rock, the mountain, the building, they're moving, Ondine, they're ... they're alive. That's what Testin saw in 1914 ... And now I think it's my turn ...
Ondine, I have to go back in. Let me into the baths tonight. I have to get to the bottom of this.
I don't think it's a good idea, Pierre ... You're not your normal self ...
You have to help me one last time ... Then I'll leave you alone. I'll disappear ...

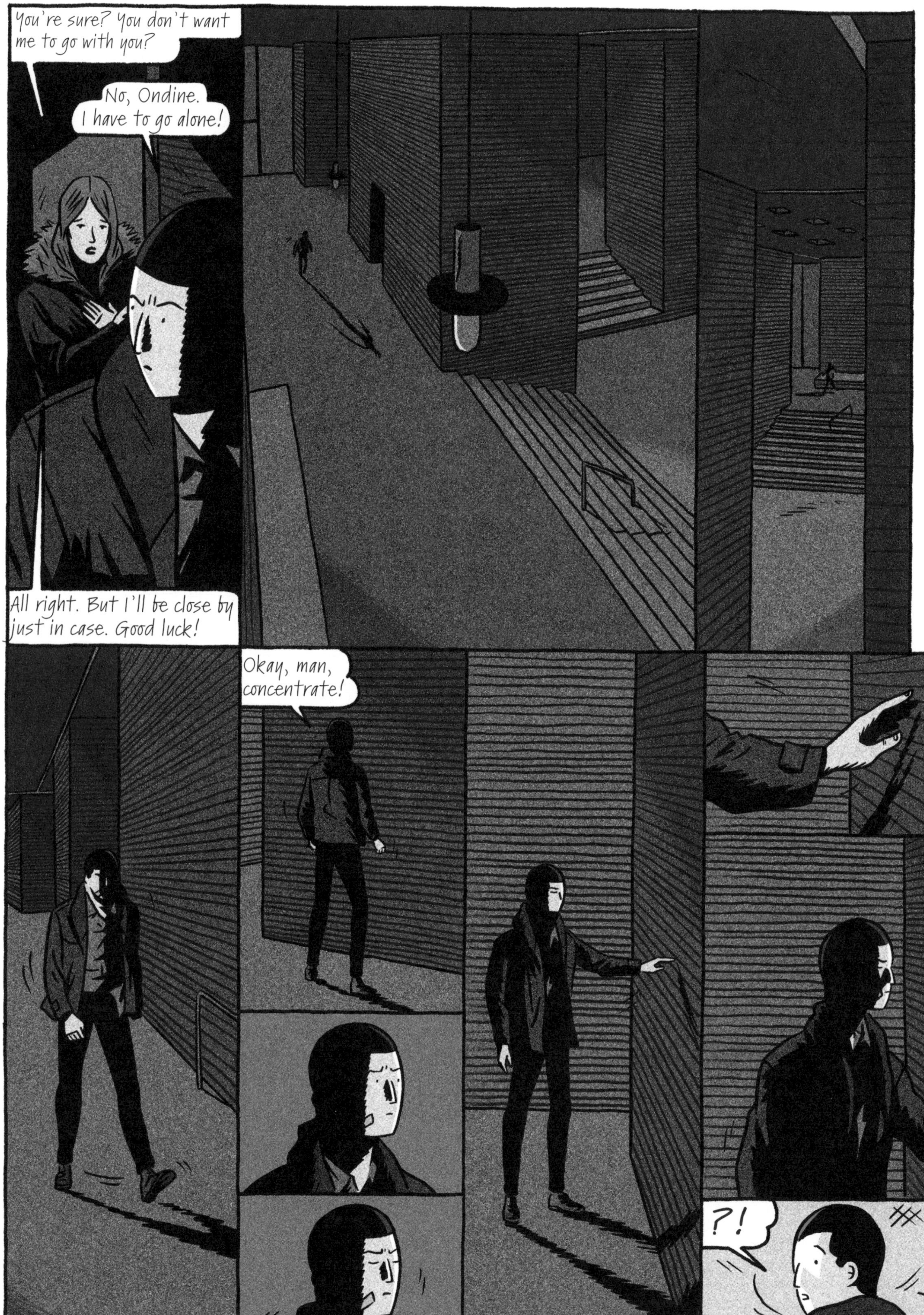
You're sure? You don't want me to go with you?
No, Ondine. I have to go alone!
All right. But I'll be close by just in case. Good luck!
Okay, man, concentrate!
?!

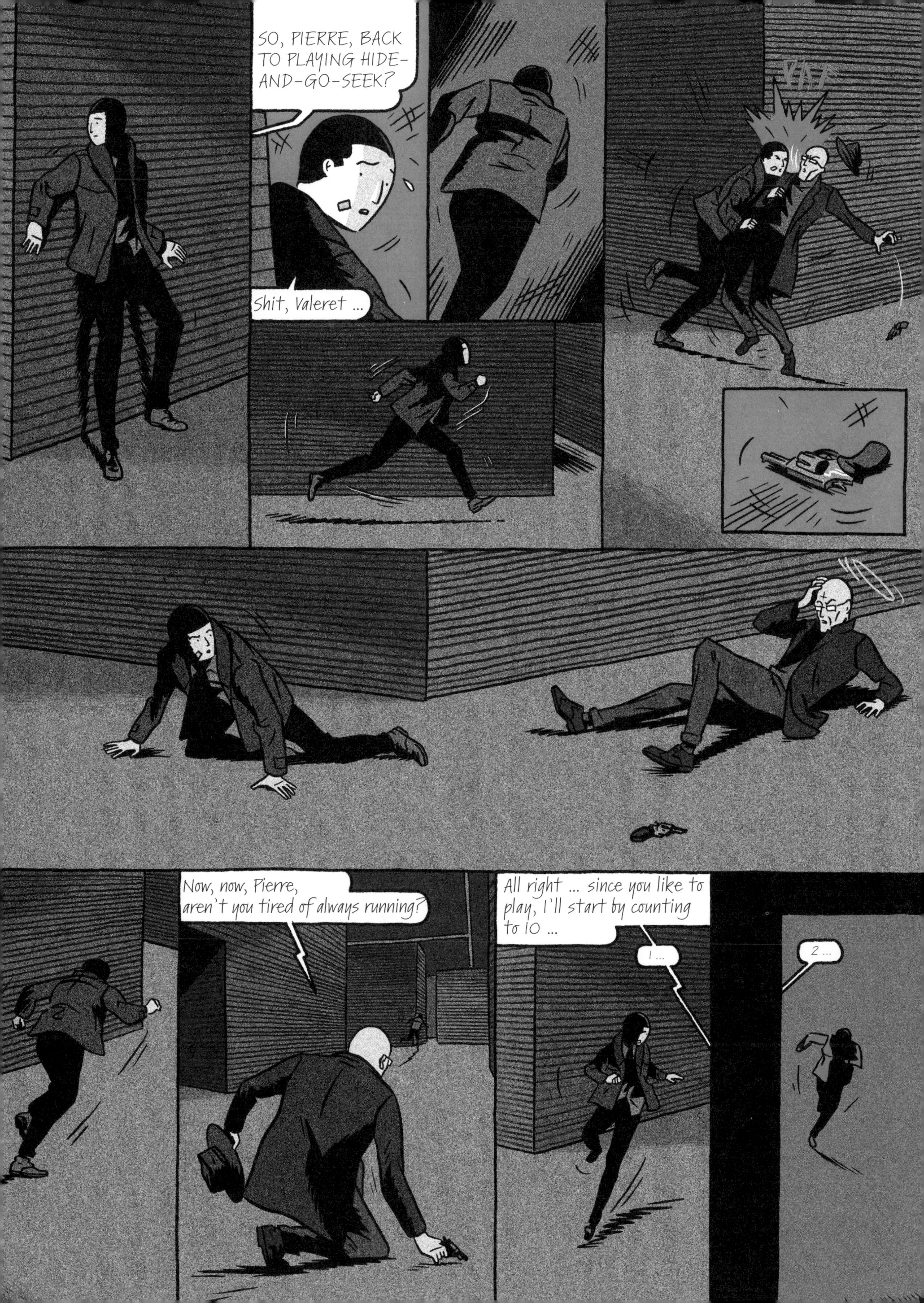
SO, PIERRE, BACK TO PLAYING HIDE-AND-GO-SEEK?
Shit, Valeret ...
Now, now, Pierre, aren't you tired of always running?
All right ... since you like to play, I'll start by counting to 10 ...
1 ...
2 ...

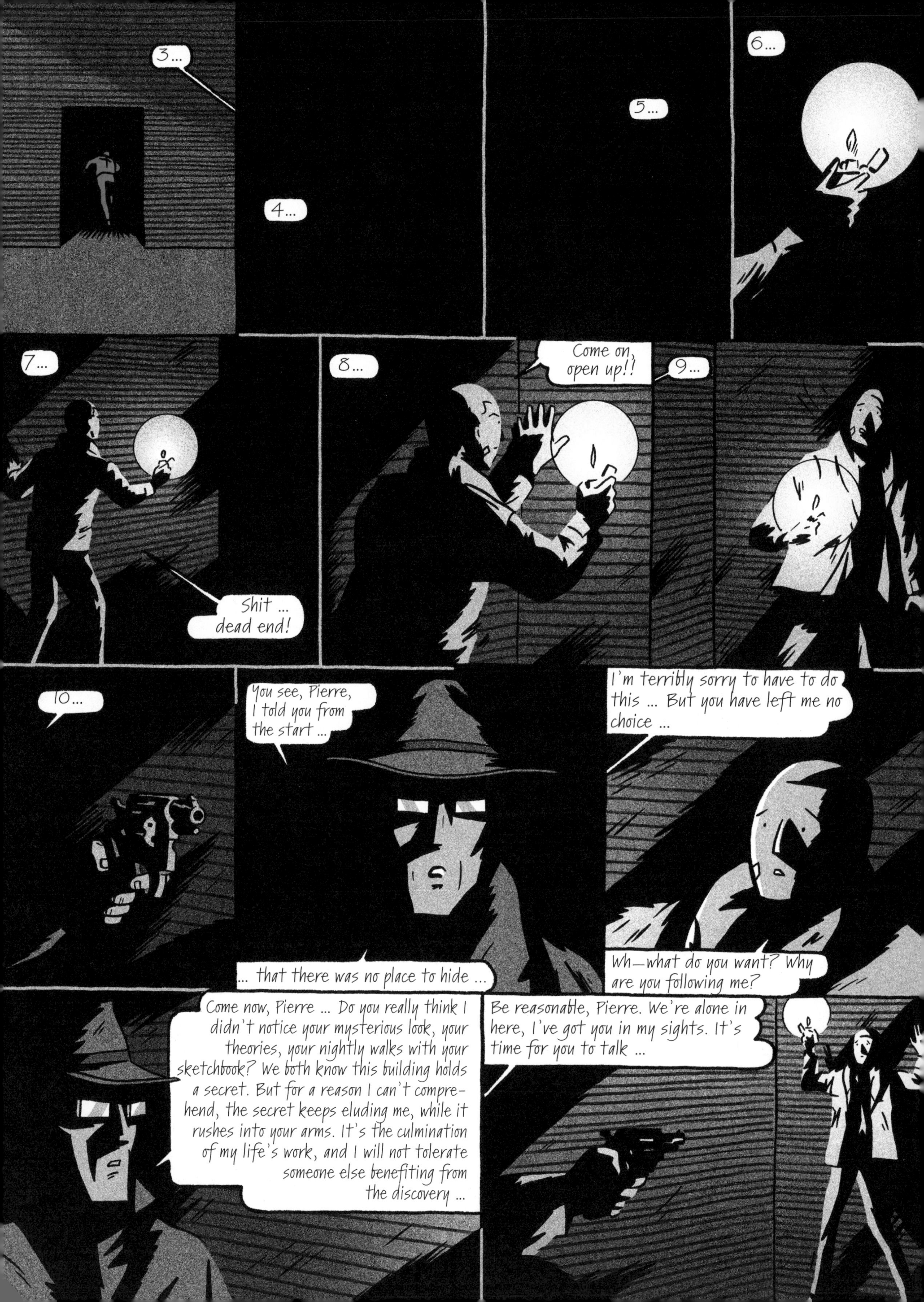
3...
4...
5...
6...
7...
Shit ... dead end!
8...
Come on, open up!!
9...
10...
You see, Pierre, I told you from the start ...
... that there was no place to hide ...
I'm terribly sorry to have to do this ... But you have left me no choice ...
Wh—what do you want? Why are you following me?
Come now, Pierre ... Do you really think I didn't notice your mysterious look, your theories, your nightly walks with your sketchbook? We both know this building holds a secret. But for a reason I can't comprehend, the secret keeps eluding me, while it rushes into your arms. It's the culmination of my life's work, and I will not tolerate someone else benefiting from the discovery ...
Be reasonable, Pierre. We're alone in here, I've got you in my sights. It's time for you to talk ...

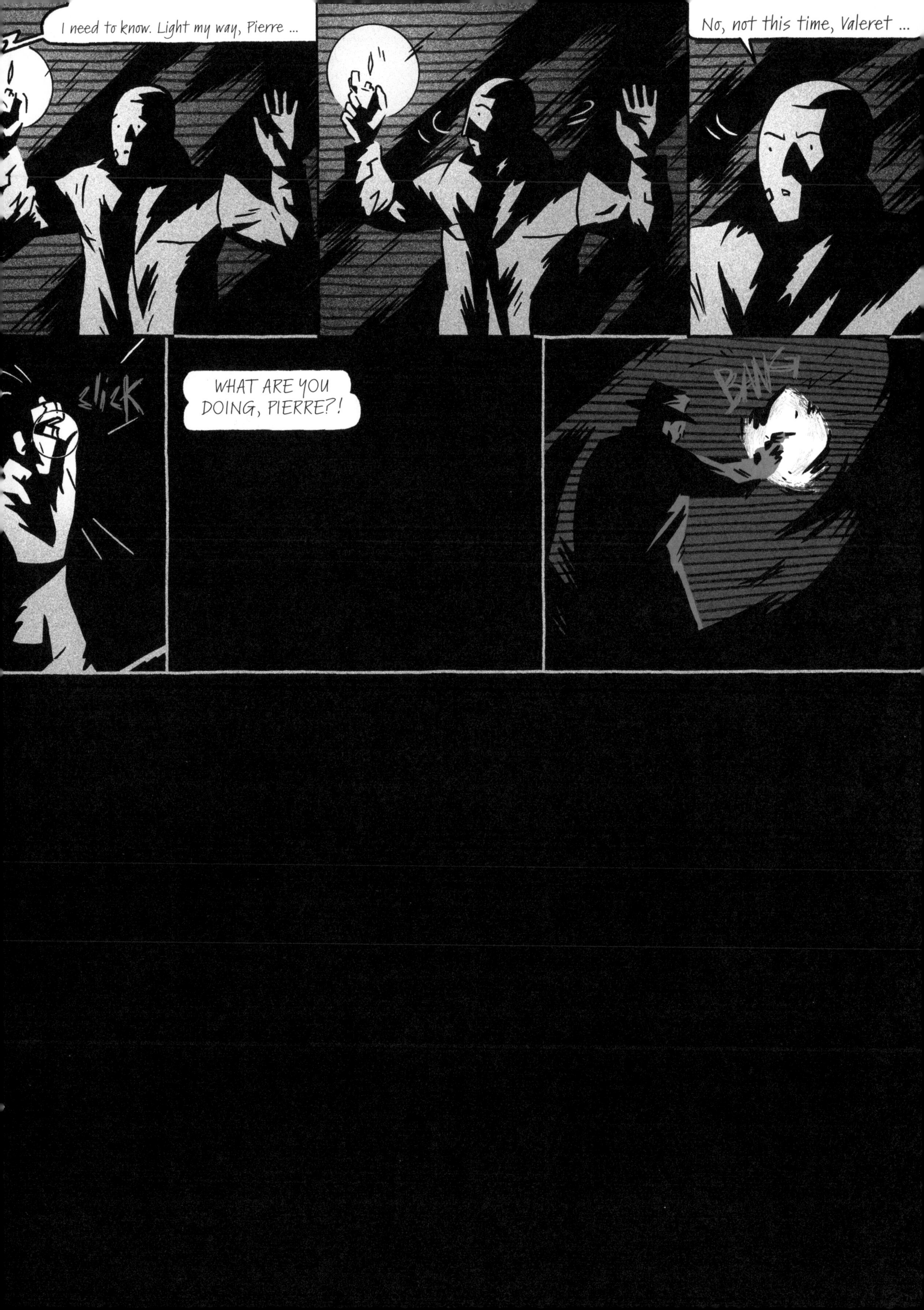
I need to know. Light my way, Pierre ...
No, not this time, Valeret ...
CLICK
WHAT ARE YOU DOING, PIERRE?!
BANG

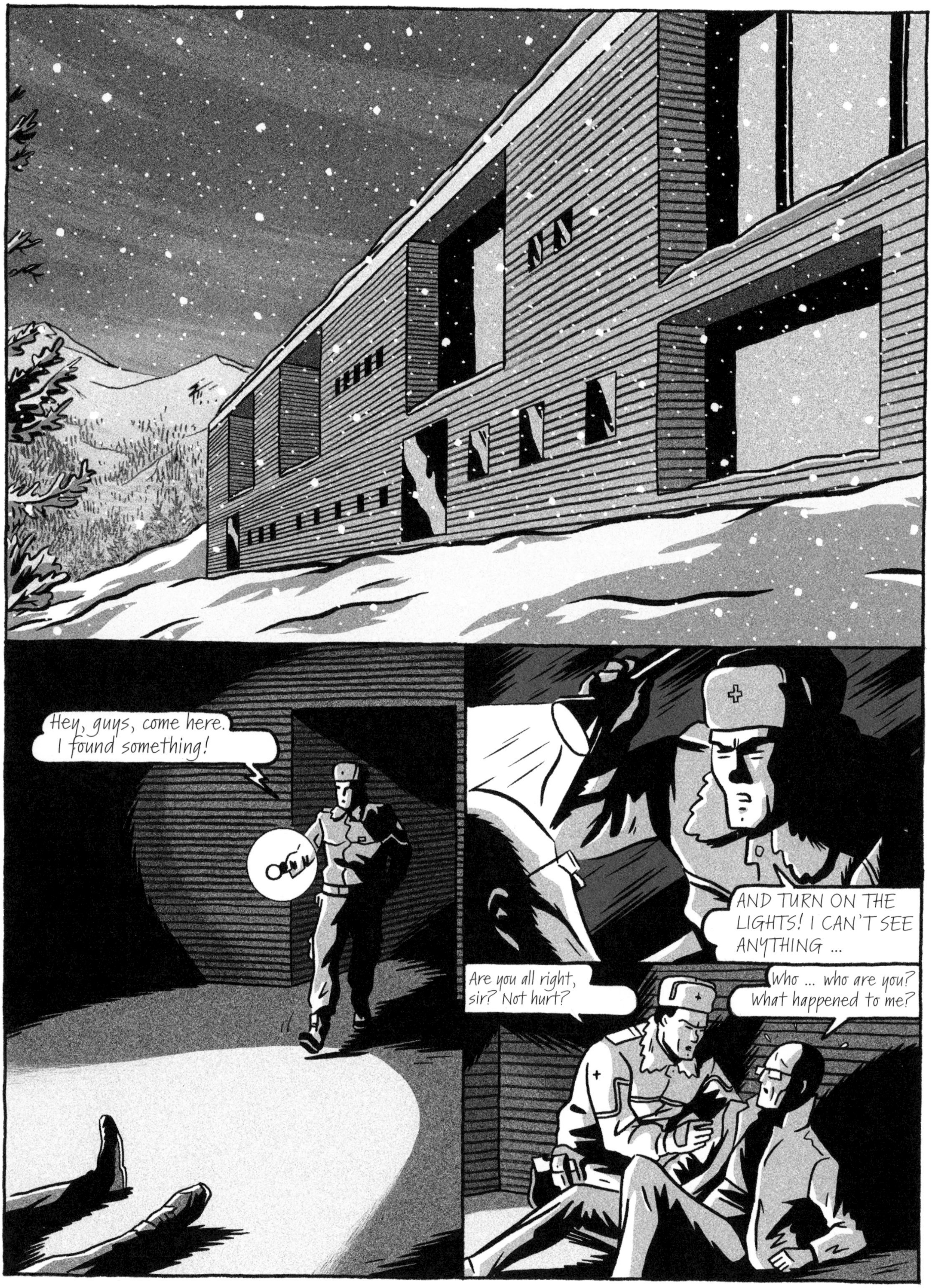
Hey, guys, come here. I found something!
AND TURN ON THE LIGHTS! I CAN'T SEE ANYTHING ...
Are you all right, sir? Not hurt?
Who ... who are you? What happened to me?

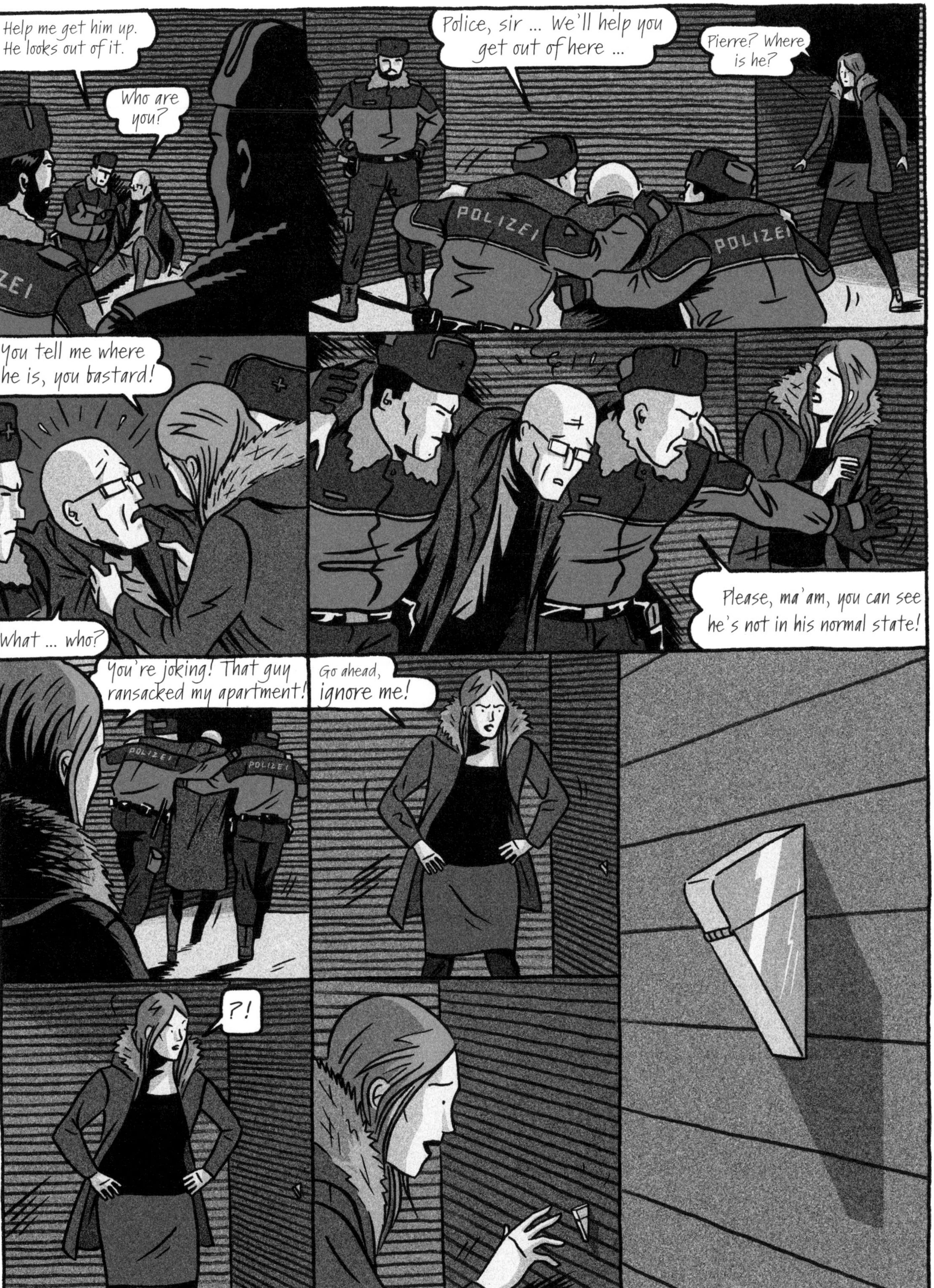
Help me get him up. He looks out of it.
Who are you?
Police, sir ... We'll help you get out of here ...
Pierre? Where is he?
POLIZEI
POLIZEI
You tell me where he is, you bastard!
What ... who?
Please, ma'am, you can see he's not in his normal state!
You're joking! That guy ransacked my apartment!
Go ahead, ignore me!
?!

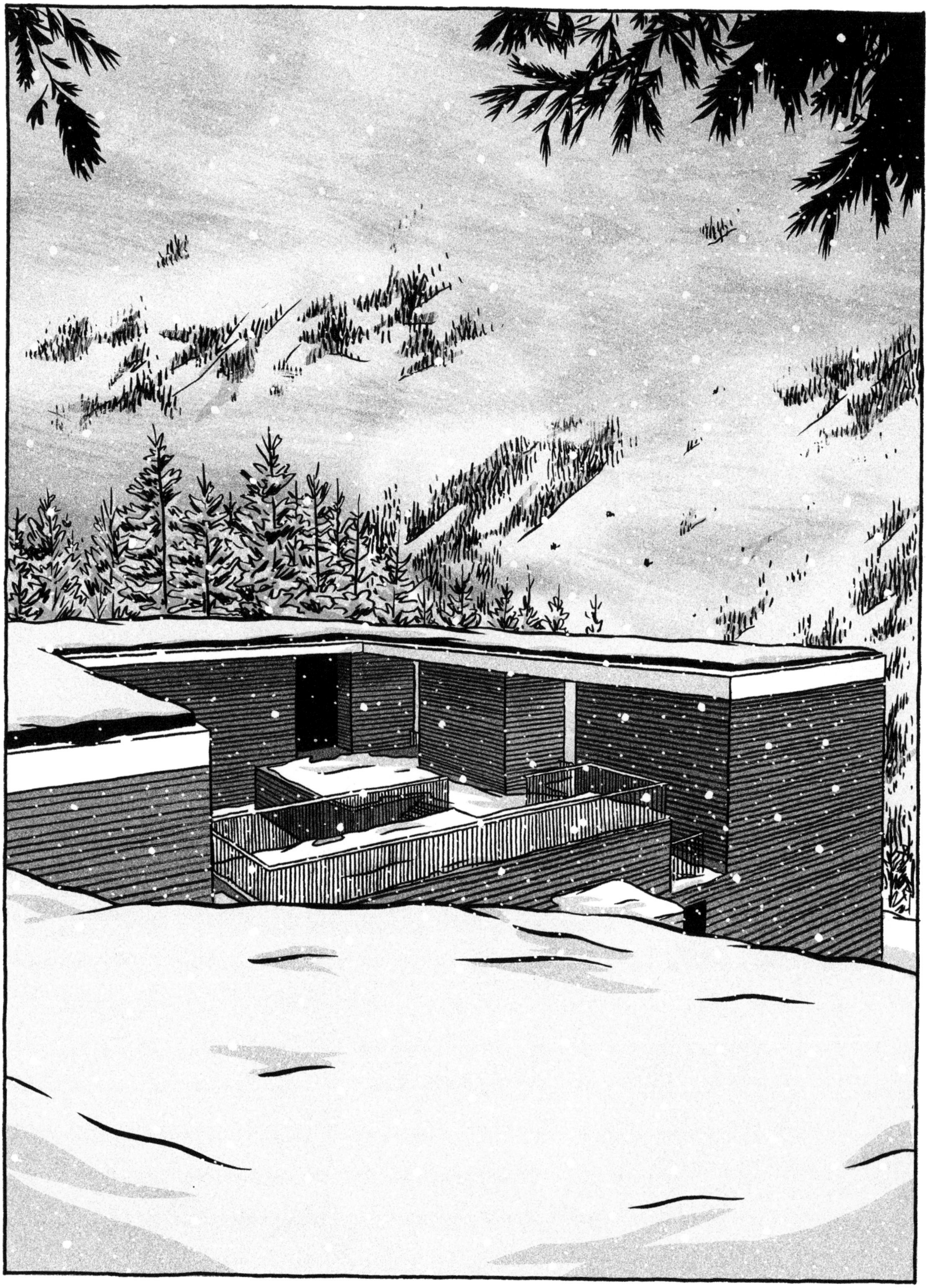

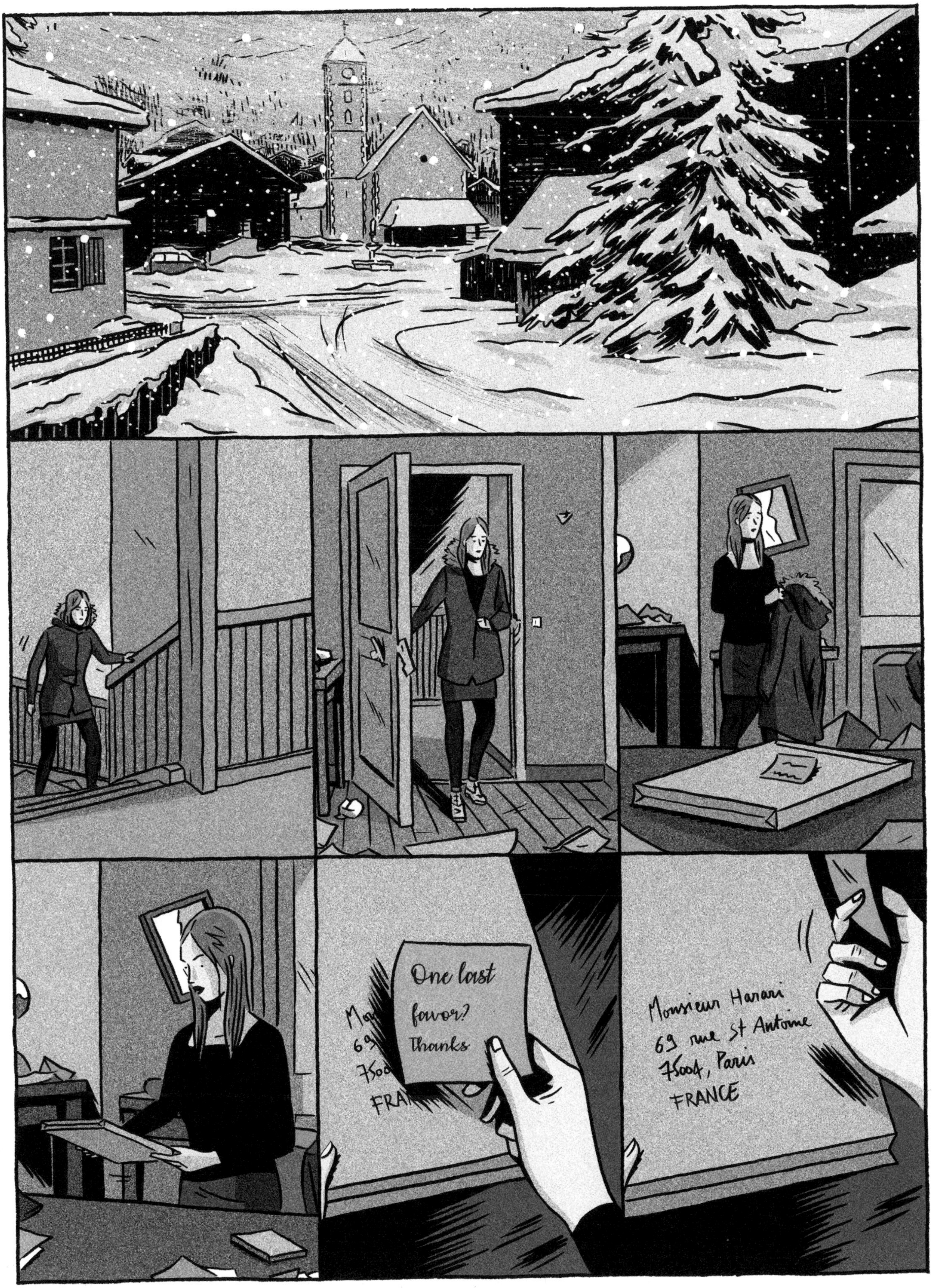
One last
favor?
Thanks
Monsieur Harari
69 rue St Antoine
75004, Paris
FRANCE

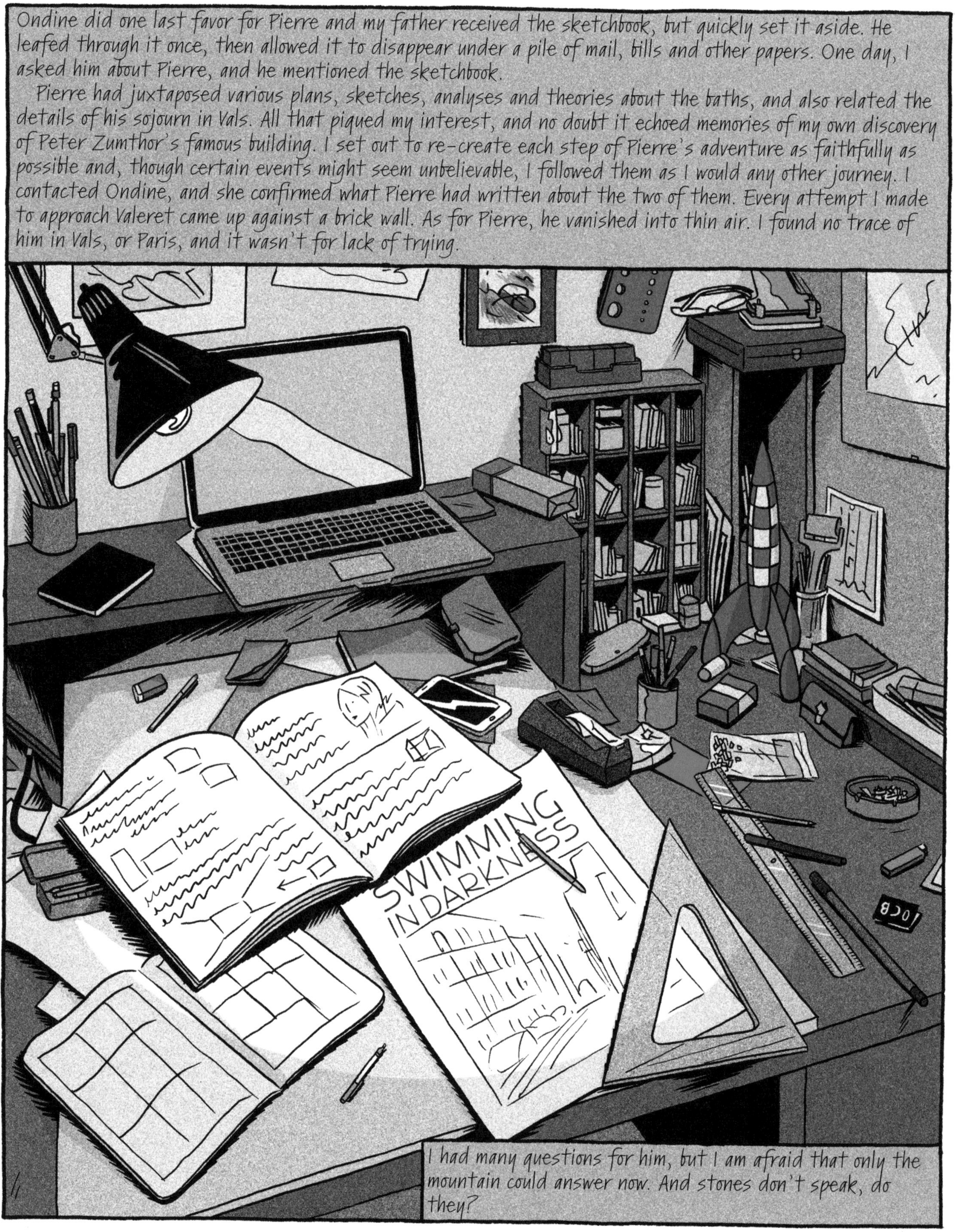
Ondine did one last favor for Pierre and my father received the sketchbook, but quickly set it aside. He leafed through it once, then allowed it to disappear under a pile of mail, bills and other papers. One day, I asked him about Pierre, and he mentioned the sketchbook.
Pierre had juxtaposed various plans, sketches, analyses and theories about the baths, and also related the details of his sojourn in Vals. All that piqued my interest, and no doubt it echoed memories of my own discovery of Peter Zumthor's famous building. I set out to re-create each step of Pierre's adventure as faithfully as possible and, though certain events might seem unbelievable, I followed them as I would any other journey. I contacted Ondine, and she confirmed what Pierre had written about the two of them. Every attempt I made to approach Valeret came up against a brick wall. As for Pierre, he vanished into thin air. I found no trace of him in Vals, or Paris, and it wasn't for lack of trying.
SWIMMING IN DARKNESS
I had many questions for him, but I am afraid that only the mountain could answer now. And stones don't speak, do they?

THE END

Lucas Harari was born in 1990 in Paris, where he still lives, and has a degree in decorative arts with a special interest in printed works. He self-published fanzines before working as an illustrator for book publishers and others. *Swimming in Darkness* is his first book.

David Homel is a writer, journalist, filmmaker and translator, and the author of seven novels. He has translated many French-language books into English and is a two-time recipient of the Governor General's Literary Award for Translation. He lives in Montreal.

TRANSLATION OF GERMAN TO ENGLISH

Page 21:
Fahrscheinkontrolle bitte.
Ticket inspection, please.

Entschuldigung.
Pardon.

Es ist ein Zweite-Klasse-Ticket!
This is a second-class ticket!

Sie sind hier in der erste Klasse.
Here you're in first class.

Page 24:
Nächster Halt ist Ilanz!!
Next stop is Ilanz!!

Ilanz! Zwei Minuten Aufenthalt!!
Ilanz! Two minutes' stop!!

Page 25:
Ausgang
Exit

Page 27:
Guten Tag!
Hello!

Hallo Jungs! Ist Christian wiederschon verschwunden?
Hi guys! Has Christian disappeared again?

Wie üblich ist er nach zwei Gläsern Bier in der Toilette eingeschlafen!
As usual, after his second beer, he's fallen asleep in the toilet!

HAHA, und er träumt von fliegende Kühe! HA HA HA!
HAHA, he's probably dreaming of flying cows! HA HA HA!

Christian! Es gibt einen Kleiner, der Englisch sprechen will!
Christian! There's a kid who wants to speak English!

Das ist er wieder und anscheinend aufgewacht!
Here he is, and apparently he woke up!

Page 28:
Ach so!
Oh, right!

Wetten, dass er es schafft, dass er ihm ein Bier spendet.
I'm betting that he gets him to buy him a beer.

Page 32:
"Das Valser Wasser!"
"The Vals water!"

"Der Mund des Berges"
"The Mouth of the Mountain"